T0215721

# Continuous Delivery with Visual Studio ALM 2015

Mathias Olausson
Jakob Ehn

Apress®

**Continuous Delivery with Visual Studio ALM 2015**

Copyright © 2015 by Mathias Olausson and Jakob Ehn

This work is subject to copyright. All rights are reserved by the Publisher, whether the whole or part of the material is concerned, specifically the rights of translation, reprinting, reuse of illustrations, recitation, broadcasting, reproduction on microfilms or in any other physical way, and transmission or information storage and retrieval, electronic adaptation, computer software, or by similar or dissimilar methodology now known or hereafter developed. Exempted from this legal reservation are brief excerpts in connection with reviews or scholarly analysis or material supplied specifically for the purpose of being entered and executed on a computer system, for exclusive use by the purchaser of the work. Duplication of this publication or parts thereof is permitted only under the provisions of the Copyright Law of the Publisher's location, in its current version, and permission for use must always be obtained from Springer. Permissions for use may be obtained through RightsLink at the Copyright Clearance Center. Violations are liable to prosecution under the respective Copyright Law.

ISBN-13 (pbk): 978-1-4842-1273-8

ISBN-13 (electronic): 978-1-4842-1272-1

Trademarked names, logos, and images may appear in this book. Rather than use a trademark symbol with every occurrence of a trademarked name, logo, or image we use the names, logos, and images only in an editorial fashion and to the benefit of the trademark owner, with no intention of infringement of the trademark.

The use in this publication of trade names, trademarks, service marks, and similar terms, even if they are not identified as such, is not to be taken as an expression of opinion as to whether or not they are subject to proprietary rights.

While the advice and information in this book are believed to be true and accurate at the date of publication, neither the authors nor the editors nor the publisher can accept any legal responsibility for any errors or omissions that may be made. The publisher makes no warranty, express or implied, with respect to the material contained herein.

Managing Director: Welmoed Spahr
Lead Editor: James DeWolf
Development Editor: Douglas Pundick
Technical Reviewer: Colin Dembovsky and Anthony Borton
Editorial Board: Steve Anglin, Gary Cornell, Louise Corrigan, James T. DeWolf,
     Jonathan Gennick, Robert Hutchinson, Michelle Lowman, James Markham,
     Matthew Moodie, Susan McDermott, Jeffrey Pepper, Douglas Pundick, Gwenan Spearing
Coordinating Editor: Melissa Maldonado
Copy Editor: Mary Behr
Compositor: SPi Global
Indexer: SPi Global
Artist: SPi Global

Distributed to the book trade worldwide by Springer Science+Business Media New York, 233 Spring Street, 6th Floor, New York, NY 10013. Phone 1-800-SPRINGER, fax (201) 348-4505, e-mail orders-ny@springer-sbm.com, or visit www.springer.com. Apress Media, LLC is a California LLC and the sole member (owner) is Springer Science + Business Media Finance Inc (SSBM Finance Inc). SSBM Finance Inc. is a **Delaware** corporation.

For information on translations, please e-mail rights@apress.com, or visit www.apress.com.

Apress and friends of ED books may be purchased in bulk for academic, corporate, or promotional use. eBook versions and licenses are also available for most titles. For more information, reference our Special Bulk Sales–eBook Licensing web page at www.apress.com/bulk-sales.

Any source code or other supplementary materials referenced by the author in this text is available to readers at www.apress.com. For detailed information about how to locate your book's source code, go to www.apress.com/source-code/.

# Contents at a Glance

# Contents

# About the Authors

**Mathias Olausson** works as the ALM practice lead for Solidify, specializing in software craftsmanship and application lifecycle management. With over 15 years of experience as a software consultant and trainer, he has worked on numerous projects and in many organizations. Mathias has been a Microsoft Visual Studio ALM MVP for six years and is active as a Visual Studio ALM. Mathias is a frequent speaker on Visual Studio and Team Foundation Server at conferences and industry events, and he blogs at http://blogs.msmvps.com/molausson.

**Jakob Ehn** is a Microsoft Visual Studio ALM MVP and a Visual Studio ALM Ranger. Jakob has over 15 years of experience in commercial software development and currently works as a senior consultant at Active Solution, specializing in Visual Studio ALM.

Jakob is a co-author of the *Pro Team Foundation Service* and *Team Foundation Server 2012 Starter* books. He actively participates in the MSDN forums and contributes to different open source projects in the Visual Studio ALM space. You can find Jakob blogging at http://geekswithblogs.net/Jakob or tweeting at @JakobEhn.

# About the Technical Reviewers

**Anthony Borton** is a senior ALM consultant/trainer for Enhance ALM, an Australian-based company specializing in helping organizations successfully adopt ALM best practices. He is a Microsoft Visual Studio ALM MVP, a Microsoft Certified Trainer, and the author of nine courses focusing on DevOps and TFS 2015.

**Colin Dembovsky** is a senior ALM developer for Northwest Cadence based in Cape Town, South Africa. After completing an MSc in Computer Science at Rhodes University, he worked as a developer (first in Linux using C++ and moving to .NET and C#) and later as a systems architect. He left development work to start ALM consulting, and has been an ALM MVP since 2011. He is passionate about helping teams improve the quality of their software, and do it more efficiently. Besides consulting and training, Colin is a frequent guest speaker. He regularly blogs at http://colinsalmcorner.com and can be found on Twitter at @colindembovsky.

When he is not working on a TFS server somewhere, he is playing guitar or mandolin and recording in his home studio, or entertaining his wife and two kids.

# Introduction

Building good software is challenging. Building high-quality software on a tight schedule can be close to impossible. Continuous Delivery is an agile and iterative technique that enables developers to deliver solid, working software in every iteration. Continuous Delivery practices help IT organizations reduce risk and potentially become as nimble, agile, and innovative as startups.

Although not sufficient in itself, having a powerful set of tools that lets you implement practices such as Continuous Integration, deployment pipelines, and release management certainly will help you go a long way. With the Visual Studio 2015 ALM suite of tools there is now a very compelling offering that covers all areas when it comes to implementing Continuous Delivery. Also, as this book will show, these tools are open and extensible by nature, meaning that you don't have to use every part of the suite if you don't want to.

## About This Book

This book does the following:

- Explains the concepts of Continuous Delivery.

- Shows how to implement a Continuous Delivery process using a modern development platform based on Visual Studio 2015, Team Foundation Server, Visual Studio Online, and Microsoft Azure.

- Gives you practical guidance and ready-to-use recipes to help you build your own Continuous Delivery pipeline.

## What You Will Learn

- What Continuous Delivery is and how to use it to create better software more efficiently using Visual Studio 2015.

- How to use Team Foundation Server 2015 and Visual Studio Online to plan, design, and implement powerful and reliable deployment pipelines.

- Detailed step-by-step instructions for implementing Continuous Delivery on a real project.

# Who This Book Is For

Continuous Delivery with Visual Studio ALM 2015 is for any development team that wants to deliver software faster while retaining a high quality. While all of the practical examples and scenarios are implemented using the Visual Studio ALM tool suite, the book contains plenty of general guidance on implementing Continuous Delivery that is useful for any development and operations team.

# CHAPTER 1

■ ■ ■

# Introduction to Continuous Delivery

This book is about helping you build great software. There are lots of things to get right in order to be successful, and we've found it very valuable to have a software factory in whch to build our software. Continuous Delivery helps you get both the process and the tools to quickly deliver software without sacrificing quality.

It can be challenging to get all parts working together, so in this book we will focus on how to do things rather than the theory behind the ideas. This way you can get up to speed and create your own factory in which to build software. We will walk you through a complete end-to-end scenario from the code to a released product, with build automation, deployment, environment management, and automated testing in between.

The tool we will use to implement these ideas is the Visual Studio 2015 family. Visual Studio has been around for a long time but in the last releases it has become a very compelling solution for implementing a Continuous Delivery process. Chapter 2 gives you an overview of the product family.

First, we want to give you a quick start into Continuous Delivery and all the practices involved in getting a release out to production. We will start with the terminology around Continuous Deployment in this chapter and then quickly move on to the implementation of a Continuous Delivery process.

---

■ **Note** If you want more background and the theory of the concepts we describe in this book, we recommend that you pick up a copy of *Continuous Delivery: Reliable Software Releases through Build, Test, and Deployment Automation* by Jez Humble and David Farley (www.amazon.com/dp/0321601912).

---

# Continuous Integration

> *"Continuous Integration is a software development practice where members of a team integrate their work frequently; usually each person integrates at least daily – leading to multiple integrations per day."*

> —Martin Fowler

The term Continuous Integration (CI) was introduced by Martin Fowler and is now the de facto standard in agile projects. Having worked on a project with a CI process in place, it is really hard to imagine how a project could actually work without it. Of course it can, but an agile project requires new ways of working, and just like Scrum is said to be all about common sense, so also is CI. But there are several problems with agile development from a deployment perspective, such as the following:

- **Testing**: In an agile project, you need to do testing earlier and more often since software is built incrementally in short iterations.

- **Cross-functional teams**: Ideally the team should be self-organized, meaning more people need to be able to deploy software.

- **Shippable product at every iteration**: Manual routines used to work, but now it is not ok to spend one week on installation tasks if the sprint is two weeks.

Continuous Integration can help to resolve these issues. In fact, agile practices have a solution for this: use the retrospective to find ways to improve. Next, we will look at how you can get going with improvements.

## Why Implement Continuous Integration?

Even if the all of the above makes sense, it can still be hard to justify the work to implement it. So instead of just having a gut feeling that this is a good practice worth the time required to set it up, we have listed our favorite reasons below. Continuous integration will do the following:

- Reduce risks

- Reduce manual routines

- Create shippable software

- Improve confidence in the product

- Identify deficiencies early

- Reduce time spent integrating code and troubleshooting integration problems

- Improve project visibility

To better visualize the difference between using CI and not, take a look at Figure 1-1. With a manual process, the cost is pretty constant, as is the benefit. You can quickly get started but the model scales poorly, so when you add more people to the team it costs more (since everyone is doing similar tasks). Also, the benefit will decrease because of the reasons above. CI, on the other hand, will cost more initially and the benefit will be low until enough of the work has gone over to the CI process, which is when the effect of CI will switch the graphs. The result: you get much more benefit at a lower cost the more you use CI.

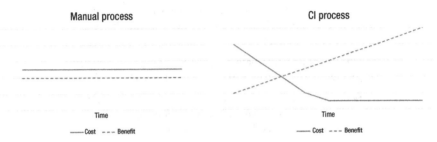

**Figure 1-1.** *Cost/benefit from using continuous integration*

Still, even with the good arguments for why CI makes sense, we occasionally hear concerns like the following:

- **Maintenance overhead**: *I will need to maintain the build environment and the CI solution.* Yes, you will. But show us any factory that works without maintenance. Why should a software factory be any different?

- **Effort to introduce**: Sure, it will take some time to get the process started. For a new project, not so much; for an existing solution, you may need to add CI capabilities incrementally for a good return on investment.

- **Quality of current solution**: Some may argue that the current process is too poor to automate, but these are the very processes that most require CI, and quickly!

- **Increased cost**: *New hardware for the build infrastructure will need to be acquired.* But think about the savings you will get by raising quality and identifying problems much earlier in the process.

- **It duplicates work**: *With CI, you need to automate what you already do manually.* Well, yes, initially you do, but the goal should be to share as much as possible of the work that developers and testers do anyway. For instance, the build system should use the same project files the developer uses locally, and the developer can use the deployment script to update the local machine when a new version needs to be installed locally. So now CI doesn't duplicate work; it actually reduces it!

To get continuous integration working, the team needs to agree on the rules around the process. If the rules are not followed, there is a potential risk that the quality of the result will degrade and people will lose confidence in the process. We recommend using the following rules as a starting point:

- **Check in often:** The CI process needs changes to work. The smaller the changes you can commit, and the more specific the changes are, the quicker you can react to things that go wrong.

- **Do not check in broken code:** Checking in often is great, but don't overdo it. Don't check in code until it works, and never check in broken code. If you need to switch context, shelve or stash the source code for a while.

- **Fix a broken build immediately:** If you happen to break something, it is your responsibility to fix it. Always take responsibility for the code.

- **Write unit tests:** The system needs to know what works and what does not work. Unit tests and other inspection tools should be used to make sure the code does more than just compile.

- **All tests and inspections must pass:** With inspections in place, you must pay attention to the results. Use feedback mechanisms like email or a build status board to make people aware when something is broken.

- **Run private builds:** If you can do a test build before check-in, in you can avoid committing things that don't work.

- **Avoid getting broken code:** Finally, if the build is broken, don't get the latest code. Why work on code that doesn't work? Instead, use the version control system and specifically get the latest version that worked.

## Build Automation

Build automation is the core step in the CI process. The automated build system is typically used to drive the CI process and not just do compilation and execute unit tests. An automated build should be possible to trigger by anyone (having permissions to do so) at any time, and it should be possible to set up a schedule for the builds (such as nightly builds). The build process should also publish the build results at a central location so people have easy access to the releases.

Automating the build process is not always a trivial task but the benefits it gives are many, including the following:

- **Saves time:** With a build server the developers don't need to wait for a build cycle; they can simply queue a build and continue working. You will also save time by removing manual steps.

- **Reduces errors when assembling the software:** By automating the process you get a consistent way of building the product.

- **Predictable results**

- **Helps you learn about problems early**

- **Reduces dependency on individuals managing the build process**

Any new project should implement automated builds since having the foundation in place from the start makes it so much easier to just do the right thing.

One important thing to think about when setting up the build automation solution is speed. You want a snappy CI process so that you can react to problems quickly. If the build is slow, people will not sit around and wait for it to complete; they will instead switch to do other work. If the build fails a while later, the developer will have to change context again, which both takes time and increases the risk of messing things up. Also, aim to fail fast. If a problem is found in the CI process, it is often meaningful to stop the build right away.

When implementing automated builds, you also need to think about what kind of build you need in which scenario. It is common for development teams to not just have one build setup for a branch, but instead more likely all of the following:

- **Continuous Integration Builds**: Lightweight to give feedback quickly, often incremental with limited testing.

- **Private Builds**: Test the changes to be committed before actually checking them in.

- **Nightly Builds**: Complete builds with more exhaustive testing.

- **Release Builds**: Complete builds that you intend to release to production.

What you end up with will most likely depend on how you develop. In Chapter 5, we will discuss best practices for how to structure the code to make it easy to build and release. In Chapter 7, we go deep into the hows of creating a build automation process.

# Unit Testing

Making sure the code compiles is of course main part of the CI process. But code that compiles doesn't tell you if the code does the right thing. Unit tests provide a great way to ensure the code is correct according to its use-cases, and the CI system is a great solution to run the tests often so you quickly can learn if a problem has been introduced in the codebase.

A good unit test runs quickly without dependencies outside of the component it's testing. When used together with code coverage analysis, you get a fine instrument to automatically test application logic and ensure that the code has good test coverage. Of course, if you are into test-driven development where the tests are developed before the application code, then you would expect a high coverage metric from the start. But regardless of testing style, the unit tests are key to the CI process, so encourage developers to write tests by giving them feedback from each build.

In Chapter 11, we will look at automated testing and apply it to the continuous delivery mindset.

## Inspection

Having all of the steps in the CI process integrated is great but how do you know if something goes wrong? Compiler errors and failing tests can easily be trapped and visualized. But what about code quality? Can you, for instance, fail a build if the code coverage for unit tests is below the level agreed upon? Or if the code has become more difficult to maintain over time, can you get notified of that? The Continuous Integration process is often thought of as the heartbeat of the project, and this is something you can take advantage of for inspection. Some inspections should lead to immediate action: for example, compiler errors should fail the build. Others can be reported to a central location so that you can look at the trends later on, like code metrics and overall build status. Chapter 8 goes into the details on how to manage product quality and technical debt using various inspections and metrics.

## Feedback

The last step in the process is to have a good way to notify the team about what works and what needs to be fixed. A good feedback system will give you ways to know about an issue immediately so that you can fix it before it grows into a big problem. You can try to be as creative as possible here to make the build result visible to the team in a good way, like displaying the current status on a build monitor or by sending out email alerts.

In fact, wouldn't it be great to have this kind of information available as part of the project status on the team's home page? Figure 1-2 shows how builds can be pinned to the home page in the TFS Web Access.

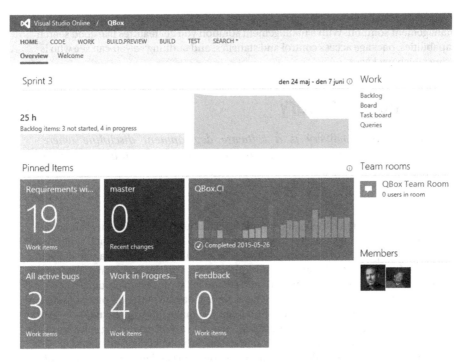

**Figure 1-2.** *Continuous feedback from the build process using TFS Web Access*

# Packaging

The idea of designing for deployment (in other words, building the software so it's easy to deploy) is a great idea. The way you package the product can make a big difference in how quickly and flexibly you can deploy the solution. Talk to the operations people to understand what packaging option works best in the environment where the product will be installed. A WebDeploy solution may be a great way to deploy a web site for some, whereas others may prefer a simple file copy solution. Some like a binary database deployment model like DacPac, and others prefer running SQL scripts. So take the time to understand the requirements and streamline the build process to produce the best packages for the solution at hand. A big portion of Chapter 7 deals with artifact packing.

# Publishing to an Artifact Store

Once the build has been produced, the final step is to make it available for others to consume. Proper artifact management is an important part of the release management process, particularly because it enables you to build once and deploy many times.

You can use built-in solutions such as publishing to a file share or publishing the build back into TFS. As simplistic as these solutions are, when used together with TFS build you still get many features of an artifact repository, like retention policies and a way to find available builds. You can take this to the next level if you use an artifact management solution. With a management solution you get features like good search capabilities, package access control and statistics, and auditing so you can see who is using which packages.

# Continuous Delivery

> *"Continuous Delivery is a software development discipline where you build software in such a way that the software can be released to production at any time"*

—Martin Fowler

Continuous Integration is great, and it provides a framework for efficiently validating software in a predictable way. But to get the most out of it, you need to look at how it fits into the overall process of delivering software. In an agile project, you want to deliver working software at every iteration. Unfortunately, this is easier said than done; it often turns out that even if you implement CI and get the build process to produce a new installation package in a few minutes, it takes several days to get a new piece of software tested and released into production. So how can you make this work better?

Not surprisingly, the key here is process. In order to deliver working software faster, you need a good cohesive set of tools and practices. So you need to add planning, environment management, deployment, and automated validation to get a great solution for your product, and this is just what Continuous Delivery is about.

## The "Null" Release Cycle

To start defining your delivery process, you can start by asking a simple question.

> *How long does it take to release one changed line of code into production?*

The answer is most likely, much longer then you want it to. We call this period the "null" release cycle, and it can be a great way to understand and tune the release cycle.

So what stops you from improving the process? First, you must know more about how you release your product. Even in organizations that follow good engineering practices, the release process is often neglected. A common reason for this is simply because releasing software needs collaboration across different disciplines in the process. To improve the situation, you need to sit down as a team and document the steps required to go from a code change to the software released into production. Figure 1-3 shows a typical delivery process; in practice, work happens sequentially, just like in the picture.

*Figure 1-3.* A typical delivery process

When you have come this far, you now know a lot more about the delivery process, which means you can start optimizing the process.

1. Look at the steps in the process that take the most time and see what can be done to improve them.

2. Look at the steps in the process that most often go wrong and understand what causes these problems.

3. Look at the sequence of the steps and think about if they need to be run sequentially or if they can run in parallel.

Having looked at the process and asked the questions, we now have possibility to improve the process, as shown in Figure 1-4.

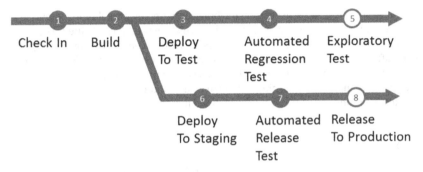

*Figure 1-4. An optimized delivery process*

In this model, we have changed the process so that most steps are automated by implementing automated tests as well as automated build and deployment. Releasing to production automatically is not for the faint-hearted so this would be triggered manually, but it uses the same automated scripts as the automated deploy to test and staging environments. We do, however, believe it can be possible to automate even release to production, especially if we have had this working from the first iteration of the project. By doing so, we build up confidence for the process; having seen it work throughout the development cycle should make us trust the process even in this critical stage. We have also parallelized the acceptance test and preparation of the production environment. By doing this in parallel we can push the release to production as soon as the acceptance tests are green, instead of the traditional stage to production first after the acceptance tests have passed.

# Release Planning

For you to deliver software in a deterministic way, you need to have a planning process that works with the conditions you have when developing the software. It's important to manage dependencies between project activities as well as software components. If you fail with the planning, some components may not be ready for release when you want to deliver yours. In Chapter 4, we will look at how you can manage the release process, including planning, metrics, and reporting.

# Release Pipelines

A delivery process can take a long time to complete. In order to give quick feedback, you can use a pipeline concept to separate different phases in the process. This way each phase can give feedback to its stakeholder as soon as that stage is complete, without having to wait for the whole sequence to complete. Figure 1-5 shows a typical deployment pipeline.

**Figure 1-5.**  *A deployment pipeline*

The commit stage takes care of creating the binaries to deploy the solution, potentially something that's done every time a change to code or configuration is committed. The rest of the pipeline is there to prove that the binaries are ready to be released by running a number of different tests. If the release candidate passes all tests, it can be released into an environment. The deployment pipeline should use different environments through the various stages, so for instance dev testing is done in a development environment and user acceptance testing is done in a QA or pre-production environment.

# Environments

When you look at the delivery process and build your deployment pipeline, it becomes apparent that you must have good control over how your environments are managed. First, you should have dedicated environments for each release and stage. This does not necessarily mean that you need dedicated machines; you just need to make sure to manage dependencies in a good way and you can build environments using the same machines. To deliver quickly you must control how environments and machines are managed. If you can script this, you can version control the configuration, which makes it possible to automate environment management. Chapter 9 goes into the details of environment creation and management.

# Release Management and Deployment

Continuous Delivery provides a great practice in producing updates in a controlled and effective manner. But without an intentional release management discipline, you can lose much of its value. What you need to add to the picture is how the release planning ties into the deployment process and know what features you want to deploy where and when.

In an agile project, you have a good situation when it comes to release management, since the first thing you do is create a product backlog and continuously groom the backlog as part of the project cycle. In other words, the backlog is your release plan. If you don't do agile development, you need to use other means to create the release plan so that you know which features you are going to deliver when.

With the release plan in place you can now design your delivery process to support the difference phases in the project. If you need concurrent development, you can implement a branch strategy to support this. With multiple branches you can add continuous integration builds to keep the code clean and your environments up-to-date and so on. Based on the release plan and the continuous integration process you can even automate the release notes for every release you do.

In Chapter 10, we will dive deep into the implementation of deployment and release management solutions.

## Automated Release Validation

When the software has been deployed, you can run tests on it. The commit phase of the build process runs the unit tests, but for integration and regression tests you must run those tests in a realistic environment with proper test data available. Ideally, you want to have a process where you can run automated build verification tests after every deployment in order to verify that the software works well enough for your testers to spend time testing it. After that, you can add more automated regression tests as you find value for; the process of running them as part of the continuous integration process will be the same. We will cover testing in Chapter 11.

# Continuous Deployment

So Continuous Integration is all about quick feedback and validation of the commit phase, and Continuous Delivery is about establishing a mindset where you can deliver features at customer demand. Continuous Deployment is a third term that's sometimes confused with both Continuous Integration and Continuous Delivery. Continuous Deployment can be viewed as the next level of Continuous Delivery. Where Continuous Delivery provides a process to create frequent releases but not necessarily deploy them, Continuous Deployment means that every change you make automatically gets deployed through the deployment pipeline. When you have established a Continuous Delivery solution, you are ready to move to Continuous Deployment if that's something your business would benefit from.

# DevOps

Another concept we want to mention that often related to continuous delivery is DevOps. The DevOps movement has gotten lots of attention over the last few of years. But what's it all about?

DevOps can be seen as a mindset where we want to bridge the gap between development and operations. Development teams today are often focused on delivering software faster, and many times the success of a team is measured by how often they can deliver a release. The primary goal for operations teams, on the other hand, is to ensure reliable operation of the system, which is measured by the stability of the environments. Since every release will affect the operations, it's tempting to do as few releases as possible to have good uptime. This potential conflict of interests should be avoided, and that's where DevOps comes in.

DevOps is often defined as a practice where the goal is to improve the flow from development to operations by working together and understanding each other's challenges. The primary focus for a DevOps mindset is to improve practices that makes this easier to work as a team, including improving the following:

- **Communication:** To do better releases, we need to understand what every step in the process, from the idea to working software in production, is all about. And to do this well, we need talk to each other and continuously learn from each other.

- **Collaboration:** Identifying the steps in the release process is great but it's even better if we can work together throughout the process. If the development team collaborates with the operations team, they can better understand the requirements of the target environment and prepare the product for deployment. And the operations team can get heads-up for that changes are coming in the next release and prepare the environments so the release goes smoothly.

- **Automation:** The third aspect of a DevOps practice is automation. Automation can be used to make the release process more deterministic and to bridge the gap between development and production. If someone from the operations team can teach developers the values in an automated deployment script, those developers can start building deployment scripts when the product is developed. The deployment scripts can then be tried out when the product is deployed to the dev and test environments, which can give the operations team good confidence in the deployment script, which can result in better-quality releases and less time spent on hand-over to operations.

- **Monitoring:** It can be challenging to get the system built and deployed, but sometimes it's even more difficult to manage the system in its real environment. So an important DevOps practice is to work with application monitoring and insights. Part of this starts with development, where we design the systems so that monitoring is built-in from the start. This is not only about error logging and diagnostics (important and essential things, of course) but we really want to enable understanding of application behaviors, which includes both diagnostics and application usage. When developing this we can learn from operations so that the correct hooks are built in that make the system easier to maintain. The goal is to have a solution where operations can get early warnings of problems in the product, have good tools to understand the problems, and have good ways to understand application usage. In Chapter 12, we will use Microsoft Application Insights to enable full end-to-end traceability in a product to provide both operational insights and usage understanding.

# Summary

By now you should have a good understanding of what Continuous Delivery is all about. This will be a long-time commitment and, like Figure 1-6 shows, it's also a maturity process; to reach Continuous Deployment, the development team must also practice the principles of the underlying steps. But once it's in place, it will be possible to release a change in just a press of a button, which will give a completely new level of service to your organization.

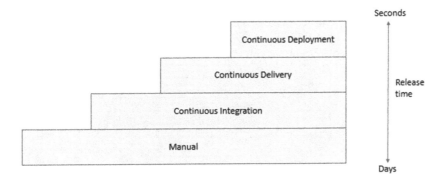

*Figure 1-6.* *Delivery maturity*

The rest of the book will explain the tools and practices you'll need to implement a Continuous Delivery process for your product.

# CHAPTER 2

■ ■ ■

# Overview of Visual Studio 2015 ALM

Visual Studio has grown from being "just" a great IDE for developing software on the Windows platform into a whole suite of tools that covers the entire lifecycle of application development on multiple platforms. When the first version of Team Foundation Server shipped in 2005, the suite was referred to as Visual Studio Team System. Now, the suite is referred to as *Visual Studio ALM*.

As shown in Figure 2-1, Visual Studio ALM supports all of the phases in the software development lifecycle, from requirement management and project planning, source control management, test management, build automation and release management, and getting information and insights into your running application from the end users.

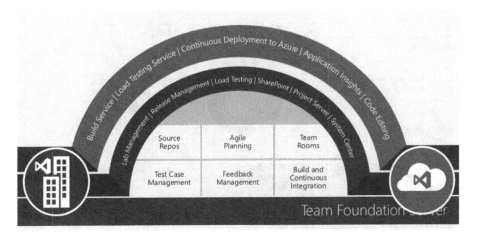

***Figure 2-1.*** *Visual Studio 2015 ALM Overview*

Even though you can (and many still do) use Team Foundation Server only for source control, the full power comes when you start using all of the tools in the suite. Since everything is integrated, not only is it easy to get started, but you also get full traceability across the project lifecycle on all artifacts.

In this chapter, we will take a brief look at the different parts of the Visual Studio ALM suite, what functionality they support, and how they are connected to each other. This will lay the foundation for the rest of the book, where you will implement Continuous Delivery for your sample application with the help of Visual Studio ALM.

# Agile Project Management

The start of most projects is collecting and prioritizing requirements. Visual Studio ALM offers out-of-the-box support for the most common process methodologies such as Scrum, Agile, and Kanban. The basic tools for implementing Scrum, such as backlog and sprint backlogs, have been available since Visual Studio 2012, but these tools have been continuously improved. The 2015 release has seen a lot of investment in the Kanban board and the task boards.

Figure 2-2 shows an example of a team dashboard in Team Foundation Server. As you can see, a lot of different information about the project can be visualized on the start page to quickly give an insight into the project status.

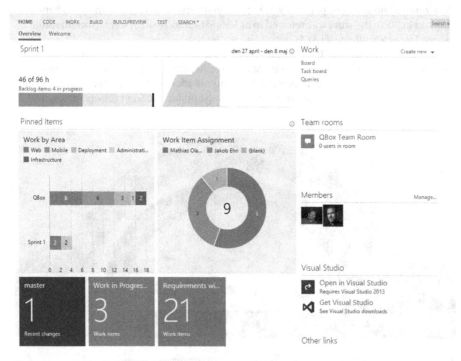

***Figure 2-2.*** *Team Foundation Server Web Access home page*

## Process Templates

Team Foundation Server ships with three different process templates that serve as a foundation for your software development process:

- Scrum
- Agile
- CMMI

These templates are "blueprints" for your project, which means that you can start by choosing the one that matches your process best, and then customize it to meet your needs.

No matter which process template you choose, you can use the different tools when managing your projects. These tools are examined in the following sections.

## Product Backlog

The product backlog is a prioritized list of requirements that you continuously refine with your stakeholders. Every team has its own backlog (if they want it), but it is also possible to aggregate these backlogs on a higher level.

Figure 2-3 shows the backlog view where you can easily create new backlog items and prioritize them by dragging each item up or down in the list.

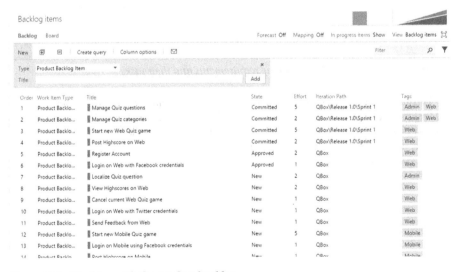

***Figure 2-3.*** *Working with the product backlog*

Depending on your development process, you might want to track bugs on the backlog, or you might want to handle them as tasks to an existing requirement. You can configure Web Access to handle both cases.

# Sprint Backlog and Task Boards

When following the Scrum methodology, a project is divided into a set of timeboxed *sprints*, each sprint being, for example, two weeks long. The product owner together with the team decides which backlog items have the highest priority; these items should be at the top of the product backlog and then assigned to the next sprint.

In the sprint, the development team works together to break down each requirement into smaller tasks that are detailed enough to estimate how many hours that particular task will take. In Figure 2-4, you can see the content of a sprint, where each requirement (in this case, one bug and one backlog item) has been broken down into a set of smaller tasks. To the right you can see the overall workload in this sprint for the team and for each team member.

***Figure 2-4.*** *The sprint backlog showing requirements and their tasks*

During the sprint, each member is responsible for updating the status of their tasks, and for grabbing new ones when they can. The status of all tasks can be viewed on the task board, as shown in Figure 2-5. Each card on the task board shows the title, who is currently assigned to the task, and the number of remaining hours.

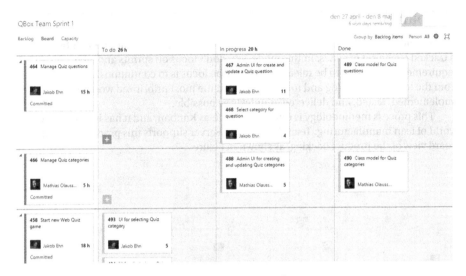

*Figure 2-5.* *The task board shows requirements across the states*

Updating the remaining hours of each task lays the foundation for the sprint burndown (shown in Figure 2-6), which is a graph that show how much work is left in the sprint and a trend line that indicates if the team is on track for the sprint or not.

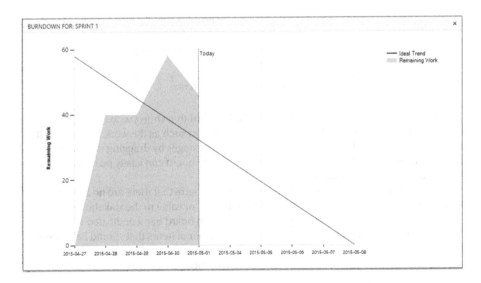

*Figure 2-6.* *A sprint burndown graph*

# Kanban Board

The product backlog can also be viewed as a board where each requirement or bug is tracked over a set of states. In this mode, you don't focus on sprints and when each requirement is planned to be released. Instead the focus is to continuously work from the top of the backlog and to make sure that the most prioritized work items get implemented, tested, and delivered as quickly as possible.

This process methodology is often referred to as Kanban, and it has its roots in the world of lean manufacturing. Team Foundation Server supports this process by using the board view of the product backlog, as shown in Figure 2-7.

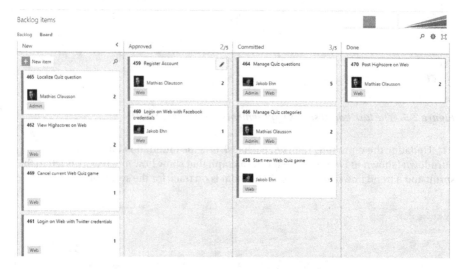

***Figure 2-7.*** *Kanban board showing the flow of requirements*

In this view, each requirement is displayed as a card that shows who is assigned what job, the currently estimated effort, and other information such as the work item id and the tags. Each card can then progress through the different stages by dragging them across the columns horizontally. The available columns in the board can easily be customized for each team to fit their process.

An important focus of a Kanban process is to make sure that there are no blocking points in the process; there should be a continuous flow of value to the stakeholders and end users. To facilitate this, every column in the Kanban board has a dedicated Work In Progress (WIP) limit that indicates the maximum number of items that should be assigned to that particular column. Also, a Cumulative Flow Diagram (shown in Figure 2-8) is available, which clearly shows the flow of value over time and can pinpoint if there are, or have been, steps in the process with low throughput.

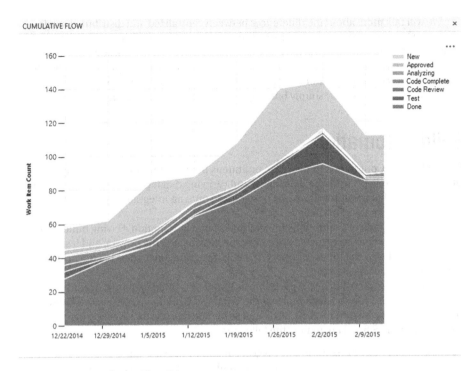

**Figure 2-8.** *Cumulative Flow Diagram*

# Source Control Management

One thing every TFS team uses is source control. Since the first version, TFS has shipped with a first-class centralized version control system that can handle any size project, including Microsoft itself. However, in the last five years the trend within software development has been strongly in favor of distributed version control, which is a paradigm shift compared to centralized VCS such as TFS, CVS, and Subversion.

It was quite a surprise when Brian Harry, program manager of Team Foundation Server at Microsoft, announced back in 2012 that Microsoft was implementing first-class support for Git within TFS and Visual Studio. What's important to understand is that this is not a Microsoft-specific variation of Git; it is a full fidelity implementation of the Git protocol. This means that you can use any Git client out there, on any platform, and use TFS as your source control provider. And you can use Visual Studio as a Git client against any hosted Git server, such as GitHub or BitBucket.

What Microsoft does bring to the table is support for *Enterprise Git*, which means things such as repository and branch security, commit policies, and integration with work items and build automation.

We will talk more about the differences between centralized and distributed version control in Chapter 5. When it comes to the process of Continuous Delivery, it doesn't really matter if you choose a distributed or a centralized version control system. What is important is that everything that is part of the automated build and deployment pipeline is stored in a versioned repository so that you at any given time can reproduce a given version of the application by simply building the same commit or changeset.

# Build Automation

A crucial part of Continuous Delivery is Continuous Integration, which is the process of taking every changeset from the developers and verifying that it compiles, that all the unit tests still work, that the application can be deployed onto an integration environment, and that the smoke tests succeed.

The cornerstone of Continuous Integration is build automation. Having builds that run on every new changeset quickly becomes the heartbeat of the project, and it should beat successfully several times every day. If it fails, the team must make it a top priority to fix the build as soon as possible.

With Visual Studio 2015, Microsoft ships a brand new build system, currently referred to as Build vNext, which replaces the Windows Workflow XAML-based build engine that shipped with TFS 2010, 2012, and 2013. The reasons for investing in a whole new version of TFS Build are mainly the following:

- **Easy customization**: The biggest pain point with the existing XAML build system was build customization. Learning Windows Workflow just to add a few simple build steps required learning a new language and toolset plus a lot of project infrastructure to get the designer experience working properly. In most cases, what developers or build managers want to do is to run scripts at a certain point in the build process. The new build system focuses on this.

- **Cross-platform support**: Supporting only Windows is no longer an option for Microsoft. The new build system comes with a cross-platform agent that runs on both Linux and Mac OSX.

- **Better use of build resources**: The new build system has no concept of a controller that is tied to a project collection. Instead, you define one or more agent pools, and then you install build agents that belong to a pool. There can be multiple build agents on the same machine, and they can belong to different pools as well.

- **Don't mess with my build output**: Another concern with the XAML-based build system was the way that it by default changed the way the output of the build ended up. One of the key principles of the new build system is that *Dev build = CI Build*, which means that there should be no difference in building your application on your local compared to the build server.

Figure 2-9 shows the web UI for creating build definitions. A build definition is simply a set of tasks that are executed in a particular order.

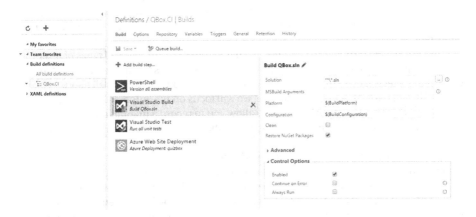

*Figure 2-9.* *Authoring build definitions in TFS 2015*

---

■ **Note** All the tasks that ship with TFS and the build agent itself are open sourced at GitHub, at `https://github.com/Microsoft/vso-agent-tasks` and `https://github.com/Microsoft/vso-agent`.

---

The new build system runs side by side with the old build system, now referred to as "XAML builds." You can even have standard build agents and XAML build agents running on the same machine. TFS will continue to support XAML builds for the foreseeable future, but don't expect any new functionality here. The message is clear from Microsoft: for all new investments that you do in TFS build automation, you should use the vNext system. If you have done a lot of customization with XAML builds, keep them around but start planning for migration.

---

■ **Note** Even though this build system is brand new, it is the recommended way to work with build automation when using TFS going forward. For this reason, we will use this system for implementing build automation in this book. Note, however, that everything we show can also be done using XAML builds.

---

# Test Management

Maintaining high quality throughout the lifecycle of the application is of course of uttermost importance. There are several ways of measuring and enforcing software quality, but no doubt a successful testing strategy and implementation is one of the most important.

As you will see throughout this book, Visual Studio ALM supports all types of tests common during the lifecycle of a project. This includes unit tests, automated acceptance tests, manual tests, and exploratory testing. Since Continuous Delivery is all about automating all parts of delivering software, we will focus on the automated tests. The testing tools in Visual Studio ALM actually allow you to record a manual test and later generate code for it that can be used as an automatic regression test to verify the same behavior.

Unit tests are developed and maintained within Visual Studio. Since the 2012 release, Visual Studio supports multiple testing frameworks such as NUnit, XUnit, and MSTest.

When it comes to manual tests, these are authored either using the web access or using a separate tool called Microsoft Test Manager. Under the hood, manual tests are defined using a work item type called Test Case, and can be grouped into test suites and test plans to match the release cycle of your project. Figure 2-10 shows a test plan with a few test suites and test cases in the web UI.

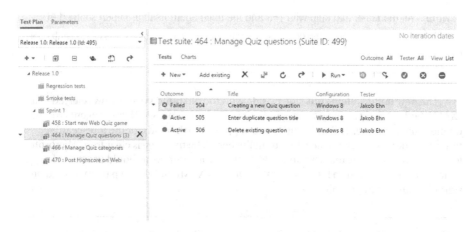

***Figure 2-10.*** *Managing test plans, test suites, and test cases*

Running the tests can also be done using either the web access or the Microsoft Test Manager (MTM) client. The biggest difference between them is that MTM can collect a lot of diagnostic information during the test run, which is very valuable if a bug is found during the test. When the tester posts a bug into TFS, the diagnostic information is automatically attached to the bug, making it much easier for the developer to understand and reproduce the bug. Figure 2-11 shows the MTM test runner in action. The MTM test runner guides the tester through the steps of a test case.

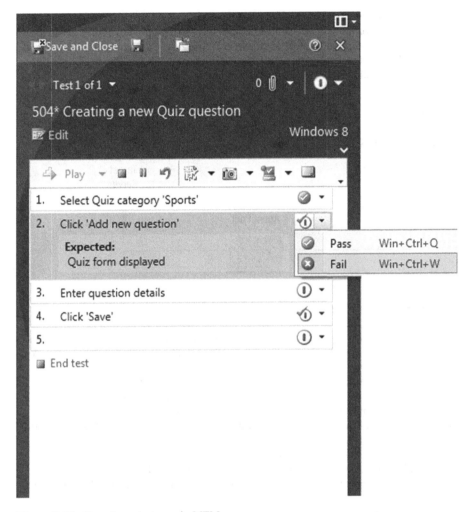

*Figure 2-11.* *Running a test case in MTM*

# Release Management

For quite some time, there was a gap in the Visual Studio ALM suite around deployment and release management. The toolset allowed you to do everything up until when you produced a set of versioned binaries and packages ready for deployment. From there you had to either roll your own or look for other vendors in the market.

That changed in 2013 when Microsoft acquired InRelease from InCycle Software Inc., which was then renamed Visual Studio Release Management.

Visual Studio Release Management provides the tools for deploying a certain version of the application components to various target servers in different environments, in a controlled and fully audited fashion, as shown in Figure 2-12. Configuration management is built into the product, letting the team define all environment-specific variables, such as database connection strings and file paths, in one secure place.

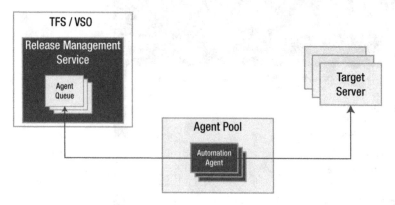

*Figure 2-12.* *Visual Studio Release Management architecture*

It also implements an approval workflow on top of the deployment pipeline that lets different roles in the organization verify and approve a deployment before it moves on to the next environment.

Since the acquisition, Microsoft has added several new features. The most important one is revamping the deployment pipeline to rely on PowerShell, and more specifically PowerShell DSC (Desired State Configuration), as the deployment mechanism. This also means that it is no longer necessary to install a deployment agent on the target machines.

Visual Studio Release Management also integrates directly with Microsoft Azure, exposing all of your existing environments and servers, making it very easy to set up automatic deployment across the different environments that are available in your Azure subscription.

In Team Foundation Server 2015 Update 1, Microsoft ships a major new version of Visual Studio Release Management that replaces the existing version. The new version is entirely web-based and uses the same task platform with the new build automation system. In this book, you will use this new version to implement a Continuous Delivery pipeline for your sample application.

We will explore Visual Studio Release Management thoroughly through the rest of this book, since release management is a foundational part of Continuous Delivery.

# Cross-Platform Support

In the last year or so, the world has realized that Microsoft is no longer the company that it used to be. They have broken down several barriers, the most noteworthy of which was the decision to open source the entire .NET Framework and related technologies on GitHub.

Microsoft has also realized that they can't force their customers to be all-in on Windows; they need to embrace more and more platforms since this is where the software industry is moving. There are many examples of this, such as the possibility to create virtual machines running Linux in Azure, and the collaboration with Docker to bring support for the popular container technology to the Windows platform.

Within the developer tools platform, there has been lots of investment in supporting cross-platform mobile development, both using the Xamarin platform built on top of Mono.NET and the Apache Cordova framework (previously known as PhoneGap), which is based on JavaScript and HTML.

At the //Build 2015 conference, Microsoft even revealed a completely new IDE called Visual Studio Code that runs on Windows, Mac, and Linux, and supports the development of modern web applications using languages such as C#, JavaScript, TypeScript, and HTML. It has IntelliSense and support for debugging. At the time of writing, it is still in preview.

Also, the new build system mentioned above has agents for running both on Linux, Mac, and Windows.

# Integration and Extensibility

Extensibility has always been important for Microsoft, and Visual Studio is built as an extension itself where everything that you use is an extension to the default Visual Studio Shell.

Team Foundation Server has had a great client object model from the start, but there have been some important pieces missing when it comes to extensibility. These pieces have been added in TFS 2015, and the extensibility story is now very strong.

## REST API

The client object model that has shipped since the first version of TFS is a set of .NET class libraries. Although the functionality was very powerful, the lack of support for other platforms and the fact that you must install Visual Studio Team Explorer to get the client object model on a target server caused a lot of problems for partners and organizations that wanted to extend TFS.

Enter the REST API. All new functionality that Microsoft currently ships comes with a REST API that can be accessed from anywhere and that uses standard web authentication protocols such as OAuth. This opens up a lot of new integration opportunities, for example in the area of mobile applications that can't use the current client object model.

Here is an example of a REST API endpoint that returns all build definitions in a team project:

```
http://TFS:8080/tfs/defaultcollection/QBox/_apis/build/definitions?api-version=1.0
```

This is a HTTP GET request against a server called TFS that returns all build definitions defined in the QBox team project. The response looks like this:

```
{"value": [{"batchSize": 1,"uri": "vstfs:///Build/Definition/3","queue":
{"queueType": "buildController","id": 3,"name": "Default Controller - TFS",
"url": "http://TFS:8080/tfs/DefaultCollection/_apis/build/
Queues/3"},"triggerType": "none","defaultDropLocation": "\\\\localhost\\
drop\\QBox","buildArgs": "","dateCreated": "2014-12-28T19:38:02.753Z","
supportedReasons": 63,"lastBuild": {"id": 119,"url": "http://TFS:8080/
tfs/DefaultCollection/e58abadf-cfef-49c5-82d8-4725b010ca9d/_apis/
build/Builds/119"},"definitionType": "xaml","id": 3,"name": "QBox.
CI","url": "http://TFS:8080/tfs/DefaultCollection/e58abadf-cfef-49c5-82d8-
4725b010ca9d/_apis/build/Definitions/3"}],"count": 1}
```

■ **Note** You can explore the full documentation for the REST API at www.visualstudio.com/integrate/.

# Service Hooks

Even though TFS supports all aspects of the application lifecycle, there are plenty of other vendors out there who deliver great solutions in the different areas of application lifecycle management. Instead of trying to force customers to stop using these solutions, TFS embraces them by allowing the end users to integrate with them instead.

This is done using *service hooks*, which enable you to perform tasks on other services when something happens in Team Foundation Server. A typical example of such an event is when someone creates a new work item or a running build is completed. This event will then execute a web request to an external system, for example to create or update a card on a Trello board or trigger a Jenkins build.

Examples of service hooks that ship with TFS 2015 include

- Trello

- Slack

- Campfire

- HipChat

- Azure

- Jenkins

There is also a general Web Hooks service that lets you integrate with any service that can be triggered by an HTTP POST request.

---

■ **Note** For a current reference list of available service hook consumers,

see www.visualstudio.com/en-us/integrate/get-started/service-hooks/consumers.

---

# Extensions (Apps)

As mentioned before, Visual Studio itself has been extensible from the very beginning. However, the most visible part of Team Foundation Server, the web access, has not been extensible at all. This has definitely changed in the 2015 release, with the introduction of *extensions*. Extensions are basically context-aware web pages that can be included at different places in the portal. These places are called extension points and can, for example, be a new tab at the top level or a new context menu item in the product backlog.

Figure 2-13 shows the Calendar extension that was published as a sample from Microsoft. This extension adds a new tab in the Home hub that shows a calendar for the team.

***Figure 2-13.*** *The Calendar web access extension from Microsoft*

---

■ **Note** Extending web access is available on Visual Studio Online, and will be shipped with TFS 2015 Update 1.

---

Looking ahead, Microsoft will provide a marketplace for web access extensions that will let end users easily locate and install third-party extensions. This is not available at the moment, but it is in the roadmap for extensibility.

# Application Insights

The last piece of the ALM puzzle is knowing how your application performs in the wild and how your users are using it. Application Insight is a cloud-based service hosted in Microsoft Azure that collects data from your applications and lets you visualize and search information within the Azure portal. Information is collected by adding an SDK to your applications that continuously sends telemetry to the portal. There are SDKs for most platforms, such as web applications, Windows store applications, Xamarin mobile applications, and Java applications. This telemetry contains detailed exception diagnostics as well as usage information, such as which pages users visit most frequently.

In addition to collecting telemetry from the application, Application Insights lets you monitor your applications from the outside by setting up simple ping messages or more complex web tests that can check if your application is accessible and if it works as expected (see Figure 2-14).

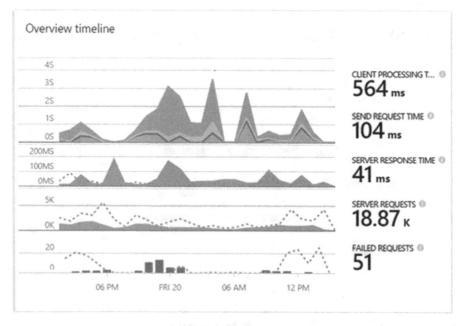

*Figure 2-14.* *Application Insights Overview timeline*

In Chapter 12, you will instrument your different application components with Application Insights and learn how this information can be accessed in the Azure portal.

# Visual Studio Online

As part of its cloud offering, Microsoft also supports Visual Studio ALM as a service. Named *Visual Studio Online*, it is an offering that contains all the parts mentioned above, but hosted in Microsoft Azure (see Figure 2-15). In addition, it offers cloud-specific services such as Cloud Load Testing, which lets you use Azure to scale up your load testing.

***Figure 2-15.*** *Visual Studio Online*

Almost everything you can do on premise using Team Foundation Server you can do on Visual Studio Online. The only major components that are missing in Visual Studio Online compared to TFS are the SharePoint team portal and the SQL Reporting Services TFS reports.

---

■ **Note** Another major limitation is that it is not possible to customize the process templates in Visual Studio Online; you can only use one of the three default templates as-is. Microsoft is currently working on this and the feature should be available in some form by the time this book is published.

You can read more about the roadmap for process customization in Visual Studio Online at http://blogs.msdn.com/b/visualstudioalm/archive/2015/07/27/visual-studio-online-process-customization-update.aspx.

---

There are a few other minor differences, and we will point them out throughout the book. If not stated otherwise, everything that we show in this book can be done either using TFS on premise or using Visual Studio Online.

## Summary

In this chapter we walked you through all of the major parts of the Visual Studio ALM suite. We have only scratched the surface of each part; the rest of the book will dive deeply into each area when you implement Continuous Delivery for your sample application using the tools and features mentioned in this chapter.

In the next chapter, you will take a brief look at the reference application QBox. You will use QBox as a baseline application for implementing Continuous Delivery using the Visual Studio 2015 ALM Suite.

# CHAPTER 3

■ ■ ■

# Designing an Application for Continuous Delivery

In this chapter we will set the stage for the examples in this book. To show you how to build a great Continuous Delivery solution, you will need some software to work with. You are going to use a fictitious application but the capabilities it implements are very real. Each chapter will add capabilities to the solution and show you in a concrete, how-to fashion how to implement the concepts using the tools in the Visual Studio 2015 platform.

## Scenario

You'll be working with QBox. Let's say it's a company that has been in the quiz business for a very long time. QBox's paper quiz products have always been appreciated by its customers. Unfortunately, the existing generation of players seems to be disappearing, and the younger generation is living in the digital world. So the decision has been made to bring QBox online. QBox has a reputation among its customers of offering a high-quality product and one that continuously comes up with new games. The development process for the new system must implement Continuous Delivery to live up to these demands so that changes can quickly be released feature by feature.

When planning the new application, you will focus on fulfilling the following high-level goals from the user perspective:

- As a player, I want to play a quiz using a web browser.

- As a player, I want to play a quiz using my phone.

- As a player, I want to see my game statistics.

- As an administrator, I want to manage players.

- As an administrator, I want to manage questions.

- As an administrator, I want to see game statistics.

Figure 3-1 shows the QBox application in action.

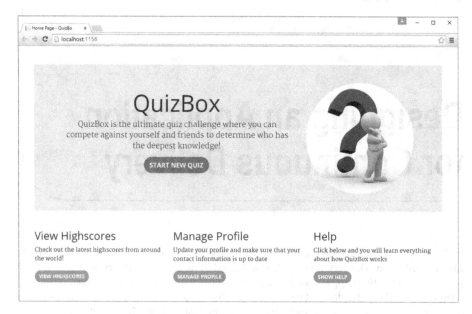

***Figure 3-1.*** *The QBox application*

# Architecture

Now that you know what the app does, let's take a look at how it's designed. The requirements for the application made us choose to have a web front end for the online application. The mobile app is developed for the three major platforms (iOS, Android, and Windows) and is made available through their respective marketplaces. To support the clients, we expose a REST API and the data is stored in a SQL Server back end. There is also an internal back-office client for administrating the system. And in the spirit of agile and Continuous Delivery we also have automated tests at various levels. Figure 3-2 shows the high-level architecture of the solution.

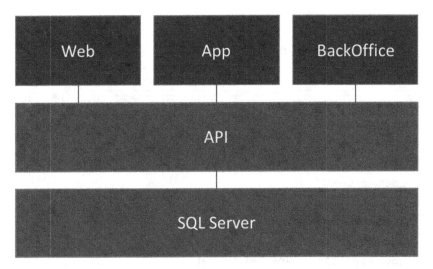

***Figure 3-2.*** *QBox architecture*

Let's take a look at the implementation. The entire QBox application is developed using a single solution. We prefer this approach since it lets all developers build the product the same way. The server build will also be configured to use the same solution. In Chapter 5, you will learn more about how to structure your code to make it easier to release feature by feature. Figure 3-3 shows the Visual Studio solution.

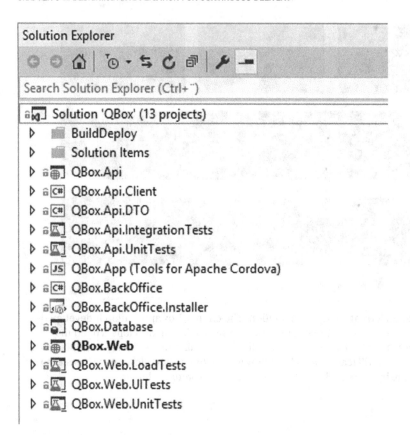

**Figure 3-3.** *The QBox Visual Studio solution*

The following is a quick description of the projects in the solution. We will go into the details of each project in later chapters when we look at how to integrate the development with the Continuous Delivery process.

- **QBox.Api**: This is an ASP.NET Web API project implementing the REST services. The API connects to the database for managing the quiz data.

- **QBox.Api.IntegrationTests**: These are integration tests for the API, implemented as Visual Studio unit tests that execute web requests against the REST API.

- **QBox.Api.UnitTests**: This is the unit test project for the API, implemented as Visual Studio unit tests.

- **QBox.App**: The mobile app, implemented as an Apache Cordova cross-platform project to target different mobile platforms using a shared codebase.

- **QBox.BackOffice**: The back-office client is a Windows application implemented using C# and WPF.

- **QBox.BackOffice.Installer**: To create an installation package for the back-office client, we use the Windows Installer XML (Wix) toolkit. Building the Wix project will produce a Windows installer MSI file. There are other options for creating installers for Windows applications; we will discuss the different packaging options in Chapter 7.

- **QBox.Database**: We use a SQL Server database project to manage the database schema, reference data, migration scripts, and more. The project produces a DACPAC file, which we will use to deploy the database.

- **QBox.Web**: The public web application is built using ASP.NET MVC.

- **Qbox.LoadTests**: We use Microsoft performance and load tests as part of the release pipeline to continuously test the performance of the system to make sure that we don't introduce performance issues when adding new functionality.

- **Qbox.Web.UITests**: The automated tests to simulate end-user scenarios are implemented as Coded UI tests and Selenium tests.

- **Qbox.Web.UnitTests**: The web application also has a unit test project. These tests are implemented using NUnit.

# System Requirements

The QBox application has the following requirements:

- **Web**: Runs on the latest versions of IE, Chrome, and Firefox

- **Back Office client**: Runs on Windows 7 and later

- **App**: iOS, Android, and Windows Phone

- **API**: IIS 8 on Windows Server 2012 or later

- **Database**: SQL Server 2012 or later

# Environments

The way the system is designed actually makes it very flexible when it comes to deployment. We can deploy the entire system on internal servers, use a public cloud, or anything in between. And we can deploy it on one or many servers depending on needs such as scalability and availability.

We decided to use Microsoft Azure to host all environments for the project. Since we want to be able to change where we run the system, we will use some Platform as a Service (PaaS) services and some Infrastructure as a Service (IaaS) services instead of relying on one particular solution. Hosting QBox in the cloud also gives us the benefit of easy access to cloud-based solutions, such as load testing in Visual Studio Online and application monitoring using Application Insights.

Figure 3-4 shows how the separation of responsibilities changes when going from an on-premises solution to a cloud-provided platform. With a good design you should be able to choose the best solution for your needs based on price, performance, availability, or any other factor that's important to you and your customers.

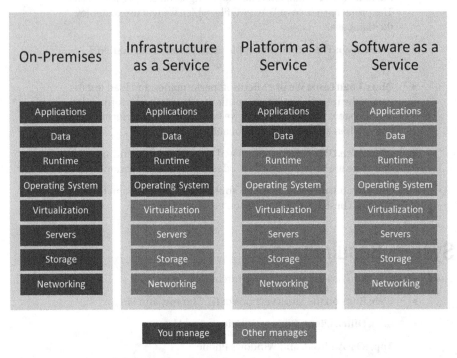

***Figure 3-4.*** *Responsibilities on-premises vs. hosted*

The mobile apps will be published to an internal store during development and testing. When a release goes to production it will be made available in the public marketplaces. The internal stores will be managed using HockeyApp (http://hockeyapp.net/), a service for mobile development provided by Microsoft.

Figure 3-5 shows how the environments are designed for the different stages in the release lifecycle.

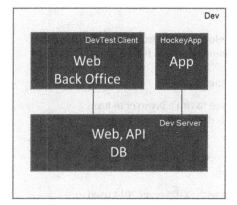
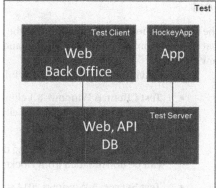
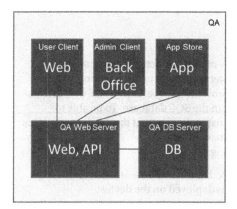
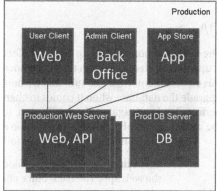

*Figure 3-5.* *Dev, test, and production environments*

Next, we'll look at the setup for each of the environments.

# Development

The development environment is used for the team's testing during development. The environment should be updated continuously.

The development environment consists of the following:

- **DevTest Client**: A Windows 7 client used to run a browser to test the web app. The back-office client is deployed on the devtest machine for testing.

- **HockeyApp**: Internally during development and testing the app can be downloaded from HockeyApp.

- **Dev Server**: A Windows 2012 server with SQL Server 2012 used to host the web application, the API, and the database.

## Test

The test environment is set up quite like the development environment; the difference is that the environment is updated on-demand when the system testers are ready to test a new release.

The test environment consists of the following:

- **Test Client**: A Windows 8.1 client used to run a browser to test the web app. The back-office client is deployed on the devtest machine for testing.

- **HockeyApp**: Internally during development and testing the app can be downloaded from HockeyApp.

- **Test Server**: A Windows 2014 server with SQL Server 2014 used to host the web application, the API, and the database.

## QA

The QA environment is set up like a smaller copy of the production environment and is updated on-demand when the acceptance testers are ready to test a new release. In this environment, we make sure that we don't throw away any existing data, but instead upgrade the database when it comes to changes in the SQL database. To be able to perform load tests against the application, we must make sure that the database contains the same amount of data as the production database does.

The QA environment consists of the following:

- **Test Client**: A Windows 8.1 client used to run a browser to test the web app. The back-office client is deployed on the devtest machine for testing.

- **HockeyApp**: Internally during development and testing the app can be downloaded from HockeyApp.

- **QA App Server**: A Windows 2014 server used to host the web application and the API.

- **QA Database Server**: A SQL Server 2014 used to host the database.

## Production

The production environment is similar to the QA environment; the difference is that there are multiple application servers. The production environment is updated when the release team is ready to do the release.

The production environment consists of the following:

- **User Client**: A Windows 7, 8, or 8.1 client used to run the web app.

- **Admin client**: The back-office client is deployed on the Windows 8.1 admin client machine for testing.

- **App Store**: The mobile apps are published to the respective marketplaces for each platform.

- **Production App Servers**: Windows 2014 servers used to host the internal web application and the API. For the public API we'll use Azure Websites.

- **Product database server**: A SQL Server 2014 hosting the database.

We will cover environment management in depth in Chapter 9.

# Summary

So now you know what the application is about. As you have seen, it is a simple application but the platform needed to support it is non-trivial. To implement a Continuous Delivery process for QBox, you will need to solve most of the challenges found in most systems today. Let's get started!

■ ■ ■

# CHAPTER 4

# Managing the Release Process

There are many things that must be done in a development project before it's possible to create a release. In this chapter, you will look at the logistics involved in planning for a release and how you can use TFS to make it easier to follow the process. By using work item tracking in TFS you get another benefit: a lot of data gets captured about the work you do, which you can use to monitor how well the work is progressing (and the process is working).

Since this book is about Continuous Delivery, we want to show how you can get to a position where you can deliver software more frequently to your customers by using good development practices. It can be difficult to decide how often to do a release. Since most development projects have a high degree of complexity (and uncertainty), it's typical that you do both research and development. Therefore, planning development projects can be challenging, so setting a fixed date may not be the ideal strategy.

How often you deliver will in the end be a decision by your product owners based on what they believe is the most beneficial to the product, the users, and the company. You must have the best tools and processes to create the release in time and with good confidence.

## Planning Your Release

In an agile project, release planning is a key event where the product owners, stakeholders, and teams come together and commit to a plan for the delivery of the next product increment. The input is a prioritized backlog, the product vision, the business objectives, and team logistics such as availability and historical velocity. The output from the planning session will be a committed list of work to be done, plus dependencies and other important information to handle during the execution of the release. We will not dive into the details of the planning work as such because there are plenty of good resources for that. Instead we will look at how you can implement these ideas for Continuous Delivery.

# Defining the Release Process

Let's start with the process at a high level. To enable Continuous Delivery, you need an agile mindset. In a small project, you could very quickly get started with a Kanban approach where you add your work to a queue (backlog) and start building and releasing as soon as you can. In most projects, however, this isn't the reality since you have dependences with other teams and products to deal with. But this doesn't mean you need to accept the waterfall-ish big-plan-up-front approach. Instead you are going to apply the small team approach at scale. There are several approaches for scaling agile, such as the SAFe framework (www.scaledagileframework.com/) or Nexus (www.scrum.org/ Resources/What-is-Scaled-Scrum). The examples in this chapter will lean towards a SAFe approach but most processes will map pretty close to what we will describe later in the chapter.

First, you need a way to manage backlogs, both for planning and for execution. The next section will explain how to use TFS to manage this. You also need to decide how to structure your work. Should you plan for the releases ahead of time or should you just work and release when you're ready? Let's call this time-boxed vs. flow-based planning.

Time-boxed planning is like Scrum, where you plan iterations (sprints) and every iteration deliver a potentially shippable product increment. You can scale this and have releases after n number of completed sprints.

Flow-based planning, on the other hand, is the Kanban system, where you put work on a queue and complete items one by one as fast as your team can manage. Put to the extreme, a completed work item automatically becomes a release (in the spirit of Continuous Deployment) but it's more common to batch up work until it makes sense to create a release.

---

■ **Note**  This is an example, so let's not get into an argument whether Scrum or Kanban is time-boxed or not. Surely any process can be used, so this is just a common way of thinking.

---

With Continuous Delivery in mind, let's use the asynchronous releases model and the practice of "develop on cadence, release on demand."

- **Develop on cadence**: Large-scale development projects need synchronization, so developing fixed iterations helps you coordinate work between teams in a predictable way.

- **Release on demand**: Even if development is made under fixed assumptions, the release cadence does not have to follow the same pattern. What works best is dependent on many things, so just because you can release often doesn't mean you should. Find the strategy that works best for your project and assume it will change.

One way to decouple releases from development is to use SAFe's notion of release trains. Figure 4-1 shows the big picture of SAFe. We will not go into the details of SAFe here but the concept of release trains can be useful when planning an agile project so let's focus on that aspect of the picture.

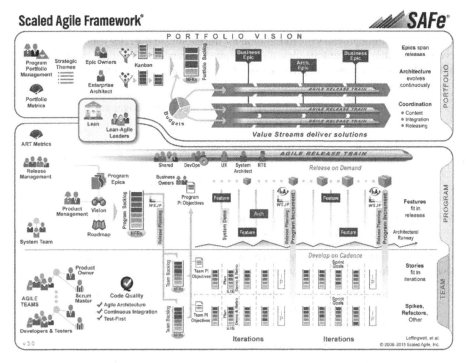

***Figure 4-1.*** *The Scaled Agile Framework (SAFe)*

The top part shows portfolio management. At this level, you set the long-term goals for development and define the release cycles (trains) to deliver value to your business. At this level, work can be tracked as Epics in the TFS Scrum template and typically managed using Kanban boards.

Next is the program management level where you focus on what needs to be done to deliver value in one release train. Here you need to coordinate work across teams to ensure a productive environment. It is also at this level that you create the releases (on demand). The work is managed using Features in TFS and is typically tracked using Kanban.

At the third level is the team. The team will focus on its part of the backlog and work to deliver features to the release train. The work is tracked using Product backlog items and Tasks, and you can use either iteration-based planning with task boards or Kanban if you prefer a more queue-based approach.

Development is a team effort, so when it comes to releasing you want a solution where anyone potentially can deploy and release the product to different environments. You want this automated as much as possible; it should be done from day one and used in all stages. Chapter 10 covers release management in depth and how to formalize the deployment and release process.

# Versioning

Software versioning provides the foundation for traceability in the release process. A version number is the unique identifier for a product version and should contain parts that can be used to understand what to expect from this version. The following is a good strategy for version number elements:

- **Major**: Incremented when significant or breaking changes are made to the product

- **Minor**: Incremented when adding backwards-compatible functionality

- **Patch**: Incremented when making backwards-compatible bug fixes

- **Build or Revision**: Optional part but useful to determine the source that produced the release

It's a good idea to apply the version to most of the work you produce during development, including the following:

- **Code**: Label the code representing the release with the version number. If you create release branches, apply the version to the branch name.

- **Work**: Assign the product version to backlog items and features to trace which version they were released in. Assign version to bugs (found in).

- **Build**: Include the version in the build name. Configure the build template to set the version in the build result (file version on executables, etc.).

- **Release**: Make the release number the version of the build to release and include the version in the release.

If you follow these principles consistently, you can correlate the different objects using the version. For instance, you can go from a file version found on a production server to the build used to produce it to the source code used in the build. This is useful in all form of analysis, such as audits or troubleshooting.

If you want to apply a new versioning strategy to your development, we recommend starting with the ideas from semantic versioning (http://semver.org/). Semantic versioning offers formalized rules to apply when comparing versions of components in a system. At the binary level, this is used to determine whether modules are compatible or not, but it's just as applicable to software compatibility questions in general.

In Chapter 7, you will apply a version strategy when building your software. This is a key component to enable good traceability in the whole development process. In Chapter 9, you will take this further when creating releases and deploying to your environments.

## Release Notes

An important part of the release process is producing the release notes. This is a document created for the end user of the product and it contains the details of the release.

With TFS it is easy to map work items to a release and use the work items to generate parts of the release notes. Together with the build or release management system, you can generate most, if not all, of the document automatically if you want to, which can make the release process consistent.

As a starting point, a release notes document should contain these elements:

- Product name

- Product version

- Date of the release

- Release summary

- System requirements

- How to obtain the release

- New features

- Fixed issues

# Building a Release Plan

In this section, you will use TFS to set up the foundation for a development environment that will support frequent releases. To do this, you need to configure a bunch of things; you need to think of how to structure your work and you may also need to consider using levels of abstraction to manage complex or time-consuming work. Then you must create the backlog for the release, which you can divide into smaller and more detailed backlogs if needed.

## Structuring the Releases

Let's start by thinking about what the release structure should look like. You will use iterations in TFS to support the release structure. Here you often have a choice between a time-box approach or a flow approach. With time-boxed planning, you create a schedule of your releases and add iterations under the releases, as shown in Figure 4-2.

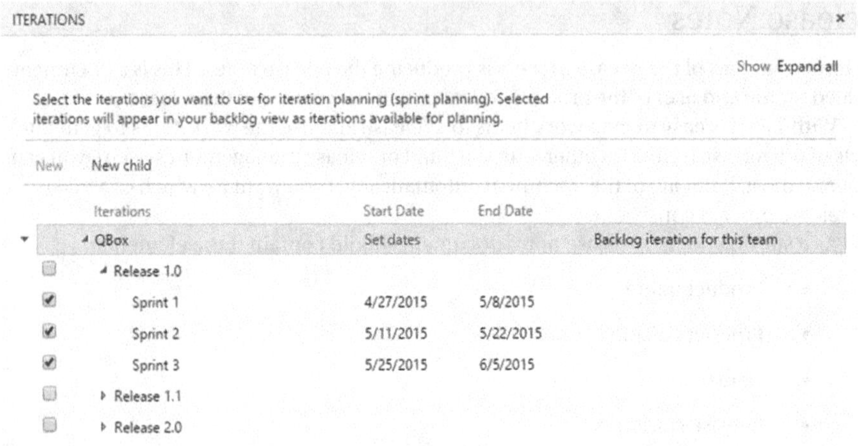

**Figure 4-2.** *Iterations for timeboxed planning*

Another way of structuring is to focus on the product increments and add sprints under them. The product increments can map to one or more epics and are planned up front. A product release is created when there is demand for it, so the release versions are not in the planning structure at all. This is a way of planning that is more optimized for Continuous Delivery. Figure 4-3 shows an example of iterations organized by product increments.

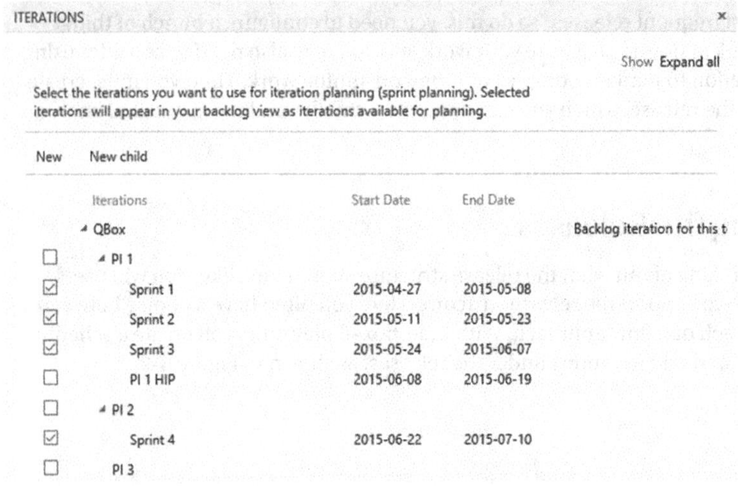

**Figure 4-3.** *Iterations for flow-based planning*

---

■ **Note**   If you want to track more information about a release, you can create a custom
work item type that represents a release. The Release work item can then hold more
than just dates; it can contain the goal for the release, release documentation, links to the
features in the release, and so on. For information on how to create a work item type, see
https://msdn.microsoft.com/en-us/library/ms404855.aspx.

---

With the time aspect of planning in place, you also want to add a way to manage
work based on functionality. In TFS, you use *areas* to do this, as Figure 4-4 shows. Add
as much hierarchy as you need but don't create a lot of areas just from speculation since
it will clutter the UI and increase maintenance. It's common to use the Areas field to
support teams in TFS; this way each team assigns work items to their area and sets that
as the default in their team settings. For a larger product, this can be limiting, especially
when multiple teams work in similar parts of the product. In that case, we recommend
using the areas to represent the functions in the product instead.

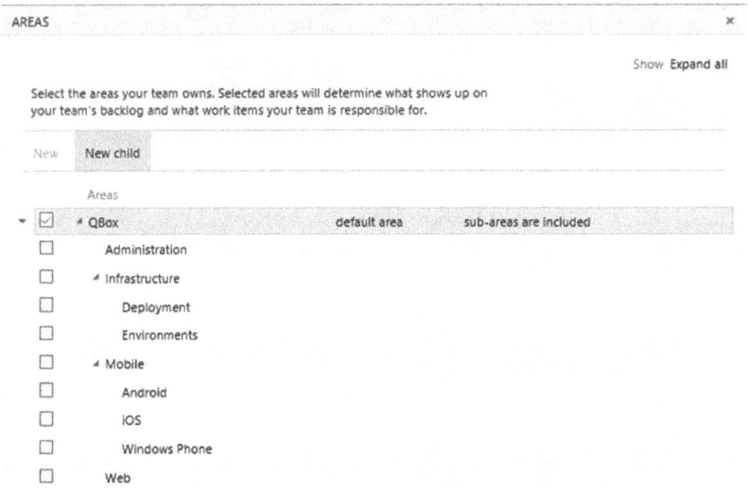

*Figure 4-4.*  *Areas for managing work by functionality*

# Enabling Scalable Release Planning

By default, work management in TFS will use a level suitable for individual teams. When
you want to do long-term release planning, this may not be sufficient. Fortunately,
you can add additional levels of backlogs to handle the scale you need in your project.
Figure 4-5 shows what the out-of-the-box backlog management tool looks like in a new
Scrum project.

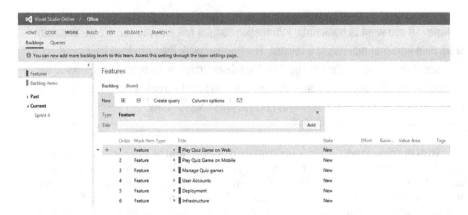

***Figure 4-5.*** *Default Scrum backlog settings*

To add an additional level to the backlog, go to the admin page for the team under Overview and Backlogs, and select the levels you want. In this case, since you're using the Scrum template, you have an additional epics level to choose from (Figure 4-6).

***Figure 4-6.*** *Selecting backlogs for the management team*

Now switch back to the Work ➤ Backlog view and hit Refresh. You will now see that the Epic level has been added as a level above Features (Figure 4-7).

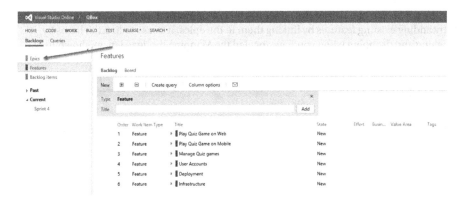

*Figure 4-7.* *Scrum backlog with the Epic level added*

# Creating a Release Backlog

After setting up the initial structure, you can start adding the work for your development. The type of work you're adding should go into the correct backlog. The following list is an example of how the different items can be regarded:

- **Epic**: Large items typically tracked at the program level; may span releases.

- **Feature**: Medium size items tracked at the project level; typically completed within a release.

- **Backlog item**: Small items tracked at the team level; completed within a sprint.

Figure 4-8 shows a few epics added to the backlog.

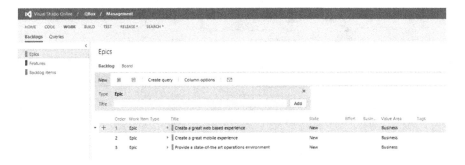

*Figure 4-8.* *Adding features to the backlog*

Next, you can detail the epics either by create features from them (using the + button) or by adding existing features by linking them to the epics. It's easy to link the items by dragging and dropping when you have toggled the Mapping mode to On, as shown in Figure 4-9.

***Figure 4-9.*** *Assigning a feature to an epic*

The result can then be listed by backlog level or you can use the relationships and see related items. Figure 4-10 displays an expanded section of the backlog, showing how easy it is to drill down to see the details of items at any level.

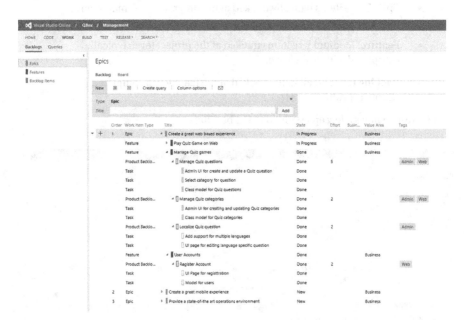

***Figure 4-10.*** *Managing a backlog from the Epic level*

# Managing Dependencies

All projects have to deal with dependencies between parts in the system. This can be simple things like the order in which items need to be implemented to more complex things like a dependency on an external contract for an integration. Regardless, you need to have a way to manage this so you have control over the dependencies.

A good way to manage dependencies between items in TFS is to use links. Just link dependent items with an appropriate link type (there are plenty to choose from so, such as the Affected By, Predecessor, or Successor link types). If you work a lot with dependencies, you may even want to add a custom link type for that.

Just linking items doesn't make them very visible as having dependencies. There is no specific feature in TFS to manage this, but one way to handle it is to take advantage of a new feature called *work item styles*. Styles allows you to define a formatting rule that gets applied to work items based on the state of the work item. Let's add a customization so that items tagged with Dependency show in red on the board.

Open the settings (⚙) for the board and select Styles. Add a new style with a rule where tags containing the word Dependency are assigned the color red. Figure 4-11 shows the completed style for highlighting items with dependencies on the board.

***Figure 4-11.*** *Creating a work item style for dependencies*

If you look at the board now, you can see how items tagged with Dependency show clearly (Figure 4-12).

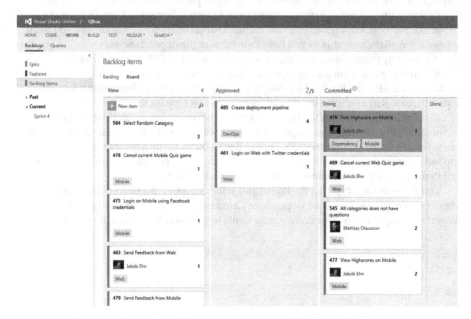

***Figure 4-12.*** *Board showing items with dependencies in a different style*

# Creating Team Backlogs

When using TFS for release planning, it can be a challenge to get a good overview of all the work that is going on in the project. To address this, you can create a team that represents smaller units that each own a part of the backlog. This way you can have one team that manages the release plan and several feature teams responsible for the development of functionality in their specific area. Each team can have its own settings and customizations to make the experience even better.

To add a team, go to the team project administration page (Figure 4-13).

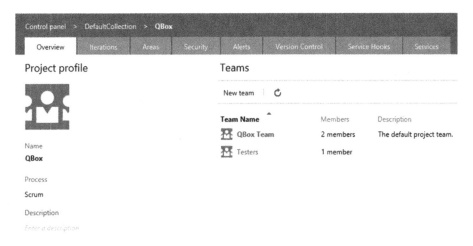

***Figure 4-13.*** *Team project administration*

Select the New team option and fill out the dialog (Figure 4-14). Make sure to un-check the Team Area check box; you don't want the tool to create an area for the team because you will choose which areas you're interested in later. This is a subjective thing, so if you want to assign work items to a team and don't see a use for many levels of areas for your teams, go for the areas by team setting.

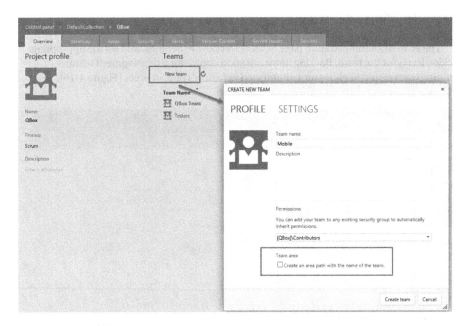

***Figure 4-14.*** *Adding a new team*

Next, assign backlog levels, areas, and iterations for your team. From the Home page, select the team (Figure 4-15).

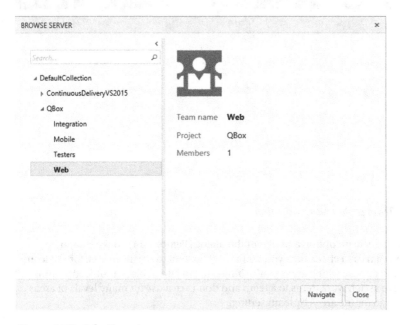

***Figure 4-15.*** *Selecting a team*

The go to the administration page, select Overview ➤ Settings, and set the appropriate backlog levels for the team. Backlog items are good choice for a development team; a planning team would likely be more interested in features and/or epics (Figure 4-16).

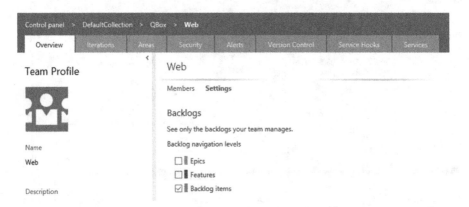

***Figure 4-16.*** *Selecting backlog levels for a team*

You should also select the iterations (Figure 4-17). Make sure to select the leaf levels or the sprints will not show in the backlog.

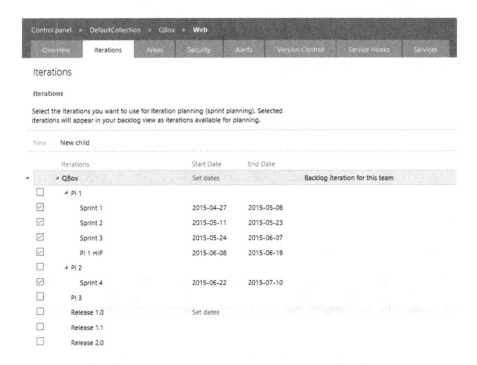

***Figure 4-17.*** *Selecting iterations for the team*

And finally select the areas the team is responsible for (Figure 4-18).

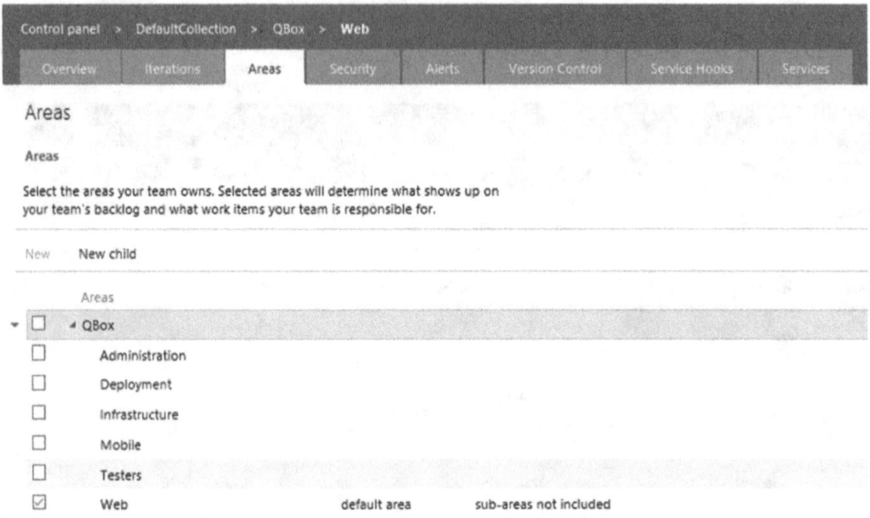

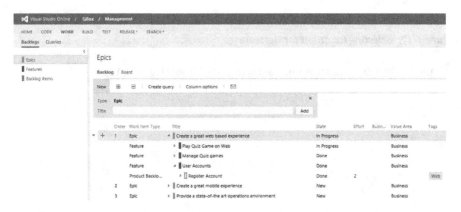

*Figure 4-18. Selecting areas for the team*

With the team feature you now have a good way to let the product planners have one view (Figure 4-19) where they can see all the work to be done at a high level. As shown in the example, the management team is not using any iterations since they may not be relevant to their work.

*Figure 4-19. Backlog view for the Management team*

The Web team now has its part of the backlog in focus (Figure 4-20). As you can see, they have selected iterations because that is very central to the way they work.

*Figure 4-20.* *Backlog view for the Web team*

# Monitoring the Release Process

Now that you have a process for managing your releases, you need to make sure it's working. Feedback and data visualization are very important parts of the process, so you need to understand what TFS can do to help make it easier to capture data from the process.

The metrics that are most useful will depend on what is most important to you; this will also change over time. In general, it's a good idea to track the current state of work, if there are any blocking items, and if there are any queues preventing you from delivering at a good pace. Cycle times are another metric that is useful for understanding behaviors in the release work, which can help improve the process. Let's take a look at how to use TFS to visualize things that are important to you.

## Work Status

The first thing is keeping track of the current work status. This is important at any level of planning, and you can use the same tool in TFS to manage it. Most people prefer visual feedback and use the boards, but you can use work item queries to create status reports. In the latest updates of the Kanban and task boards, there are many enhancements. For instance, you can add custom fields, custom columns, and avatars. Figure 4-21 shows an example of a Kanban board with custom swim lanes and columns.

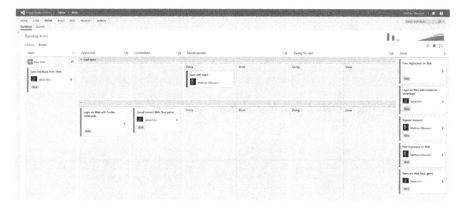

*Figure 4-21.* *Using backlog columns and lanes for good work status monitoring*

59

# Blocked Work

The next thing to watch out for is impediments or blocked work. In TFS, you can solve this in different ways. Some work item types have a Blocked field; in other cases, you can use a tag to annotate blocked items.

To quickly identify blocked items, you can again take advantage of work item styles. Let's add a style to color all blocked items orange.

Open the board settings and select the Styles tab. Add a new styling rule with the rule criteria set to match blocked items, Blocked = Yes in your case, and give it an appropriate color. Figure 4-22 shows the style dialog with the Blocked rules applied.

***Figure 4-22.*** *Adding a card style*

The blocked items are now shown in the defined style on the board (Figure 4-23).

***Figure 4-23.*** *Backlog with showing a blocked item*

You can also track blocked items using a work item query (Figure 4-24).

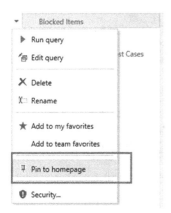

***Figure 4-24.*** *Work item query for blocked items*

The result from the query can be turned into a tile by adding it to the team's homepage, as shown in Figure 4-25.

***Figure 4-25.*** *Adding a work item query to the homepage*

If you go back to the homepage, you now have the Blocked Items query pinned item (Figure 4-26).

***Figure 4-26.*** *Blocked items as a tile on the homepage*

# Throughput

The third metric you want to track is how much work you have completed over time in order to see if you are improving or not. You can also use this flow metric to look for queues in the system in order to understand and avoid bottlenecks in the process. The cumulative flow diagram, CFD, is a great tool to manage throughput. In Figure 4-27, you can see how work moves over time and how much work you have at any given point in time.

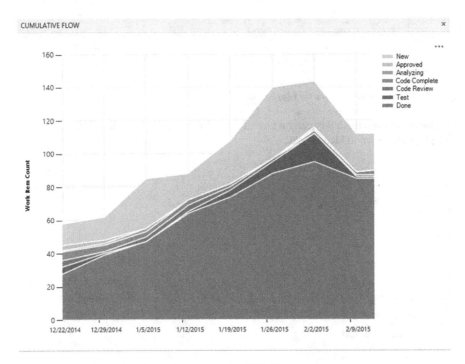

*Figure 4-27.* *Measuring throughput using the CFD diagram*

# Cycle Time

The last metric we want to touch on is cycle times. Cycle time analysis is similar to throughput analysis, but it focuses on how long it takes to move work from one state to another, not just looking at how much work you have in the queue, like in the CFD diagram. From a DevOps perspective, it's a good idea to measure time spent in states related to development/operation activities. If you want to improve the dev/test flow, you would look for time spent in these activities instead.

Other relevant cycle time metrics are mean time to repair (MTTR), the time on average it takes from when a problem has been identified until the resolution is in production. For a Continuous Delivery scenario, tracking mean time to delivery (MTTD) lets you analyze if you are improving time to delivery.

In TFS, it's more difficult to visualize this data since you need to do calculations to get the result. To analyze cycle times, you first need to define between which states you want to track time and then calculate the time spent for matching work items over time. If you're interested in the MTTD metrics, you define the time span to analyze. Then you select all Done work items between those dates. For each work item, calculate the time spent between states Approved to Done and finally calculate the average per week. Fortunately, you can get the data from the TFS warehouse (this works with TFS and not VSO) using a SQL query like this:

```sql
SELECT
        RIGHT
        (
                '0'
                -- Number of the week inside the year
                + CAST(DATEPART(wk, [Microsoft_VSTS_Common_ClosedDate])
                        AS VARCHAR)
                -- Separator
                + '/'
                -- Year
                + CAST(DATEPART(yyyy, [Microsoft_VSTS_Common_ClosedDate])
                        AS VARCHAR)
                -- Maximum length of the returned value (format: WW/YYYY)
                , 7
        ) AS [Week]
        -- Average Cycle Time in days, per each week
        ,AVG(
                DATEDIFF(dd, [Microsoft_VSTS_Common_ActivatedDate],
                        [Microsoft_VSTS_Common_ClosedDate])
                )
                AS [Average Cycle Time in days]
FROM
        [dbo].[CurrentWorkItemView]
WHERE
        [ProjectPath] = '\DefaultCollection\Sprint 3'
        AND [System_WorkItemType] = 'Product Backlog Item'
        AND [System_State] = 'Done'
GROUP BY
        -- Grouping by week and year to calculate the average
        DATEPART(wk, [Microsoft_VSTS_Common_ClosedDate]),
        DATEPART(yyyy, [Microsoft_VSTS_Common_ClosedDate])
ORDER BY
        -- Ordering by year and week number
        DATEPART(yyyy, [Microsoft_VSTS_Common_ClosedDate]),
        DATEPART(wk, [Microsoft_VSTS_Common_ClosedDate])
```

Figure 4-28 shows how Excel can be used to show the cycle time using the query above.

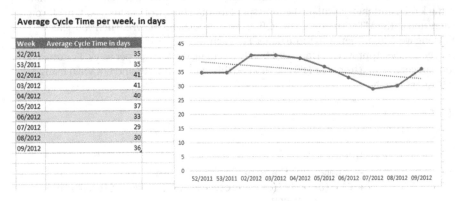

**Average Cycle Time per week, in days**

| Week | Average Cycle Time in days |
|------|---------------------------|
| 52/2011 | 35 |
| 53/2011 | 35 |
| 02/2012 | 41 |
| 03/2012 | 41 |
| 04/2012 | 40 |
| 05/2012 | 37 |
| 06/2012 | 33 |
| 07/2012 | 29 |
| 08/2012 | 30 |
| 09/2012 | 36 |

*Figure 4-28.* *Graph showing average cycle times per week*

# Summary

Planning a release is a challenging task that should not be taken lightly. At the same time, if you want to get your project going and not get stuck in lengthy process work, you should try to build on experience. Use existing patterns and solutions whenever possible. We believe there's a lot of goodness in a mindset where we develop on cadence and release on demand. This lets the team adjust the release pace as requirements change. We also favor automation, which has a lot of benefits, such as repeatability, speed, and self-service.

When you have your (initial) process in place, make sure you have good tooling to make if efficient. With the areas, iterations, and teams concepts in TFS, you can manage work at all levels in the product development process. Use the TFS customization points to make the backlogs even easier to use; add colors, columns, and lanes to make it fun to work with. Finally, define and monitor key metrics. Using metrics will help you visualize the release process and help you stay on track.

And remember that this is an iterative process, so make sure to continuously improve the process and tooling.

# CHAPTER 5

# Source Control Management

Version control is at the very heart of team software development. Organizations that are not using revision control in software development should be rare today.

Putting your changes into revision control gives you full traceability of all changes done to the application over time, allows you to roll back undesired changes, and enables parallel development using branches. You can also safely delete files that are currently not needed without having to worry if you might need them later. This is one reason that there should never be any code that is commented out. If the code is not needed, delete it. If it turns out that it actually was needed, you can easily restore it from version control history.

When it comes to version control tooling today, there are two major types that you can use: *centralized* and *distributed* version control. We'll start this chapter with a short overview of these types and how they differ. Team Foundation Server supports both types, with Team Foundation Version Control (TFVC) for centralized version control and Git for distributed version control, so we will take a look at these two in more in detail. The rest of the chapter will discuss branching and dependency management, and how these concepts relate to Continuous Delivery.

## Centralized vs. Distributed Version Control

Looking back at the history of version control systems, one can categorize them into three different generations[1]:

- **First Generation**: Lock-based version control systems working on one file at a time. Examples here are RCS and SCCS.

- **Second Generation**: Centralized version control, which supports working on multiple files at a time. Merging must be done before committing the changes to the server. Examples here include CVS, SourceSafe, Subversion, and Team Foundation Version Control.

- **Third Generation**: Distributed version control where every developer has a full copy of the source repository locally. Commits are done locally, and merging is done when the committed changes are flowed to or from the server.

---

[1]Eric Sink, A History of Version Control, `http://ericsink.com/vcbe/html/history_of_version_control.html`

Today the majority of version control systems in use belong in the second generation. But during the last decade there has been a strong momentum towards distributed version control, especially in the open source community where the workflow of distributed version control is a very natural fit.

In centralized version control systems, all changes must be checked into a shared server repository in order to share them with the rest of the team. To work efficiently, the developers need to be connected to the server most of the time. Due to its centralized architecture, it is possible to enforce very fine-grained security permissions, such as allowing a subcontractor to view and edit only parts of the source tree.

In a distributed version control system, every developer has their own copy of the source code, including full history. They can share changes between each other without any need to share them through a central server. This is one of the major reasons for its popularity in the open source community. One flipside is that since each developer must have the entire repository with full history locally, applying permissions and auditing is not as powerful as it is with centralized version control. For many enterprises, this is the main reason to not adopt distributed version control.

Although no central server is strictly necessary in order to work with DVCS, all but the smallest teams designate a central server repository to be the integration point, from which build automation will fetch the source code and run automated builds and tests. Without this, it is simply not possible to practice Continuous Integration. It also enables things like making backups at a regular basis.

Now, let's take a look at the two types of version control offered by TFS. When talking about these different types of version control in TFS, it should be noted that both version control types have almost full feature parity when it comes to ALM integration. Since Git is a relatively new addition to TFS, there are still some differences in this area, but for all new ALM features that are being added to TFS, Microsoft is committed to supporting both TFVC and Git.

---

■ **Note** You will sometimes see that the first version of a new feature might only support TFVC or Git, but this is more a sign of Microsoft applying the *crawl-walk-run* approach for new features than an indication of any version control type being favored over the other.

---

# Team Foundation Version Control

The first version of TFS shipped with a centralized version control system. Up until TFS 2013 this was the only kind of version control that was supported in TFS, so it was often just referred to as "TFS." With the addition of Git in TFS (see below) we now refer to this type of version control as *Team Foundation Version Control (TFVC)*.

TFVC revolves around the notion of *workspaces*. A workspace is the local copy of the team's codebase, and is mapped to one or more nodes in the source control tree. There are two kinds of workspaces, *server* and *local*:

- **Server**: Stores all information about the state on the server. All team members must publicly check out the files that they are working on, and must be connected to the server most of the time. Server workspaces can handle huge amount of files but have several drawbacks including poor offline handling and can often cause conflicts when developers are doing changes locally.

- **Local**: Team members can get a copy of the workspace and then work offline up until the changes needs to be checked in. Most operations are faster compared to server workspaces. The only real drawback is that the performance degrades as the number of files in the workspace increases.

Branching in TFVC is a server-side operation and the branches are path-based, meaning that different branches are mapped to different paths in the workspace. Therefore it is possible to switch between branches without checking in any changes. In general, branching in TFVC is considered to be a lot more "heavy" when compared to distributed version control systems like Git and often causes hard-to-resolve merge conflicts. There is some merit to these opinions but there are thousands of developer teams that successfully uses TFVC for large application development projects successfully. By following good developer practices such as checking in often and regularly merging the changes back to master, you should be able to do this without having too much trouble with merge conflicts.

The main strengths of TFVC are that it can support very large codebases without any problem, and that it allows very fine-grained control over permissions, down to individual files.

---

■ **Note**  For more information about Team Foundation Version Control, see
https://msdn.microsoft.com/en-us/library/ms181237.aspx.

---

# Git

Git is a distributed version control system, and was originally implemented by Linus Torvalds to support working with the Linux kernel. For the last five years, Git has been the major player when it comes to distributed version control systems. In Visual Studio 2012, Microsoft implemented first-class support for Git in TFS; it also added client support for Git in Visual Studio.

In Git, code is stored in *repositories*. To start working with a Git repository, the developer first *clones* the repository, which pulls down the entire repository with full history. Then all changes are made locally and are committed to the local repository.

To share changes done in a local repository with other developers (usually through a designated central repository), the local commits are pushed to the remote repository. After this, other developers can pull down the latest changes to their local repositories.

Branches in Git are a very lightweight operation. All changes (commits) in Git are stored as snapshots, and a branch is simply a pointer to a specific commit in the history graph. This means that switching branches in Git is just a matter of changing the pointer, which is a very fast operation. However, it also means that branches are path-independent, so any changes in a branch need to be committed before switching branches.

Again, we should emphasize that the Git implementation in TFS is a full fidelity implementation of the Git protocol, meaning that you can use any Git client on any platform to work against a Git repository in TFS. The only limitation at the moment is that TFS and VSO do not support the SSH network protocol. This is currently being investigated by Microsoft, so hopefully it will be supported in the near future.

---

■ **Note**  In TFS 2015 Update 1, Microsoft added the capability to add Git repos to an existing TFVC team project. Many companies have existing large team projects (using TFVC) with extensive version control and work item history, and up until this update they had to create a new team project and migrate the existing information to this new team project.

---

Git's main strengths are its support for committing locally, the ability to work fully offline, and its strong ecosystem of tooling across all of the main operation systems.

## Version Control and Continuous Delivery

When it comes to implementing Continuous Delivery, there really isn't a big difference which type of version control you are using. To implement Continuous Integration, you must designate a master/trunk branch somewhere to be the integration point from which your continuous integration server will pick up the changes. Whether this is a TFVC path or a Git repository in TFS doesn't matter that much.

Make sure you understand the pros and cons of the different types of version control, taking things such as the team experience, auditing, and security regulations into consideration when you select the type of version control for your projects. But no matter if you choose TFVC or Git, you will be able to apply Continuous Integration and Continuous Delivery using the practices and tools shown in this book.

---

■ **Note**  For more discussion on the differences between TFVC and Git, and some guidelines that may help you select the one most appropriate for your team, see https://msdn.microsoft.com/en-us/Library/vs/alm/code/overview.

---

# Branching and Continuous Delivery

The concept of branching and merging is central when it comes to version control. There are several reasons why a developer would decide to create a branch, such as

- To work on a new feature or bug

- To stabilize a new release

- To work on a larger refactoring

However, there is a tension between branching and Continuous Integration. The core of Continuous Integration is, as the name implies, to integrate continuously, preferably on every check-in. Creating a branch contradicts this purpose since you are not integrating your changes with the rest of the team every time you check in. Branching gives you isolation, but the downside is that you are postponing the merging operation that eventually must be done in order to integrate the changes. Most developers have experienced "big bang" merges where a branch that might have lived for several weeks or even months finally is merged back to main, leading to hundreds of conflicts. This is the opposite of Continuous Integration!

To implement Continuous Delivery and reap the benefits of it, you must make sure that you do integrate continuously, so you need to either avoid branching or keep your branches as short-lived as possible.

But how can you implement changes and new features to your codebase and still release frequently? First of all, you want to make sure that the quality of the code that goes into the master branch is as high as possible. We will discuss a few techniques that can be applied at the source control level, before the change is merged to master.

But then there are the changes that are part of a bigger change, perhaps a new feature. You obviously don't want to release incomplete or untested features to your users, so you need to find a way to make changes to your code and make sure that these changes are not visible to the users until they are complete. There are two popular patterns for doing this, *feature toggles* and *branch by abstraction*. We will discuss both patterns.

## Working on Mainline

Working towards Continuous Delivery and Continuous Deployment, where every check-in is automatically deployed all the way to production, means that you must take several measures in order to make sure that your changes do not break the mainline.

---

■ **Note**   The term *mainline* refers to the branch from which release builds are produced. Other common names for this are *trunk* or *master*.

---

In Chapter 10, you will look at implementing a deployment pipeline, which will take the changes through several stages before reaching the production environment. Each of these stages will apply different kinds of verifications, such as compilation, running unit tests, deploying the application to test and staging environments, and performing analysis on the codebase. If any of these stages do not succeed, the pipeline will stop and the change will not make it into production.

With regards to source control management, there are several things you can do in order to secure your master branch from potentially breaking code. The things that we will discuss here are a mixture of tooling and design patterns, but they all serve the same purpose: to keep the mainline deployable.

## Embracing Code Reviews

Keeping the main line stable often means that you need to increase the number of people that look at the code before it gets committed into the master branch. Using pair programming during development is a great practice, but applying a more formal code review process can also be very beneficial.

When using Git, the code review process is best done using *pull requests*. A pull request is made by creating a local branch where the changes are made. When complete, the local branch is published to the server from where a pull request can be created. This triggers a workflow in which one or more reviewers can look at the changes, comment on them, and either accept or reject the pull request. If the pull request is accepted, the changes in the branch are merged into the master and the original topic branch is (by default) deleted. Figure 5-1 shows an example of a pull request.

***Figure 5-1.*** *Pull request*

In the left part of the screen, all the changed files are listed in a hierarchical view. Note that a pull request can often contain several commits, but the pull request will merge these into one list of changes. The column in the middle contains the discussion that is done around the changes, both from the developer and the reviewers. When adding comments, reviewers can scope them to the whole pull request, a file, or an individual line within a file.

■ **Note**   Read more about conducting pull requests in Visual Studio Online and TFS at http://blogs.msdn.com/b/visualstudioalm/archive/2014/06/10/git-pull-request-visual-studio-online.aspx.

In Team Foundation Version Control, the concept of pull requests does not exist. Instead, you can request a code review using the My Work hub in Visual Studio Team Explorer, as shown in Figure 5-2.

***Figure 5-2.***  *Requesting a code review*

As part of requesting a review, you can select one or more reviewers and then submit the request. This will create a new shelveset in TFVC that the reviewers can inspect and comment on. Once complete, the shelveset can be unshelved and checked into the main branch.

Note that these techniques, pull requests and code reviews, serve the same purpose of having one or more reviewers approve the changes *before* they are committed to the master branch, thereby lowering the risk of bugs or other non-desirable code changes making it into the deployment pipeline.

# Applying Branch Policies

You can further improve the quality of the code that is committed to master by applying branch policies. These are currently available for Git repos only and their purpose is to evaluate different policies when code is pushed to a particular branch. Below we list the branch policies that are currently available in TFS, but we expect that more policies will show up over time.

## Code Review Requirements

This policy is used to enforce the use of pull requests for the entire Git repository or only for parts of it. Applying this policy will enforce that all changes going into your master branch must be done using pull requests. Figure 5-3 shows an example where a minimum of two reviewers must approve the pull requests, but only if there are changes below the path /QBox.Web/ in the Git repository.

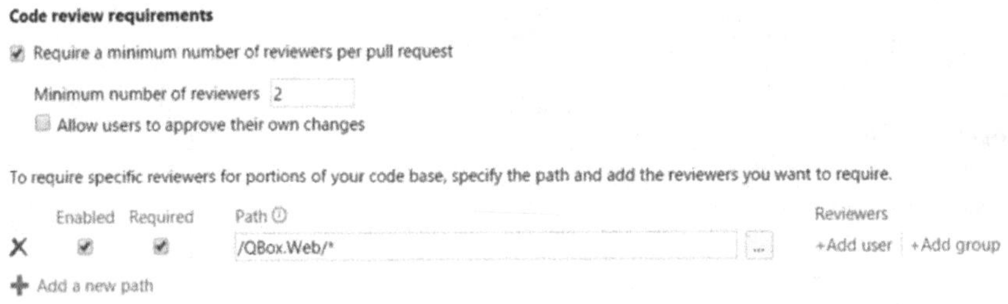

**Figure 5-3.** *Code review requirements*

## Automatically Build Pull Requests

This policy allows you to, in addition to running a pull request workflow as described above, also designate a particular build that must complete successfully in order for the pull request to be merged to master.

When this policy is enabled, a build will be queued when the pull request is created, and if the build fails, the pull request will automatically be rejected. Figure 5-4 shows an example of how this is configured.

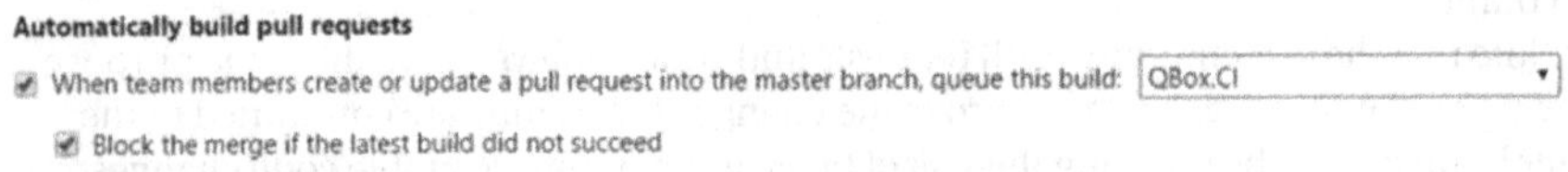

**Figure 5-4.** *Automatically build pull requests*

## Work Item Linking Requirements

The last branch policy that can be applied is not about the code itself, but is instead about enforcing that the change that is being done has a corresponding work item. This allows you to assert that no unplanned work is going into the master branch. You can configure if you want to block the merge of the pull request if there are no linked work items, as shown in Figure 5-5.

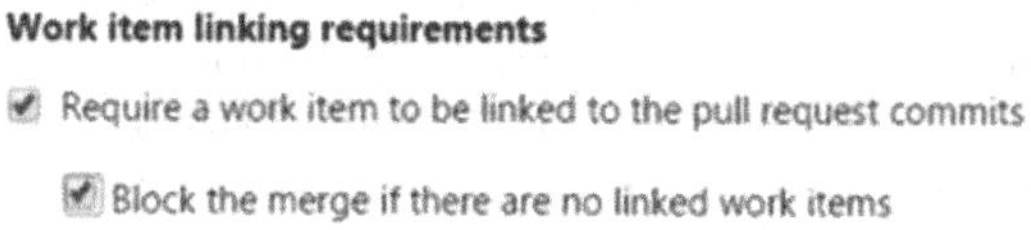

**Work item linking requirements**

☑ Require a work item to be linked to the pull request commits

☑ Block the merge if there are no linked work items

***Figure 5-5.*** *Work item linkinq requirements*

# Feature Toggles

A feature toggle is basically a conditional expression that lets you dynamically run or not run some parts of your code base, thereby enabling or disabling a certain feature. The value for the condition is usually stored in a database or in a configuration management system and can be dynamically changed. This lets you enable or disable a feature on the fly, either for all users or for just a smaller set of users depending on your implementation and business needs.

Here is an example of a C# implementation of a feature toggle, taken from the FeatureToggle repository available at GitHub at https://github.com/jason-roberts/FeatureToggle:

```
var toggle = new ShowMessageToggle();
if (toggle.FeatureEnabled)
{
    Console.WriteLine("This feature is enabled");
}
else
{
    // to disable the feature:
    // <add key="FeatureToggle.ShowMessageToggle" value="false"/>
    Console.WriteLine("This feature is disabled");
}
```

Feature toggles have several advantages in addition to letting you keep working on the mainline. It lets you implement A/B testing by enabling a new feature to some users but not to all. Then you can evaluate how the new feature is received and used, and make follow-up decisions based on that information.

■ **Note**   We will discuss A/B testing and canary tests in more detail in Chapter 11.

Microsoft uses feature toggles extensively for the development of Visual Studio Online to enable testing of new features to a smaller group of people before enabling them for everyone.

There are some drawbacks with feature toggles. The first one is that there is obviously always a risk that you will introduce an incomplete or untested feature to end users by mistake. In the worst case, this can cause security leaks or data corruption. Another potential risk is that the codebase over time becomes cluttered with feature toggles, making it harder to maintain. To reduce this risk, make sure that you enforce a policy to remove the feature toggles once they have been fully deployed into production; otherwise your code base can get swamped over time with conditional statements.

■ **Note**   For more information about feature toggles, see
`http://martinfowler.com/bliki/FeatureToggle.html`.

There are several different open source .NET frameworks for implementing feature toggles, such as FeatureSwitcher, FeatureToggle, and FeatureBee.

## Branch by Abstraction

An alternative to using feature toggles is to use a design that lets you gradually implement new functionality in the codebase, while the old functionality is still there and running. Once you are done, you switch the implementation and remove the old code.

This pattern is usually referred to as *branch by abstraction*, which is a bit misleading since it is about *not* creating a branch but instead implementing the changes in the main branch by introducing an abstraction layer. You start off by introducing one or more interfaces that abstract the existing functionality. Then you rewrite all the client code to use the new interfaces. Once this is done, you can start writing a new implementation for the interface that will implement the new functionality. This technique allows you to gradually add new functionality to the existing codebase and release it regularly.

■ **Note**   Jez Humble has a great post about branch by abstraction at
`http://continuousdelivery.com/2011/05/make-large-scale-changes-incrementally-with-branch-by-abstraction/`.

Note that not all changes can be implemented this way; particularly, UI changes can be tricky to abstract. When doing UI changes, if possible try to implement a new UI that lives side by side with the existing one, and switch to the new one when ready. For web applications, you can specify a new route for the new UI (/application/admin/new, for example).

# Branching Strategies

There is a famous quote that says, "Save your creativity for your product, not your branching strategy." This quote has a lot of merit to it: it is easy to create a branch but the work of merging it back to its parent branch can cause a lot of extra work and headaches over time.

If you do decide to use branching in your team, you should decide upon a model that servers a clear purpose and is understood by every team member. Here we will discuss a couple of branching strategies that are very common.

It should also be noted that when we talk about branches and strategies for them, we mean long-lived, published branches. When using Git, it is very common to create a local branch for every change that is being done. This is a good practice, and does not collide in any way with the principles of Continuous Integration.

## Branch by Release

The most common branching strategy is to create a branch for every release. Once all development is done and most of the testing has been completed, a release branch is created from main/trunk to stabilize the codebase. Once this is done, the new version is deployed to production and the release branch is tagged (Git) or labeled (TFVC) with a corresponding tag/label. This branching model is shown in Figure 5-6.

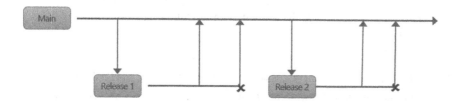

*Figure 5-6. Release branching*

This branching strategy lets the team start working on the next release while the current release is being tested and stabilized. Every change that is committed to the release branch is merged back to main as soon as possible so that you don't lose any changes that are being done during stabilization.

## Branch by Feature

Another branching strategy that can be combined with branch by release is known as branch by feature, or feature branching. This strategy, shown in Figure 5-7, focuses on the development of new features by working on them in an isolated branch, typically named after the feature that is being worked on.

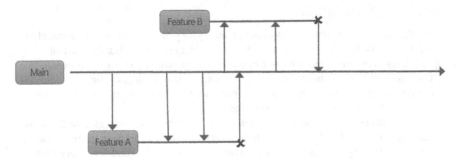

**Figure 5-7.**  *Feature branching*

If you are using TFS, you can create a feature branch for every feature or user story work item that is being assigned to you.

This strategy potentially lets the team select which features should be part of the release. If a certain feature is not ready in time for release, or maybe the team decides to scrap the entire feature, the branch is simply not merged back into the main branch. This does require that the application design is clearly separated and modularized; otherwise a change in one feature will affect other features, and this cherry picking of features will not be possible.

The downside of this branching strategy, as we will discuss in more detail later, is that it postpones integration to the main, thereby not following the principles of Continuous Integration.

---

■ **Note**   There has been a lot of discussion about feature branches and Continuous Delivery. Jez Humble has a nice write-up about it at `http://continuousdelivery.com/2011/07/on-dvcs-continuous-integration-and-feature-branches/`.

---

## GitFlow

GitFlow is a branching strategy for Git that was created by Vincent Driessen (`http://nvie.com/posts/a-successful-git-branching-model/`). It relies on two permanent branches, master and develop. The master branch stores the official release history and the develop branch holds the integration points for all features. The feature branches are created from the develop branch and then merged back once they are finished. When it is time to stabilize a release, a release branch is created from the develop branch. When the release is ready to ship, it gets merged to master and also back to develop. See Figure 5-8.

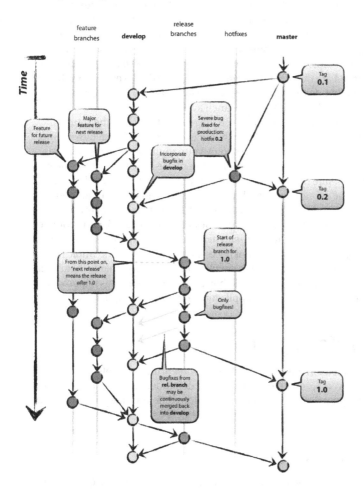

***Figure 5-8.*** *GitFlow*

Since GitFlow is based on a strict naming convention and a workflow, it is very suitable for tooling support. Vincent Driessen implemented a collection of Git extensions that allow developers to easily follow the GitFlow workflow using specific GitFlow commands. These extensions are available at `https://github.com/nvie/gitflow`.

Other tools that support GitFlow include SourceTree from Atlassian and the GitFlow for Visual Studio extension available from the Visual Studio Gallery.

A common objection of the GitFlow branching pattern is that it is too complex for many teams. One might argue that the reason for the success of GitFlow is that by imposing a strict naming convention and a well-defined workflow, it generally makes it easy to understand and follow.

## Branching and Deployment Pipelines

A key principle of deployment pipelines is that you should build your binaries once and then deploy them across your different environments. You use build automation to create binaries, install packages, and any other artifacts necessary for deploying your applications. You then push these artifacts to some kind of artifact repository, for example to TFS server storage. The deployment pipeline will fetch these files later and deploy them using deployment scripts to each environment. This ensures that the binaries that were tested and approved are the same that will eventually be deployed into production.

If you are using the "working on mainline" approach, it is easy to hook up the deployment pipeline, since there is only one branch available.

When using branch by release, you must use the release branch as the source of the deployment pipeline, since this is the branch that eventually will be deployed into production. Often, however, you will need to deploy your application to dev and test environments before you enter the release stabilization phase. We suggest that you set up a similar deployment pipeline from your master branch that will deploy the bits onto dev and test servers. But these are not the same binaries that will end up in production.

For the branch by feature strategy or variations on it, like GitFlow, you have an additional problem in that new branches are constantly created, making it more complex to deploy them onto testing servers. We recommend that you try to keep the feature branches as short-lived as possible. For example, it is not necessary to implement the whole feature in one feature branch; you can break it up into smaller increments and merge them back to master (or develop, in the case of GitFlow) as soon as they are done. This requires, of course, that the increments don't break the application and that it is shippable.

# Dependency Management

All but the simplest application has dependencies to other artifacts. Implementing Continuous Integration requires you to manage these dependencies in an efficient and structured manner. You can divide the dependencies into different categories, covered in the next sections.

## Third-Party Dependencies

First of all, you don't want or need to implement all functionality yourself. Quite often the functionality you need is available as (for example) a third-party library. This dependency can sometimes be in the form of source code but most of the time it is binary dependencies. These dependencies are typically not updated that often; only when a new version is available that contains new features or bug fixes that you really need should you update these dependencies.

# Source Control Dependencies

As an application grows in size over time, you start looking for ways to break it up into smaller pieces to manage the complexity that inevitably occurs. One way to do this is to break up the source code into smaller solutions and then reference projects between solutions. This means that solution A can reference one or more projects from solution B and solution C.

Using source code dependencies can be advantageous in periods when there are a lot of simultaneous changes in many parts of an application, but generally it creates a lot of complexity since you must make sure that all paths point correctly, and changes to projects require all dependent solutions to be recompiled, even if the interface did not change.

# Component Dependencies

A better way to break up an application is to extract parts of it into smaller self-contained solutions from which you create one or more library packages. Then you change the original project to reference these binaries created by this library instead of the source code. This kind of dependency is very similar to a third-party dependency; the only real difference is the frequency in which it is updated. Often every new version of an internal dependency should be integrated with client applications. A new version of a library needs to be published somewhere where the dependent applications can pull it down and build against it.

# Sharing Dependencies

If you are producing dependencies, you must also decide how to distribute these dependencies to the applications that use them. The most common options are to either commit the artifacts back to version control, or to package them and distribute them using a package management system like NuGet. This latter option is in most ways superior to the first one, but we will cover both options here.

## Branching

If you have source code dependencies or binary dependencies in a TFVC project, you can use this technique. Branch the dependency from where it is located in source control to a location below the dependent application. Figure 5-9 shows branching a dependency called *CommonLibrary* into a folder below the solution root of the application called Dependencies\CommonLibrary. This way, the dependency is automatically downloaded with the rest of the source code of the application.

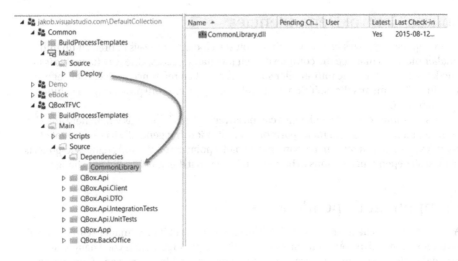

*Figure 5-9.* *Branching dependencies*

In this case, the dependency is binary, so there is a folder called Deploy beneath the CommonLibrary application where typically an automated build would check in a new version of the library.

Now, all references to the dependency are of relative dependency. To update the dependency to a new version, a new merge is done. The team that develops the client application can decide when to update to a newer version.

## Workspace Mappings

Another way to include the dependency, if you are using TFVC, is to include the source control path to the dependency in the workspace mapping. An example of this is shown in Figure 5-10, where you have a workspace mapping for an application; in addition, there is a mapping for the CommonLibrary\Deploy folder that is pulled down into the Dependencies\CommonLibrary folder, located beneath the application folder. So you will end up with the same relative structure as you did with the branching solution.

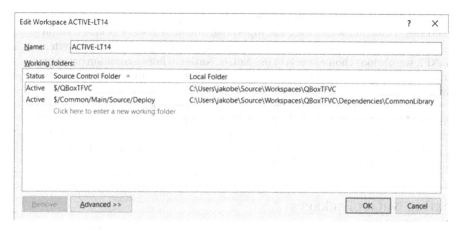

*Figure 5-10. Workspace mappings*

A key difference with this approach compared to the branching approach is that when a new version of the shared library is pushed, it will automatically be pulled down to the client application as part of the workspace. This might not always be desired.

Also, the extra workspace mappings must be set up for every team member and also for every build definition, which can quickly become tedious and error prone.

If you do select to share dependencies using source control in TFVC, we recommend that you use the branching approach instead.

## Git Submodules

If you are using Git, there is a feature called *submodules* that can be used for this purpose. Submodules allow you to keep a Git repository as a subdirectory of another Git repository. This lets you clone another repository into your project and keep your commits separate.

Git submodules have worked well for many teams, but are generally considered to be a somewhat complicated and potentially error-prone solution, so make sure that you and your team fully understand how they work before deciding to use them.

---

■ **Note**    Learn more about Git submodules at https://git-scm.com/book/en/v2/ Git-Tools-Submodules.

---

## NuGet

Committing generated artifacts to source control has several drawbacks. For one thing, it can quickly increase the size of the repository. This is especially important when using Git, since you are pulling down the entire history of the repository. Another problem is that when you commit the generated binaries back to source control as part of an automated build, you end up with a new commit or changeset id. This means that you can no longer unambiguously trace the application binaries back to a unique commit id.

A better way to distribute binaries is to do it using a package management system. For .NET, the obvious choice here is to use NuGet. NuGet defines a common package format in which all files of the packages are included together with a manifest file that contains metadata about the packages and any dependencies it might have.

One big advantage with a package management system like NuGet compared to just using regular binary references is the dependency management. This enables package developers to specify which other NuGet packages their packages depend on. When the package is installed by a developer in their local solution, all the dependencies are automatically downloaded, with the correct version.

## Sharing NuGet Packages

NuGet has a public gallery, available at www.nuget.org. At this moment, it contains around 400,000 packages and is growing at a steady rate.

For enterprise development, you typically don't want to distribute shared libraries through the public NuGet gallery. There are several different options available for hosting internal NuGet packages. We will discuss a few of these here. Then we will look at how to incorporate your extra NuGet package feeds into your projects.

## Shared Folders

The simplest option is to simply set up a network share that is available for all developers and the build agent servers. The upside is that it does not require any addition infrastructure. The downside is that it won't easily be available outside the company network; it does not scale very well since it is just a list of files.

## Internal Feed Server

As part of the NuGet project, there is a NuGet.Server package, shown in Figure 5-11, that implements the NuGet server functionality of exposing a file directory as a feed that is consumable by any NuGet client.

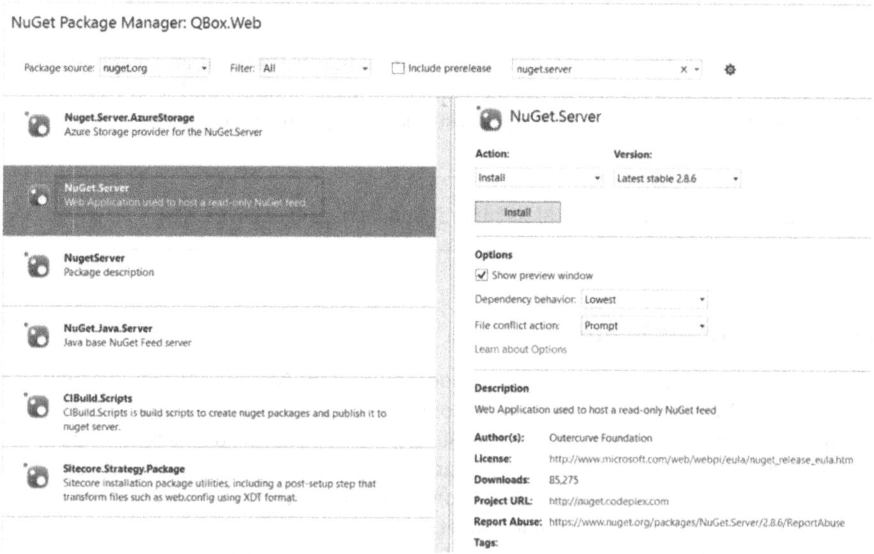

*Figure 5-11.* *NuGet Server package*

Creating your own NuGet server application is as easy as creating a blank ASP.NET web application, and then adding the NuGet.Server package to it. After deploying the web application to an IIS instance, it will have a feed available at `http://SERVER:PORT/nuget`. The path from where the NuGet packages will be read from is configured using an `appSetting` called `packagesPath`, as shown in Figure 5-12.

```
<appSettings>
    <!-- Set the value here to specify your custom packages folder. --
>
    <add key="packagesPath" value="C:\MyPackages" />
</appSettings>
```

*Figure 5-12.* *Configuration of the NuGet packages path*

## MyGet

MyGet provides hosted feeds for NuGet, Npm, Bower, and Vsix artifacts. It is free for open source projects; for private feeds and some additional services there is a monthly fee. MyGet also contains additional developer services such as build services integration, package mirroring, and package dependency analysis.

---

■ **Note** Learn more about MyGet at www.myget.org.

---

## ProGet

Another option for hosting NuGet feeds is ProGet from inedo. ProGet is an on-premise NuGet package repository server. It too has extra features including build server support, multiple feed support, package caching, and support for granular security.

---

■ **Note** Learn more about ProGet at `http://inedo.com/proget/overview`.

---

## Accessing NuGet Feeds

Regardless of which of the above tools you choose to host the NuGet packages, you will need to add the NuGet feed URL in order to consume packages from it. This is done using the NuGet Package Manager in Visual Studio, where you can add extra package sources. By default, there is one entry here that points to the public NuGet gallery feed URL (`https://api.nuget.org/v3/index.json`). Adding extra package sources here will instruct NuGet to not only evaluate NuGet.org for packages but also any additional sources. As shown in Figure 5-13, you can add any number of package sources, and you can also prioritize them. By keeping the most common package sources at the top, the package restore operation will run as fast as possible.

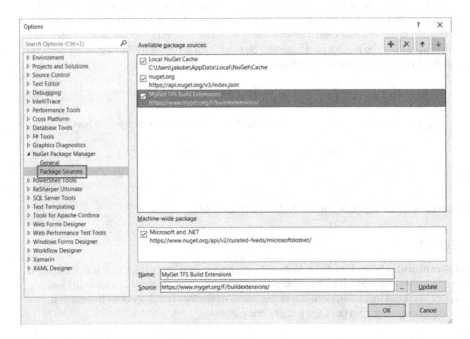

*Figure 5-13.* *Adding NuGet package sources*

Note that one of the package sources points to a MyGet public feed; this is the URL format of a MyGet feed.

---

■ **Note**    In Chapter 7 we will discuss how to create and publish NuGet packages as part of an automated build in TFS.

---

## Committing NuGet Packages to Source Control

A common question that causes a lot of debate is if one should commit the downloaded NuGet packages to source control or not. NuGet has the ability to dynamically download the required packages as part of the build (using the nuget restore command). This allows you to only store the NuGet configuration files in source control; the binaries will be pulled down when the solution is compiles.

Some of the problems with committing binaries to source control have already been discussed in this chapter. The upside of having everything in source control is that you only need a simple get on the source repository and you will have everything you need to build the system. With NuGet restore, you must remember to compile the solution at least once before you can work offline. (NuGet caches every package that is downloaded so it will not be fetched if it already exists on disk.)

Another potential problem with relying on dynamic NuGet restore is the hard dependency that exists on the public NuGet gallery. Although not frequent, it has gone offline on a couple of different occasions, causing build servers all over the world to fail.

# Summary

In this chapter, you explored the role of source control management in Continuous Delivery. You looked at different types of version control, and the ones that are supported in Team Foundation Server and Visual Studio Online. Then you looked at branching, which is a very important concept in source control management, and in particular how it relates to Continuous Delivery. Dependency management is another important topic, so we talked about how to reference internal and external dependencies and available options when it comes to sharing NuGet packages.

In the next chapter, you will take a look at PowerShell, which is the primary tool of choice when it comes to build and deployment scripting on Windows.

# CHAPTER 6

■ ■ ■

# PowerShell for Deployment

PowerShell has become one of the most important tools for any successful deployment solution on the Microsoft stack today. In essence it's a task automation and configuration framework. It's a scripting language built on the .NET Framework so we get great integration with the platform, and it's easy to extend using both C# as well as PowerShell itself.

This chapter is intended as a quick start into PowerShell to give you enough background to get started. We will focus on the aspects of PowerShell that you will use in the delivery pipeline; there will be many more examples in the coming chapters as well.

Today there are two styles of PowerShell: traditional procedural PowerShell and Desired State Configuration, which, as the name implies, is used to declare the intended state of a system rather than the steps to take to achieve that state. Both are useful when managing deployments, so we will take a look at both here.

## PowerShell

As stated, PowerShell is a scripting language, so it has all the usual language constructs such as if-then-else conditions, loops (while, do, for, foreach), structured error handling, and variables.

Let's start with a quick example. The following is a PowerShell script that prints the memory usage of all Notepad processes:

```
<# Print the memory usage of a process #>
$processName = 'notepad'
Write-Host "Looking for process '$processName'."

$processes = Get-Process -Name $processName

if($processes.Count -gt 0)
{
    foreach ($process in $processes)
```

```
    {
        # Note the use of paranthesis to specify evaluation order.
        Write-Host "Process id $($process.Id) is using $($process.VM) memory."
    }
}
else
{
    Write-Hos "Process not running."
}
```

This piece of PowerShell script shows a lot about what you can do with PowerShell, for instance:

- Strings are declared using single or double quotes.

- Variables are defined using the $ sign.

- Comparisons use special operators (-lt, -gt) instead of < or >. This is because < and > are used to send output to a stream in PowerShell.

- Control blocks are specified using curly braces, { }.

- Comments are either written using # or between <# ... #> blocks.

If you have PowerShell on your system (and most likely you do), you can start a PowerShell command window and run your PowerShell commands or scripts as shown in Figure 6-1.

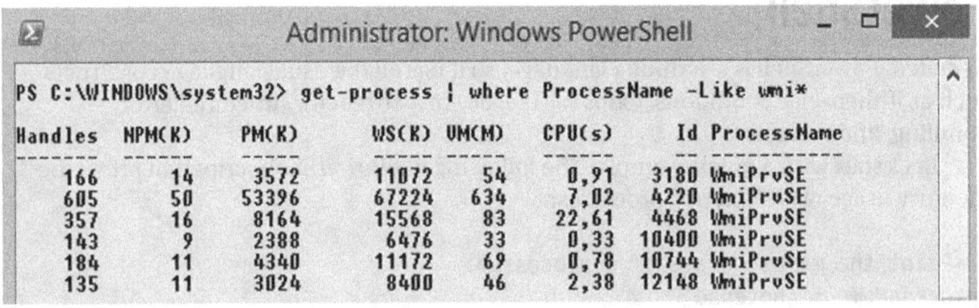

```
Administrator: Windows PowerShell

PS C:\WINDOWS\system32> get-process | where ProcessName -Like wmi*

Handles  NPM(K)    PM(K)     WS(K) VM(M)    CPU(s)      Id ProcessName
-------  ------    -----     ----- -----    ------      -- -----------
    166      14     3572     11072    54      0,91    3180 WmiPrvSE
    605      50    53396     67224   634      7,02    4220 WmiPrvSE
    357      16     8164     15568    83     22,61    4468 WmiPrvSE
    143       9     2388      6476    33      0,33   10400 WmiPrvSE
    184      11     4340     11172    69      0,78   10744 WmiPrvSE
    135      11     3024      8400    46      2,38   12148 WmiPrvSE
```

*Figure 6-1.* *The PowerShell command prompt*

If you want a convenient and powerful editor, you can use the PowerShell ISE (Integrated Script Environment), shown in Figure 6-2.

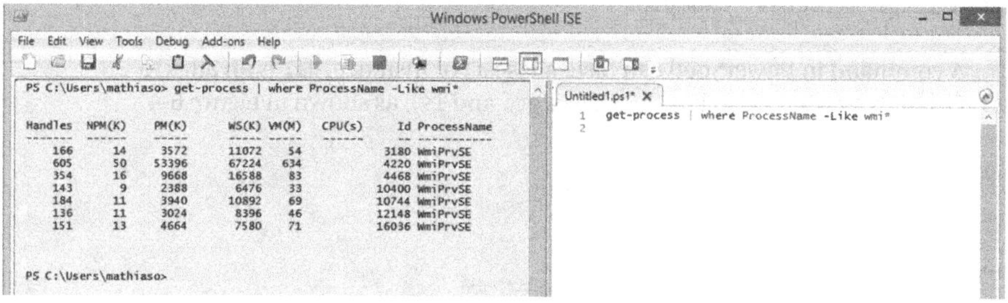

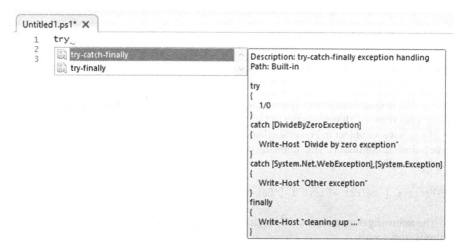

***Figure 6-2.*** *The PowerShell Integrated Scripting Environment (ISE)*

ISE provides a lot of capabilities, like autocomplete, IntelliSense, and integration with the help system. A nice little nugget is Ctrl + J, which pops up a list of script templates that help you write code more quickly and with fewer typos. This is shown in Figure 6-3.

***Figure 6-3.*** *Using script templates in ISE*

A great way to quickly get up to speed with PowerShell is to use the help system on objects you want to learn more about. For instance,

```
Get-Help Get-Process
```

shows what the Get-Process command can do. Add -examples or -detailed to the end of the command to see examples or details, respectively, like so:

Get-Help Get-Process -examples

A command in PowerShell can have aliases. For instance, dir is an alias to Get-ChildItem (which also has the aliases gci and ls), as shown in Figure 6-4

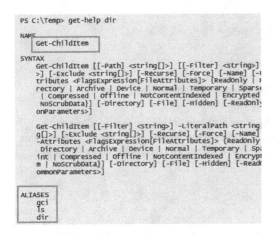

**Figure 6-4.** *Aliases in PowerShell*

An alias is useful both for mapping to existing conventions as well as to speed up typing. You create an alias using the Set-Alias PowerShell command.

If you have an object in PowerShell and you want to know more about it, you can use the Get-Member command. The following command shows the capabilities of a System. Diagnostics.Process object:

Get-Process | select -First 1 | Get-Member

The following output shows the result of the command; you can see it has properties, methods, and events:

```
TypeName: System.Diagnostics.Process
```

| Name | MemberType | Definition |
| ---- | ---------- | ---------- |
| Handles | AliasProperty | Handles = Handlecount |
| Name | AliasProperty | Name = ProcessName |
| NPM | AliasProperty | NPM = NonpagedSystemMemorySize64 |
| PM | AliasProperty | PM = PagedMemorySize64 |
| VM | AliasProperty | VM = VirtualMemorySize64 |
| WS | AliasProperty | WS = WorkingSet64 |
| Disposed | Event | System.EventHandler Disposed(System.Object, System.EventArgs) |
| ErrorDataReceived | Event | System.Diagnostics.DataReceivedEventHandler ErrorDataReceived(System... |
| Exited | Event | System.EventHandler Exited(System.Object, System.EventArgs) |
| OutputDataReceived | Event | System.Diagnostics.DataReceivedEventHandler OutputDataReceived(Syste... |
| BeginErrorReadLine | Method | void BeginErrorReadLine() |
| BeginOutputReadLine | Method | void BeginOutputReadLine() |
| CancelErrorRead | Method | void CancelErrorRead() |
| CancelOutputRead | Method | void CancelOutputRead() |

# Cmdlets

Here's a term you'll often see in PowerShell documentation and scripts: a cmdlet is a lightweight command in the PowerShell environment. It's a convenient extensibility model that provides a function with enhanced capabilities and integration with the PowerShell runtime, such as parameter binding (named parameters, parameter validation) and access to implicit variables like -whatif to simulate a command or -verbose to get detailed logging.

You can create cmdlets directly in a PowerShell script. To do so you only need to annotate a script with the [CmdLetBinding] attribute. If you want full control over what your command does, you can also write a cmdlet in code. A good starting point if you are interested in writing your own cmdlets in C# is the article "Writing a Windows PowerShell Cmdlet" at https://msdn.microsoft.com/en-us/library/dd878294.aspx.

# Getting Output

There are plenty of ways to send messages back to the user. Typically, you use the Write-* commands. One thing to be aware of is that Write-Host outputs directly to the screen whereas Write-Output writes to the pipeline. For this reason, never use Write-Host in your build or deployment scripts.

You can also echo the content of a variable to the output stream by simply using the variable. The following code outputs the content of the $PSVersionTable:

```
PS C:\Temp> $PSVersionTable
```

```
Name                          Value
----                          -----
PSVersion                     5.0.10240.16384
WSManStackVersion             3.0
SerializationVersion          1.1.0.1
CLRVersion                    4.0.30319.42000
BuildVersion                  10.0.10240.16384
PSCompatibleVersions          {1.0, 2.0, 3.0, 4.0...}
PSRemotingProtocolVersion     2.3
```

If you want to format the output, there are several options among the Out-* commands. For example, Out-GridView sends the output to a table in a separate window. If you want more control, there are the Format-* commands. Format-List, for instance, shows each property of an object on a separate line.

There are also a few shorthand operators for redirecting output; these are explained in Table 6-1.

*Table 6-1.* *PowerShell Output Operators*

| Operator | Description |
|----------|-------------|
| > | Redirects pipeline output to a file, overwriting the current content. |
| >> | Redirects pipeline output to a file, appending to the existing content. |
| 2> | Redirects error output to a file, overwriting the current content. |
| 2>> | Redirects error output to a file, appending to the current content. |
| 2>&1 | The error messages are written to the output pipe instead of the error pipe. |

If you want to make it easy for the user of your script to see important data, you can control the text color using the –Foreground and –BackgroundColor properties. The following code writes out all processes with a working set of greater than 200MB in a red foreground color:

```
Get-Process | ForEach-Object {
    if($_.WorkingSet -gt 200MB) {
        Write-Host $_.Name, $_.WorkingSet -ForegroundColor Red
    }
    else {
        Write-Host $_.Name, $_.WorkingSet
    }
}
```

# PowerShell Pipeline

As seen in the example above, you can write PowerShell in a procedural way. You can also use the PowerShell pipeline, where output from one cmdlet can be passed to another. This is a very efficient way to chain different activities and get a script that has a very fluent look. There is, of course, a risk that the script will become difficult to maintain since more compact code can be harder to read.

The following is an example of a series of PowerShell commands running in a pipeline. It first lists all running processes, filtered by name like note*, then selects a few properties from the result items, sorts them by working set (descending), and finally shows the results in an autosized table:

```
Get-Process |
    Where-Object { $_.Name -like 'note*' } |
        Select-Object WS, CPU, ID, ProcessName |
            Sort-Object WS -Descending |
                Format-Table -AutoSize
```

It gives this result:

```
    WS       CPU   Id ProcessName
    --       ---   -- -----------
11931648 0,078125 9716 notepad
11714560  0,09375  704 notepad
```

Things to note from the example:

- The $_ variable represents the current object in the pipeline.

- You use Where-Object to filter data.

- Select-Object lets you choose what data is used (including options to take the first or last n items).

- Sort-Object sorts the result.

# Error Handling

Just like in any piece of software, things can go wrong, and PowerShell is no different. A good error handling principle will make your script work in a predictable way. This is very important in a deployment scenario since you typically need to stop or revert a step in the process if something goes wrong.

PowerShell supports two ways of handling errors: the traditional error code approach found in most scripting environments and the structured exception handling found in modern development languages. Here are a few rules of thumb for handling errors in PowerShell:

- Whenever an error occurs, it's logged in the $error variable. It's a collection, so if multiple errors occur, they are all there.

- If you call an external process, the $LastExitCode will be set. Typically 0 means success and other numbers represent an error.

- A script or a function should either be set in the $lastexitcode or throw an exception to signal to the caller that an error occurred.

- Use verbose logging (i.e. Write-Verbose) to report details about an error. Try to include as much information as possible, but make sure not to leak sensitive information.

- Try to make the logs readable, for instance by using the Format-List command.

Here's an example of a generic try-catch-finally clause that rethrows the exception:

```
try
{
    1/0
}
catch
{
    # Output the error state from the $_
    $_ | Format-List -Force
}
finally
{
    Write-Host "cleaning up ..."
}
```

The exception information is written like this:

```
Exception               : System.Management.Automation.RuntimeException:
                          Attempted to divide by zero. ---> System.
                          DivideByZeroException: Attempted to divide by zero.
                              --- End of inner exception stack trace ---
                          at System.Management.Automation.
                          ExceptionHandlingOps.CheckActionPreference
                          (FunctionCon text funcContext, Exception exception)
                          at System.Management.Automation.Interpreter.
                          ActionCallInstruction`2.Run(InterpretedFra
                          me frame)
```

```
                              at System.Management.Automation.Interpreter.
                              EnterTryCatchFinallyInstruction.Run(Interp
                              retedFrame frame)
                              at System.Management.Automation.Interpreter.
                              EnterTryCatchFinallyInstruction.Run(Interp
                              retedFrame frame)
TargetObject             :
CategoryInfo             : NotSpecified: (:) [], RuntimeException
FullyQualifiedErrorId    : RuntimeException
ErrorDetails             :
InvocationInfo           : System.Management.Automation.InvocationInfo
ScriptStackTrace         : at <ScriptBlock>, <No file>: line 3
PipelineIterationInfo    : {}
PSMessageDetails         :
cleaning up ...
```

# Functions

In your scenarios, you will often use a basic approach to structuring your code using layers of scripts. The benefit of this is that the scripts are used as they are; there is no need to go through a packaging process. There are other options, including creating PowerShell modules, which we will not cover in this book. To do this, you first need to refactor your scripts to use functions that you can call. A PowerShell script can contain one or more methods, and you can use them all, once the script has been loaded in your PowerShell session.

A function can have typed arguments. If you want to specify if a parameter is required, you need to declare the function with a [CmdLetBinding] attribute, like so:

```
function CreateWebSite()
{
    [CmdletBinding()]
    param(
        [parameter(Mandatory=$true)]
        [string]$name,
        [int]$port = 1000)

    Write-Host "Creating website $name on port $port."
}
```

To include functions from another script you use "dot-sourcing." In other words, the file is imported using a . notation. This function can then be called in several ways, with or without named parameters. The following example is included the CreateWebSite.ps1 script from the Lib folder, parallel to the folder where the executing script is saved.

95

```
. .\Lib\Web\CreateWebSite.ps1

CreateWebSite "My Web Site" 100
CreateWebSite -name "My Web Site" -port 100
CreateWebSite -name "My Web Site"
```

## PowerShell Drives

PowerShell offers an interesting concept for accessing data from providers in a uniform and familiar way called PowerShell drive, or PSDrive. A PowerShell drive can be read just like the file system, so commands like Get-ChildItem work the same on a FileSystem provider as on a Registry provider.

If you want to see what PowerShell drives you have access to, just call Get-PSDrive:

```
Get-PSDrive
```

| Name | Used (GB) | Free (GB) | Provider | Root |
| ---- | --------- | --------- | -------- | ---- |
| Alias | | | Alias | |
| C | 73,31 | 27,79 | FileSystem | C:\ |
| Cert | | | Certificate | \ |
| D | 13,44 | 1,74 | FileSystem | D:\ |
| Env | | | Environment | |
| F | 0,89 | 0,00 | FileSystem | F:\ |
| Function | | | Function | |
| HKCU | | | Registry | HKEY_CURRENT_USER |
| HKLM | | | Registry | HKEY_LOCAL_MACHINE |
| Variable | | | Variable | |
| WSMan | | | WSMan | |

You can then use the drive providers just like a regular drive. For instance, if you want to see the current list of environment variables, do the following:

```
PS C:\Temp> ls env:
```

| Name | Value |
| ---- | ----- |
| ALLUSERSPROFILE | C:\ProgramData |
| APPDATA | C:\Users\mathi\AppData\Roaming |
| ChocolateyInstall | C:\ProgramData\chocolatey |
| CommonProgramFiles | C:\Program Files\Common Files |
| CommonProgramFiles(x86) | C:\Program Files (x86)\Common Files |
| CommonProgramW6432 | C:\Program Files\Common Files |
| COMPUTERNAME | WIN-9B074AI755I |
| ComSpec | C:\WINDOWS\system32\cmd.exe |
| DNX_HOME | %USERPROFILE%\.dnx |

To get a list of the variables in the current scope containing the word in, do the following:

```
PS C:\Temp> ls variable:\*in*
```

```
Name                        Value
----                        -----
OutputEncoding              System.Text.SBCSCodePageEncoding
WarningPreference           Continue
InformationPreference       SilentlyContinue
```

## Sample Script/Template

It's a good idea to have a shared template to ensure the scripts get a common structure and get documented in a consistent way. The following script contains the parts we think are most important for getting started with a new script quickly: documentation, a function body, and error handing:

```
<#
.Synopsis
        Short description of the purpose of this script
.Description
        Extensive description of the script
.Parameter X
    Description or parameter X
.Parameter Y
    Description or parameter Y
.Example
        First example of usage of the script
.Example
        Second example of usage of the script
#>

function MyFunction()
{
    <#
    .Synopsis
            Short description of the purpose of this function
    .Description
            Extensive description of the function
    .Parameter X
        Description or parameter X
    .Parameter Y
        Description or parameter Y
```

```
.Example
        First example of usage of the function
.Example
        Second example of usage of the function
#>
[CmdletBinding()]
param($x, $y)

try
{
    1/0
}
catch
{
    # Output the error state from the $_
    $_ | Format-List -Force
}
finally
{
    Write-Host "cleaning up ..."
}
}
```

If you want to know more about commenting your PowerShell code, run the following help command:

```
Get-Help about_Comment_Based_Help
```

---

■ **Note**    You may get an error that the help system needs to be updated. You can update help with the `update-help` command.

---

## Testing and Debugging Your Scripts

Testing and debugging PowerShell scripts can be a bit tricky since there isn't a traditional IDE in which to work. We recommend using these simple techniques to debug your scripts:

- Always parameterize scripts so that they can be tested locally.

- Use `Write-Debug` to output information to the console.
  Note that the debug output will not be displayed unless the
  $DebugPreference variable is set to "Continue."

- Use the ISE, set breakpoints in the code, and use the debugger.

- Break down the script into smaller units and test each
  individually.

Sometimes when developing a script you can end up with a situation where an old version of a function is affecting the result. If you want to check which functions are loaded in your session, you can use the PSDrive function provider:

```
ls function:
```

For instance, if you want to see if MyFunction has been loaded, do this:

```
PS C:\Temp> ls function:\my* | Format-Table -AutoSize

CommandType Name        Version Source
----------- ----        ------- ------
Function    MyFunction
```

If you then want to remove a function, it can easily be removed using the normal remove-item command:

```
Remove-item function:\MyFunction
```

If you really want to make your PowerShell code shine, you can apply the same unit test approach to PowerShell as to any other programming language. While it's more that we can cover in this book, we recommend taking a look at Pester, a BDD-based testing framework for PowerShell (https://github.com/pester/Pester).

# Common Scenarios

When starting with a new technology like PowerShell, we've found it very efficient to have a set of resources to build upon. Earlier in the chapter we talked about the importance of structuring the PowerShell assets, so the intention is that the examples in the next sections can be used as they are but are also great candidates to include in your library of reusable scripts.

If you want more examples and inspiration, the Microsoft TechNet article "A Task-Based Guide to Windows PowerShell Cmdlets" at https://technet.microsoft.com/en-us/library/dd772285.aspx is a good start.

## Working with the File System

Let's start by exploring the file system. We'll also give you examples that show how to manage files and file content.

### List XML Files Recursively in a Folder

Do you want to search a folder recursively for XML files?

```
Get-ChildItem -Filter "*.xml" -Recurse
```

## List All Sub-Directories in a Folder

This example illustrates that you can use the Get-ChildItem command to find files, folders, or both:

```
Get-ChildItem -Directory
```

## Copy All Files from One Folder to Another Recursively

The following is another basic example, but make sure to include the -recurse parameter or the content of the scripts folder will not get copied:

```
Copy-Item c:\scripts c:\backup -recurse
```

## Find (and Remove) All Files Older Than 10 Days

Here's an example where you first select the files, then pipe the results to a where filter that selects only files created earlier than 10 days, and finally sort the result by CreationTime:

```
Get-ChildItem -Path .\ -Force |
    Where-Object { !$_.PSIsContainer -and $_.CreationTime -lt (Get-Date).
AddDays(-10) } |
    Sort-Object -Property CreationTime
```

If you want to delete the files, just pipe the result to Remove-Item:

```
| Remove-Item -Force
```

## Find Files Larger Than 1GB

Similar to the last example, this one finds all files larger than 1GB on the system drive. Note the convenient constant for GB.

```
Get-ChildItem "$env:SystemDrive\" -File -Recurse |
    Where-Object { $_.Length -ge 1GB }
```

---

■ **Note**    This command will typically raise a large number of unauthorized exceptions for many of the system directories on the C: drive.

---

# Get the First and Last 10 Lines in a File

When working with log files it's very practical to have a way to read only the first or last part of the file. Get-Content has both options, as shown here:

```
Get-Content .\log.txt -TotalCount 10
Get-Content .\log.txt -Tail 10
```

# Replace a String in a Text File

There are many ways to do a pattern match in a string. This one is very easy to use if you want to replace a string in a file:

```
(Get-Content .\web.config) -replace 'debug="true"', 'debug="false"'
```

If you want to save the file, pass it to Set-Content:

```
| Set-Content -Path .\web.config
```

# Load a File as XML, Replace a Value, and Save It

If you prefix a variable with [xml], it will be loaded as an XML document and you will get access to the usual DOM methods, like SelectNodes or the DocumentElement. Another really nice thing in ISE is that you can access the document elements using dot (.) notation. If you first load the document into a variable (select the Get-Content line and press F8), it will even provide you with IntelliSense (see Figure 6-5).

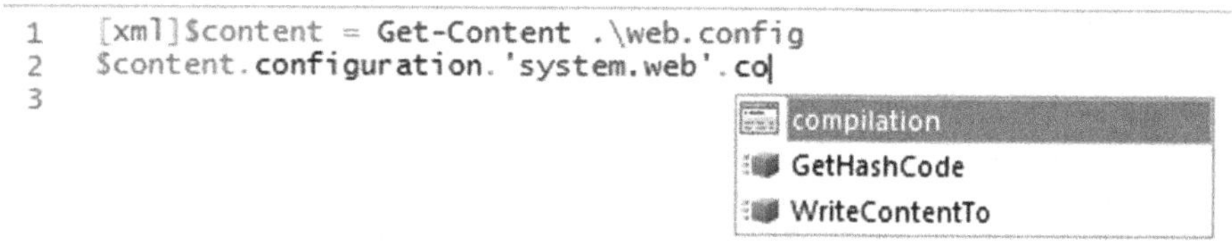

```
1    [xml]$content = Get-Content .\web.config
2    $content.configuration.'system.web'.co|
3
```

compilation
GetHashCode
WriteContentTo

***Figure 6-5.*** *Using XML in PowerShell*

So to update the debug setting from true to false in this web.config file, do this:

```xml
<?xml version="1.0" encoding="utf-8"?>
<configuration>
  <system.web>
    <compilation debug="true" targetFramework="4.5" />
    <httpRuntime targetFramework="4.5" />
  </system.web>
</configuration>
```

You only need these lines of PowerShell:

```
[xml]$content = Get-Content c:\temp\web.config
$content.configuration.'system.web'.compilation.debug = "false"
$content.Save("c:\temp\updated.web.config")
```

## Loading a CSV File

Let's say you've got this CSV file you want to process:

```
Order ID;Order Date;Customer;Status
1;2015-05-01;Annies Bakery;Processed
2;2015-05-26;Bobs Biscuites;Delayed
3;2015-06-02;Chris Pankakes;Processed
```

Of course there's a function to load CSV files! Just call Import-Csv and you can access the fields in the file just like you did with XML files (Figure 6-6).

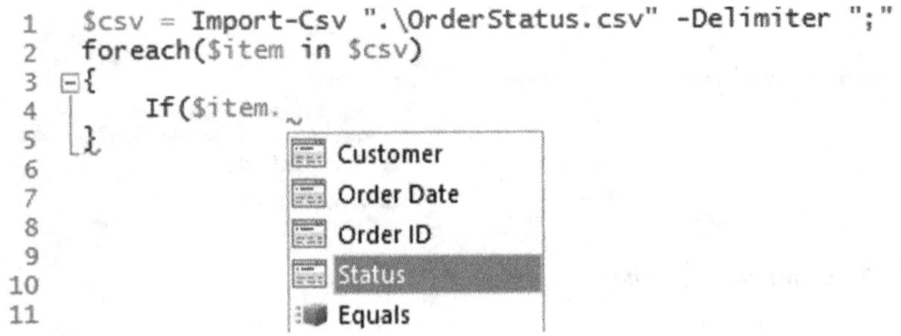

*Figure 6-6.* *Using CSV files in PowerShell*

## List File Version Information

Version information is an important part of traceability in the deployment process, so it can be practical to use PowerShell to get the values from files. From a file item you can query for the VersionInfo object, and you can then select the properties you're interested in. The following example prints out the information fields for Visual Studio 2015:

```
(Get-Item "C:\Program Files (x86)\Microsoft Visual Studio 14.0\Common7\IDE\
devenv.exe").VersionInfo |
    Select-Object -Property CompanyName, FileVersion, ProductVersion,
    ProductName
```

```
CompanyName             FileVersion       ProductVersion   ProductName
-----------             -----------       --------------   -----------
Microsoft Corporation   14.0.23107.0      14.0.23107.0     Microsoft® Visual
                        built by: D14REL                   Studio® 2015
```

If you want to know more about which other fields are available in the VersionInfo object, just pipe it to Get-Member:

```
PS C:\Temp> (Get-Item "C:\Program Files (x86)\Microsoft Visual Studio 14.0\
Common7\IDE\devenv.exe").VersionInfo | Get-Member

    TypeName: System.Diagnostics.FileVersionInfo

Name              MemberType    Definition
----              ----------    ----------
Equals            Method        bool Equals(System.Object obj)
GetHashCode       Method        int GetHashCode()
GetType           Method        type GetType()
ToString          Method        string ToString()
Comments          Property      string Comments {get;}
CompanyName       Property      string CompanyName {get;}
FileBuildPart     Property      int FileBuildPart {get;}
FileDescription   Property      string FileDescription {get;}
FileMajorPart     Property      int FileMajorPart {get;}
FileMinorPart     Property      int FileMinorPart {get;}
FileName          Property      string FileName {get;}
FilePrivatePart   Property      int FilePrivatePart {get;}
FileVersion       Property      string FileVersion {get;}
InternalName      Property      string InternalName {get;}
IsDebug           Property      bool IsDebug {get;}
IsPatched         Property      bool IsPatched {get;}
IsPreRelease      Property      bool IsPreRelease {get;}
IsPrivateBuild    Property      bool IsPrivateBuild {get;}
IsSpecialBuild    Property      bool IsSpecialBuild {get;}
Language          Property      string Language {get;}
LegalCopyright    Property      string LegalCopyright {get;}
```

```
LegalTrademarks     Property        string LegalTrademarks {get;}
OriginalFilename    Property        string OriginalFilename {get;}
PrivateBuild        Property        string PrivateBuild {get;}
ProductBuildPart    Property        int ProductBuildPart {get;}
ProductMajorPart    Property        int ProductMajorPart {get;}
ProductMinorPart    Property        int ProductMinorPart {get;}
ProductName         Property        string ProductName {get;}
ProductPrivatePart  Property        int ProductPrivatePart {get;}
ProductVersion      Property        string ProductVersion {get;}
SpecialBuild        Property        string SpecialBuild {get;}
FileVersionRaw      ScriptProperty  System.Object FileVersionRaw {get=New-
                                    Object System.Version -ArgumentList @(...
ProductVersionRaw   ScriptProperty  System.Object ProductVersionRaw {get=New-
                                    Object System.Version -ArgumentList...
```

# Managing Processes

In this section, you'll take a look at some useful commands for managing processes, including running a command on a remote machine.

## List Running Processes Sorted by Name

Here's a commonly used PowerShell command, Get-Process, which gives you information on processes running on a system:

```
Get-Process | Sort ProcessName
```

If you want to get processes on a remote machine, just add -ComputerName to the argument list:

```
Get-Process -ComputerName MyServer | Sort ProcessName
```

## Kill a Process

The following example is something you often need in a deployment script, a command to stop a running process:

```
Get-Process -Name "Note*" | Stop-Process
```

## Run a Command

There are several ways to run PowerShell scripts. For instance, if you want to run a command declared in a string variable, you can use Invoke-Expression:

```
$command = 'Get-Process'
Invoke-Expression  $command
```

If you want to run a PowerShell script block, you can use Invoke-Command instead:

```
Invoke-Command -ScriptBlock { Get-Process }
```

And if you want to run a PowerShell script file, you can simply call the file directly:

```
.\file.ps1
```

### Run a Command on Remote Machine(s)

To run a command on a remote machine, it must have Win RM enabled and have the port to Win RM open in the firewall (default port 5985 for HTTP and 5986 for HTTPS). You can use the winrm command to configure the service. The quickconfig does a basic setup for you:

```
Winrm quickconfig
```

To run a command on a remote machine, you only need to pass the additional -ComputerName argument:

```
Invoke-Command -FilePath .\file.ps1 -ComputerName MyRemoteMachine
```

If you want to run the command on several machines, just pass them as a comma-separated list:

```
Invoke-Command -FilePath .\file.ps1 -ComputerName Machine1, Machine2
```

# Managing Windows Services

Next up, some tips on managing Windows resources.

### Show a List of Services

Use the Get-Service command to list the Windows services on your machine. If you want to filter only running services, pipe the result to the Where-Object cmdlet:

```
Get-Service | where status -eq "running"
```

### Start and Stop a Service

A common deployment scenario is to update a Windows service. Most likely you will need to first stop the service, update the installation, and then start the service again. Here's an example that stops the web server and starts it again:

```
Stop-Service -Name W3SVC
#--Update website
Start-Service -Name W3SVC
```

## Install an MSI Package

If you are using MSI packages to deploy an application, here's a script that will run the installer from PowerShell. Add all the parameters you need to run the installer silently.

```
$filePath = "client.msi"
$parameters = "/qn /norestart /i ""$filePath"""
$process = [System.Diagnostics.Process]::Start("msiexec.exe", $parameters)
$process.WaitForExit()
```

# Working with Websites

In this section, we want to show a couple of examples for managing websites in IIS.

## Create an IIS Website

The following script creates a new IIS site at three levels. It first creates the app pool, then the website, and finally the web application. And it does a few other things, too. It checks if the site folder exists. If the application already exists, it's removed, so you can ensure that the site is always created according to the script.

```
$app = 'MySite'
$path = "c:\web\$app"

# Create site if not exists
if(!(Test-Path $path))
{
    New-Item -Path $path -ItemType directory
}

# Remove site if exists
if(Test-Path "IIS:\Sites\$app\$app")
{
    Remove-Website -Name $app
    Remove-WebAppPool -Name $app
}

# Create web app pool, site and application
New-WebAppPool -Name $app
New-Website -Name $app -Port 9090 -PhysicalPath $path
New-WebApplication -Name $app -ApplicationPool $app -PhysicalPath $path
-Site $app
```

## Configure IIS Properties

This final example sets the SSL setting for the web application to required and also enables Windows authentication:

```
Set-WebConfiguration -Location "$app/$app" -Filter "system.webserver/
security/access" -Value "Ssl" -Force

Set-WebConfigurationProperty -Location "$app/$app" -Filter "system.
webServer/security/authentication/windowsAuthentication" -name Enabled
-value $true -Force
```

---

■ **Note**    For this to work you will need an SSL certificate installed on the web server and Windows authentication available as well.

---

# Using .NET

Since PowerShell is built in .NET, it's very easy to use code in a .NET assembly. You will use some techniques in the coming chapters, so here's a quick sample to show the syntax.

## Call a .NET Function

To use loaded types you only need to enclose the type in brackets ( [ ] ). For instance, [System.Diagnostics.Process] references the .NET Process type. To use the members of the type, use the :: operator. Here's the code to get the currently running process:

```
[System.Diagnostics.Process]::GetCurrentProcess()
```

# PowerShell Desired State Configuration

DSC is a new way to manage deployment and configuration of a system. Instead of the procedural, instruction-based model in traditional PowerShell, DSC uses a declarative model. PowerShell DSC was first introduced in the Windows Management Framework 4.0, and WMF 5.0 will include additional DSC content.

A DSC script contains a declarative set of resources and their desired properties. A DSC resource in itself is also a PowerShell script that encapsulates a configuration object like the file system or SQL Server.

Working with DSC can be split into two tasks: authoring DSC resources and creating DSC configuration scripts. Ideally, you will have resources for the objects you want to configure so that you can focus on the configuration scripts to manage your deployments.

PowerShell 4.0 DSC ships with the resource providers shown in Table 6-2. See `https://technet.microsoft.com/en-us/library/dn249921.aspx` for more information.

***Table 6-2.*** *DSC 4.0 Resource Providers*

| Provider | Description |
|----------|-------------|
| **Archive Resource** | Unpacks archive (.zip) files at specific paths on target nodes |
| **Environment Resource** | Manages system environment variables on target nodes |
| **File Resource** | Manages files and directories on target nodes |
| **Group Resource** | Manages local groups on target nodes |
| **Log Resource** | Logs configuration messages |
| **Package Resource** | Installs and manages packages, such as Windows Installer and `setup.exe` packages, on target nodes |
| **WindowsProcess Resource** | Configures Windows processes on target nodes |
| **Registry Resource** | Manages registry keys and values on target nodes |
| **WindowsFeature Resource** | Adds or removes Windows features and roles on target nodes |
| **Script Resource** | Runs Windows PowerShell script blocks on target nodes |
| **Service Resource** | Manages services on target nodes |
| **User Resource** | Manages local user accounts on target nodes |

WMF 5.0 will provide additional resources, such as managing a SQL Server database, Windows Firewall settings, and Windows Active Directory objects.

The DSC Resource Kit on Microsoft TechNet is also a great place to go to find resources (`https://gallery.technet.microsoft.com/scriptcenter/DSC-Resource-Kit-All-c449312d`).

To see which resources are available in your environment, just run `Get-DscResource` and PowerShell will list the resources for you.

The files are conventionally stored at two locations if you want to examine the scripts in detail:

- %ProgramFiles%\WindowsPowerShell\Modules

- %systemroot%\system32\WindowsPowershell\v1.0\Modules\PS
  DesiredStateConfiguration\DSCResources

# Using a Resource

The following example uses DSC to configure a machine as a web service. The requirement in this case is simply to ensure that the IIS role is installed with ASP.NET 4.5.

1. Create a configuration script.

```
configuration EnableIIS
{
    param
    (
        # Target nodes to apply the configuration
        [string[]]$NodeName = 'localhost'
    )

    Node $NodeName
    {
        # Install the IIS role
        WindowsFeature IIS
        {
            Ensure          = "Present"
            Name            = "Web-Server"
        }

        # Install the ASP .NET 4.5 role
        WindowsFeature AspNet45
        {
            Ensure          = "Present"
            Name            = "Web-Asp-Net45"
        }
    }
}
```

2. Run the script from PowerShell. You can call the configuration supplying the optional NodeName parameter if you want to run the script on a different machine. This will then create a MOF file for each node in the configuration.

```
EnableIIS

Directory: C:\temp\EnableIIS

Mode    LastWriteTime       Length Name
----    -------------       ------ ----
-a---   8/11/2015   8:48 PM    1622 localhost.mof
```

3.  Call `Start-DscConfiguration` and supply the path to the
    MOF file. In the example here, you provide `-Wait` to have the
    process run in a blocking mode so that you can see the result.
    You can also pass in `-Verbose` to get more detailed logging.

    ```
    Start-DscConfiguration -Path .\EnableIIS -Verbose
    -Wait -Force
    ```

## The Two Ways to Run a DSC Script

PowerShell DSC has two models of working. The default is to push a script to a target
node; this is a very easy way to get started. However, if you have many machines to
manage, it can get difficult to keep track of which configuration has been applied where.
The other DSC model is to use a server to hold the configuration and let the nodes pull
the DSC configuration from there. The pull model is also a good choice if you want to
avoid configuration drift because the nodes can be set up to check their configuration
against the pull server and update themselves if a difference is detected.

For more information about working with a DSC pull server, take a look at "Windows
PowerShell Desired State Configuration Pull Servers" at `https://technet.microsoft.`
`com/en-us/library/dn249913.aspx`.

## DSC on Linux

Configuring environments can be a challenging task. If you need to manage different
platforms with different tools, it can be overwhelming. So to make things a bit simpler,
DSC is also available on Linux, which provides the benefit of having only one tool to
manage both Windows and Linux machines. If you want to learn more about this, take a
look at "Get Started with Windows PowerShell Desired State Configuration for Linux" at
`https://technet.microsoft.com/en-us/library/mt126211.aspx`.

## Creating a Resource

Creating a custom DSC resource is out of scope for this book, but if you want to learn
more about DSC and how to create a resource, we recommend downloading the ALM
Rangers guide "PowerShell DSC for DevOps and ALM practitioners" from `https://`
`vsardevops.codeplex.com/`. You can also learn a lot from the latest WMF assets at `www.`
`microsoft.com/en-us/download/details.aspx?id=46889` or look at the scripts in the
PowerShell Gallery at `http://msconfiggallery.cloudapp.net/`.

# Summary

PowerShell is a great tool for any kind of automation on the Windows platform. With traditional PowerShell you get an extensible task execution environment, which can be used to automate your deployment steps, for instance. With PowerShell DSC you get a declarative model where you can define the intended state of a system and PowerShell will ensure it is made so. Both are excellent techniques that complement each other and can help you build a great software delivery platform.

You will learn more about PowerShell in the coming chapters where you will use it to extend the build system, configure environments, and integrate deployment tasks.

# CHAPTER 7

# Build Automation

Build automation is the cornerstone of Continuous Delivery. It is the workhorse that carries out the repetitive task of getting the source code every time you commit something and running it through a series of steps including tasks such as label/tag, versioning, compiling, unit testing, and generating the necessary deployment artifacts.

In this chapter, you will take a deep look at Team Foundation Build 2015, a brand new build system. It's been built from the ground up to offer a modern build system that makes it easy to implement build automation.

The output of an automated build is a set of artifacts that will later on be picked up by the deployment pipeline and deployed to the different target environments. Depending on what you are building, there are a lot of different options for how you can package you artifacts. We will cover the most common ones in this chapter; for each type, we will show how you can automate the creation of these artifacts using TFS Build 2015.

First, let's take a quick look at some key principles of build automation. These principles are important no matter what you are building and which continuous integration server you might be using.

## Key Principles

We mentioned a few of these key principles and practices in Chapter 1. Here we will discuss some of them in more detail.

### Keeping CI Builds Fast

Continuous Integration (CI) is all about integrating changes to your application as quickly as possible and providing feedback to the team. Feedback at this stage typically means things such as compiler information, status of unit tests, and results of code analysis.

To be able to respond to any problem caused by a change, it is important that the person responsible for the change is notified as soon as possible after the change has been committed to the source control repository. If there is a longer delay, the person might already have switched context into some other task. For larger system, it is not uncommon for the build to take several hours.

If your build is slow, you need to analyze what is taking most of the time, and what you can do to speed this up. Common resolutions include breaking up your applications in smaller parts, removing long-running integration tests, and switching to incremental builds. We will discuss how you can achieve some of these things in this chapter.

## Visualizing Build Status

Everyone on the team should be able to easily view the status of the automated builds, preferably on a large screen in every team room. In addition to making the status transparent to everyone, it also enforces the mentality of keeping the build successful. Nobody wants to be break the build when everyone can see it on the big screen!

In TFS Build 2015, you can pin build definitions to the team web access home page (shown in Figure 7-1), making the current and passed status visible to everyone in the team.

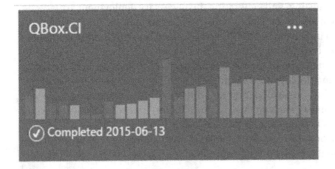

*Figure 7-1.* *Build status tile*

## Ensuring High Build Quality

To reach a high level of automation around build and deployment, you want to avoid as much manual work as possible since this will slow the process down. This increases the need of finding ways to automatically verify the quality of the code and the resulting build. Options here include running unit tests and integration tests to verify the functionality of the build, but also measuring the quality of the code itself using tools like FxCop and Code Metrics as part of the automated build. We will discuss this in more detail in Chapters 8 and 9.

## Build Once, Deploy Many

As discussed previously, building your artifacts only once is important for several reasons. Making sure that you deploy the same set of binaries to all environments avoids the risk that you introduce changes that have not been tested properly. It also means that you don't waste time and resources on building something multiple times.

In order to implement this strategy successfully, you must make sure that your binaries are environment agnostic, which means that they don't make assumptions about the environment upon which they are being executed.

This also means that you should manage environment configurations at deploy time, not at build time. Unfortunately, it is common to perform, for example, web config transformations as part of the build. Visual Studio does make it very easy to create different configuration files for different build configurations (web.debug.config, web.release.config), thereby implying that you should build your application one time for each environment, only to end up with the correct configuration file.

As this book will clearly show, this is not the recommended approach when it comes to implementing a predictable and secure release pipeline. We will use a release management tool (in this case Visual Studio Release Management) to configure and apply correct environmental settings at deploy time.

## Versioning All Artifacts

We talked about versioning previously in this book, and different strategies for versioning. No matter which strategy you choose, it is essential that you make sure that all your artifacts are versioned as part of the build. This creates traceability from the deployed binaries back to the build that produced them. It also makes it possible for applications to report their application version at runtime, which is very useful for troubleshooting.

# Build Types

As mentioned briefly in Chapter 1, you will almost always need several types of builds for a single application. In addition, you often have multiple branches per application so you will need to make sure that you cover those branches with builds as well. The different build types serve different purposes. The next few sections will cover the most common build types and their primary functions.

## Continuous Integration Build

The CI build runs every time someone commits a change to the source control repository. This means that this build can easily run more than a hundred times every day, depending on the size of your team and how often they commit their changes.

If the build fails for some reason, the developer who was responsible for breaking the build should be notified immediately, and it should be top priority to fix the build. In order to keep this feedback loop tight, you need to make sure that this build doesn't take too long.

A CI build typically performs these functions:

- Pulls down the latest source code

- Compiles all the projects

- Runs all unit tests

- Optionally deploys to a test environment

- Notifies developer/team about any failures

Note that by unit tests here we mean "pure" unit tests that can be run during the build without hitting any external systems such as databases or web services. This is one way to ensure that the CI build runs fast.

## Nightly/Integration Build

For many applications, running the whole suite of tests including integration and UI tests in the CI build takes too much time. Therefore it is a good idea to mark all integration tests in a way that makes it possible exclude them from the CI build. You will look at the details on how to do this later in this chapter.

Instead, you can run all these tests in a separate build that often is called nightly build because it runs every night. It could also be called an integration build to point out that it actually performs integration tests as part of the build.

A Nightly/Integration build performs these functions:

- Pulls down the latest source code

- Compiles all the projects

- Runs code analysis tools, such as FxCop, StyleCop, code metrics

- Runs all unit tests

- Deploys to a clean test environment

- Runs all integration and UI tests on the test environment

- Measures code coverage

## Release Build

This purpose of the Release build is to produce a set of versioned artifacts that you can later on deploy using your deployment pipeline. This build normally doesn't run on every commit; instead it is triggered manually or it can be scheduled to run every night, perhaps during acceptance testing where you want to have a fresh install every morning.

It is a good idea to make this build type dependent upon the CI and/or the nightly build, so that you make sure that all your quality gates have been fulfilled before you produce a new version for release.

A Release build performs these functions:

- Pulls down the latest code

- Labels or tags the source control repository

- Adds version information to all relevant source artifacts

- Compiles all projects

- Creates all project artifacts that are necessary for deployment, including items such as Web Deploy packages, Windows Installer files, deployment scripts, database change scripts, etc.

- Publishes all artifacts to a shared location like a network share, server repository like TFS, or a separate artifact repository like NuGet or Artifactory from where the deployment pipeline can access them later

# Team Foundation Build 2015

The history of build automation in Team Foundation Server consists of major changes. The first version, TFS 2005, launched with a build automation engine that used MSBuild as the orchestration language. This was a natural selection at the time, leveraging the existing tool of choice for building most of the projects types on the .NET platform. The build definitions were stored in source control as MSBuild projects files.

TFS 2008 introduced much improvement around authoring the build definitions, with a new user interface in Visual Studio Team Explorer for this. Trigger and drop management were improved vastly, and the build definitions were now stored in the TFS database. The actual build process was still based on MSBuild and stored in source control.

With TFS 2010, a major change was introduced when Windows Workflow became the build orchestration language. MSBuild was still used for compiling the projects, but the rest of the build automation process was realized using Window Workflow activities. For example, getting the source code, labelling the source code, associating the build with work items, etc. was implemented as separate workflow activities. The build process was designed using the standard Windows Workflow designer, and the resulting build process template was stored as XAML in source control. Although very powerful, the authoring experience suffered from complex workflow templates and lots of friction in the authoring experience. For example, to add the running of a script at some point, you needed to create a Visual Studio project with several project references. In addition, there was no efficient way to test the workflow locally.

In 2015, Microsoft shipped TFS with a completely new build automation system. It is no longer built on Windows Workflow; instead it is built around the concept of build tasks that are implemented in either PowerShell or Node.js. The authoring is now done in the web access build tab, and is just a matter of adding the necessary tasks in the correct order and setting properties on each task.

---

■ **Note** In this book, you will only look at the new build system in TFS 2015. The existing XAML build system is still available and will continue to be supported for the foreseeable future, but there will not be any investments there. We recommend that you start migrating any existing investments in XAML builds to the new build system.

---

# Architecture

Figure 7-2 shows the overall architecture of TFS Build 2015.

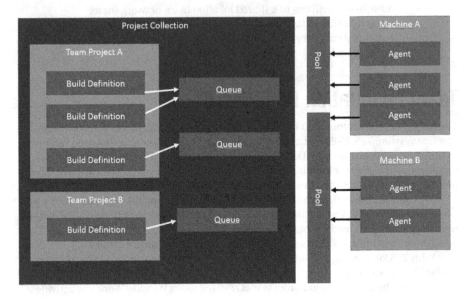

***Figure 7-2.*** *TFS Build 2015 architecture*

*Build agents* are the processes that perform the actual work. These agents can be installed side by side on any supported machine that can access the TFS server. There are no restrictions how many agents can run on a machine. On a Windows machine, build agents are typically installed as a Windows Service, but they can also run as a console application in case you need to interact with the desktop, for example when running UI tests as part of the build.

When agents are configured, they are joined to an *agent pool*. Agent pools are defined on the server level (or account level in the case of Visual Studio Online). Pools have their own security permissions, making it possible to create separate pools of agents that are locked down and only used for a specific purpose.

On the project collection level, *build queues* are defined. A build queue is basically just a way of grouping build definitions to a specific pool. Each queue belongs to a pool, and every build definition can be executed against any queue that is defined in the current project collection.

## Windows Build Agents

The Windows build agent is a standard .NET executable that is installed using XCopy deployment, and then configured using a supplied PowerShell script. This approach makes it easy to install multiple agents on the same machine, something that is not easily done with the XAML build system.

You can download the latest version of the agent installer from your TFS server administration page. This will give you a ZIP file that you can extract to a suitable location. The download link is shown in Figure 7-3.

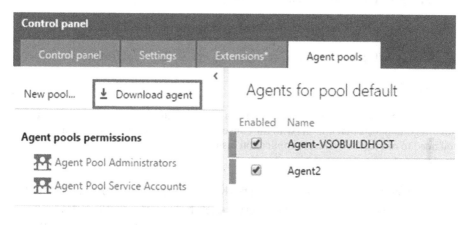

*Figure 7-3. Downloading a build agent*

When you have installed the files on your build server, you can run a PowerShell script called ConfigureAgent.ps1 to configure the agent, telling it which TFS server and pool to connect to.

---

■ **Note**   To minimize the problem of long file paths, make sure to install the agent as close to the drive root as possible, such as in c:\vsa.

---

Here is an output log from configuring a build agent to run against a Visual Studio Online account (the procedure is identical for Team Foundation Server):

```
PS C:\vsa> .\ConfigureAgent.cmd
Enter the name for this agent (default is Agent-ACTIVE-LT14) agent1

Enter the URL for the Team Foundation Server (default is )
https://jakob.visualstudio.com

Configure this agent against which agent pool? (default pool name is
'default') QuizBox

Enter the path of the work folder for this agent (default is 'C:\vsa\_work')

Would you like to install the agent as a Windows Service (Y/N)
(default is N) Y
```

Enter the name of the user account to use for the service (default is NT AUTHORITY\NETWORK SERVICE)

Installing service vsoagent.jakob.agent1...

Service vsoagent.jakob.agent1 has been successfully installed.

Creating EventLog source vsoagent.jakob.agent1 in log Application...

PS C:\vsa>

You can specify if the agent should run as a Windows Service or not. If you intend to run integration tests that interact with the console, such as CodedUI or Selenium tests, you need to run this as a console application instead.

---

■ **Note** Windows build agents are automatically updated when a new version is installed on the server. There is no need to upgrade every single build agent manually. Instead you install a new version on the server and then the agents will automatically be updated. There is also an option on the pool administration page to manually triggering an update to all build agents.

Anyone that has had to manually update build agents and controllers every time an update came out will really appreciate this auto-update feature.

---

## Cross-Platform Build Agent

In addition to the Windows build agent, there is a cross-platform build agent from Microsoft that runs on Mac OSX and Linux. This agent is built with TypeScript and runs on Node.js, thereby making it possible to run on multiple platforms.

---

■ **Note** The cross-platform agent is open sourced and available at https://github.com/Microsoft/vso-agent.

---

Before you can install and run the agent, you need to set up permissions for the account that will be running the build. First, you need to enable alternative credentials for the account so that it can connect to VSO, as shown in Figure 7-4.

*Figure 7-4. Enable alternate credentials*

Then you need to give the account permissions to add an agent to the tool. This is done by adding the user to the Agent Pool Administrators group (shown in Figure 7-5). You also need to allow the agent to listen to the build queue, by adding the agent account to the Agent Pool Service Account group.

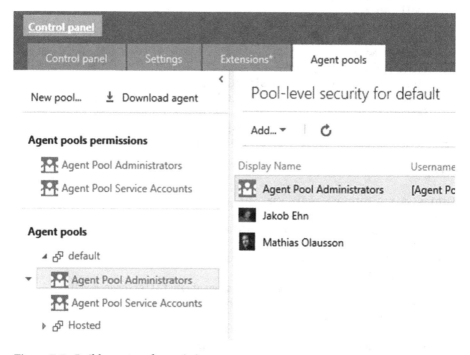

*Figure 7-5. Build agent pool permissions*

To run the agent, you only need to have node and npm installed on the system. The rest is downloaded and installed for you.

The following is an example log from configuring the cross-platform build agent to run against a Visual Studio Online account:

**Installation**

```
Mathiass-Air:~ Mathias$ sudo npm install vsoagent-installer -g
Password:
/usr/local/bin/vsoagent-installer -> /usr/local/lib/node_modules/vsoagent-
installer/bin/install.js
vsoagent-installer@0.2.14 /usr/local/lib/node_modules/vsoagent-installer
├── iniparser@1.0.5
├── svchost@0.1.2
├── minimist@0.2.0
├── node-uuid@1.4.3
├── validator@3.11.2
├── async@0.9.2
├── q@1.4.1
├── adm-zip@0.4.7
├── shelljs@0.2.6
├── vso-task-lib@0.2.5 (shelljs@0.3.0)
├── read@1.0.6 (mute-stream@0.0.5)
├── xmlreader@0.2.3 (sax@0.5.8)
├── touch@0.0.3 (nopt@1.0.10)
├── minimatch@2.0.8 (brace-expansion@1.1.0)
├── glob@5.0.11 (path-is-absolute@1.0.0, inherits@2.0.1, once@1.3.2,
│   inflight@1.0.4)
├── nconf@0.6.9 (ini@1.3.4, async@0.2.9, optimist@0.6.0)
└── svcinstall@0.2.1 (shelljs@0.3.0, plist@1.1.0)
```

**Configuration**

```
Mathiass-Air:~ Mathias$ mkdir vsa
Mathiass-Air:~ Mathias$ cd vsa
Mathiass-Air:vsa Mathias$ vsoagent-installer
Installing agent to /Users/Mathias/vsa
Copying:  /usr/local/lib/node_modules/vsoagent-installer/agent
/Users/Mathias/vsa
Copying:  /usr/local/lib/node_modules/vsoagent-installer/node_modules
/Users/Mathias/vsa
making scripts executable
Done.
Mathiass-Air:vsa Mathias$ node agent/vsoagent
Enter alternate username > olaussonm
Enter alternate password >
Enter server url > https://jakob.visualstudio.com
Enter agent name (enter sets Mathiass-Air.lan)  > mac
Enter agent pool name (enter sets default)  >
successful connect as Mathias Olausson
```

```
Retrieved agent pool: default (5)
Mathiass-Air.lan
Creating work folder ...
Creating env file ...
Saving configuration ...
2015-06-26T22:08:12.752Z: Agent Started.
```

**Running**

```
2015-06-26T22:15:11.930Z: Running job: Build (Debug,iphonesimulator)
##[Error] 2015-06-26T22:15:22.873Z: Return code: 1
2015-06-26T22:15:22.875Z: Job Completed: Build (Debug,iphonesimulator)
2015-06-26T22:15:26.017Z: Running job: Build (Release,iphonesimulator)
2015-06-26T22:15:26.973Z: Job Finished: Build (Debug,iphonesimulator)
##[Error] 2015-06-26T22:15:29.380Z: Return code: 1
2015-06-26T22:15:29.382Z: Job Completed: Build (Release,iphonesimulator)
2015-06-26T22:15:33.084Z: Job Finished: Build (Release,iphonesimulator)
```

Figure 7-6 shows a sample log from the build page when running an XCode build step.

***Figure 7-6.*** *XCode build output*

# Distributing Builds

With TFS Build 2015, it is easy to install multiple build agents, either on the same machine or on multiple machines. Often your TFS server will host many different applications from different teams and different clients. These applications might very well have different requirements when it comes to building the software.

You should always strive to include all application dependencies in source control, or use a package manager repository such as NuGet to bring these dependencies in. But sometimes this is not practical. If, for example, you are building Visual Studio extensions, you will need Visual Studio SDK on the build server, but downloading and installing it during every build doesn't make sense (even if it certainly is possible).

Therefore, you need a way to specify the capabilities of the different agents, and then make sure that your builds are executed on compatible agents. In TFS Build 2015, this is done using *capabilities* and *demands*. Capabilities can represent different features on that particular build agent, such as the version of the OS or a higher level function such as priority or team affinity. There are two kinds of capabilities, *system capabilities* and *user capabilities*.

System capabilities are generated automatically when the build agent is started, so you can't change these capabilities. System capabilities include which operating system is running on the build agent, the version of .NET Framework, and if Visual Studio is installed. User capabilities are added by the build administrator, and let you specify other types of capabilities for that particular agent. If you have one build server that is much faster than the other ones, you could add a capability to all agents on that machine called *FastBuild*.

Figure 7-7 shows the capabilities for a build agent.

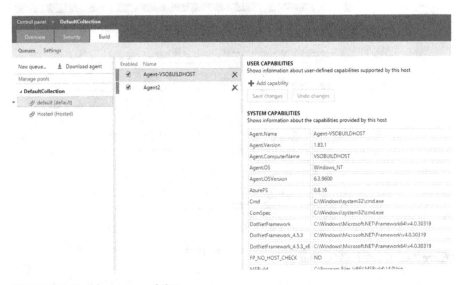

***Figure 7-7.*** *Build agent capabilities*

Agent capabilities are defined in the Build tab at the collection administration level, as shown above. Here you can create new build queues, and when an agent is installed and configured to use that specific queue, it will show up in the agent list.

The different capabilities are shown to the right, first the user capabilities followed by the system capabilities.

To assign a build definition to a matching build agent at queue time, you need to configure the demands, as shown in Figure 7-8.

| Build | Options | Repository | Variables | Triggers | **General** | Retention | History |
|-------|---------|------------|-----------|----------|-------------|-----------|---------|

| 🖬 Save ▾ | 📇 Queue build... | ⤺ Undo |
|-----------|------------------|--------|

| Default queue | default | ▾ Ċ Manage |
|---------------|---------|-----------|
| Description | | |
| Build number format | 1.0.$(Date:yy)$(DayOfYear)$(Rev:.rr) | |
| Build job authorization scope | Project Collection | ▾ ⓘ |
| Build job timeout in minutes | 0 | ⓘ |
| Badge enabled | ☐ | ⓘ |

**Demands**

| **Name** | **Type** | | **Value** |
|----------|----------|---|-----------|
| msbuild | exists | | |
| visualstudio | exists | | |
| vstest | exists | | |
| ✗ FastBuild | equals | ▾ | True |
| ➕ Add demand | | | |

*Figure 7-8. Build definition demands*

As with capabilities, some demands will be generated automatically. But how does the build definition know which demands this build definition has? This is actually derived from the tasks that have been added as build steps. For example, the *vstest* demand that you can see in Figure 7-8 has been added because you used the *Visual Studio Test* task. If you remove this task, the vstest demand would also be removed. So, each build task lists the demands as part of its manifest definition. See the section on creating custom build task later in this chapter for more details on how this works.

In addition to the generated demands, you can add more demands for the build definition. Here you have added the FastBuild demand that will match the FastBuild capability that you added before. This build will always execute on the agent called Agent1, since only this agent has this capability.

---

■ **Note**    It is also possible to force a build definition to be executed on a particular machine by using the *Agent.Name* demand. However, we recommend that you use more explicit demands to specify the reason for this demand (such as FastBuild). This makes it much clearer for others.

---

## Creating Build Definitions

If you have been using older versions of TFS Build, you will find that creating and customizing build definitions in TFS 2015 is much easier and more powerful. In this section, you will walk through all the details of creating a build definition that compiles, tests, and publishes the artifacts back to TFS.

Start by browsing to the Build hub in TFS web access and press the + button. This will open a dialog, shown in Figure 7-9, showing a list of existing build definition templates.

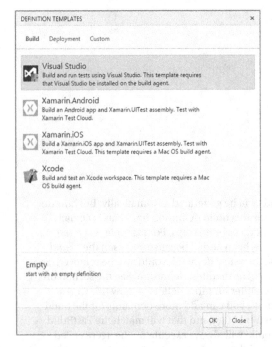

*Figure 7-9.  Build definition templates*

The definition templates are grouped into *Build, Deployment,* and *Custom.* As you will see, you have the ability to save build definitions as a custom build definition template. These templates are shown in the Custom tab in this dialog.

Select the Visual Studio template to create a new build definition based on this template. This template contains build steps for building, running unit tests, indexing the source code, and publishing the artifacts back to TFS.

Let's walk through all the available tabs of a build definition.

# Build

This is where you define the build process for your build. A build process is made up of a set of build steps that are executed in a particular order. You can add, delete, and reorder the build steps by simply dragging them to the desired place. By selecting a build step, you can configure the properties for that particular build step. Figure 7-10 shows the build steps in the selected build definition template.

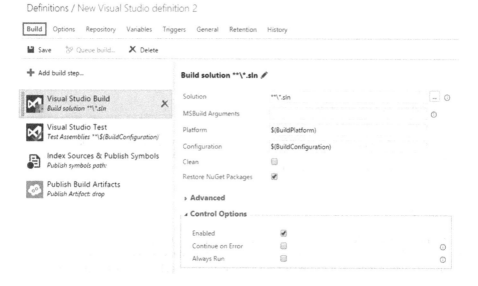

***Figure 7-10.*** *Build section*

In Figure 7-10, the Visual Studio Build step is selected, and you can see the properties of this step. Every build step has a display name that can be modified by clicking the little pencil icon next to the name. This is very useful both to make it apparent what the task is actually doing (updating version number) and when you are using multiple instances of the same task.

Select *Add build step* to view the list of available build tasks (Figure 7-11).

127

*Figure 7-11.* *Adding build steps*

As you can see, the list of tasks is pretty long and contains a lot of tasks that cover platforms other than Windows, such as Android, iOS, and Xamarin. Later in this chapter you will learn how to create custom build tasks.

## Options

Currently there is only one option available here, called MultiConfiguration (Figure 7-12). Selecting this option lets you specify one or more multipliers, which will cause the build definition to be executed multiple times with the different values of the multipliers.

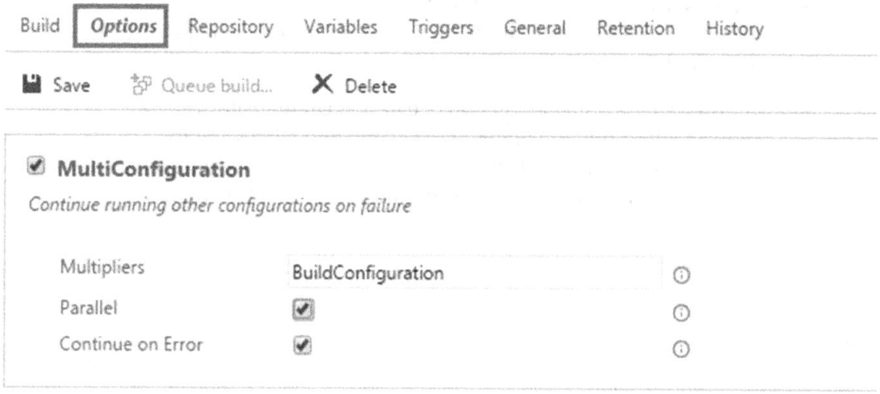

| Build | **Options** | Repository | Variables | Triggers | General | Retention | History |

▮ Save   ᵗ⁇ Queue build...   ✗ Delete

☑ **MultiConfiguration**
*Continue running other configurations on failure*

| Multipliers | BuildConfiguration | ⓘ |
| Parallel | ☑ | ⓘ |
| Continue on Error | ☑ | ⓘ |

***Figure 7-12.*** *Build options*

A common scenario for this is to use the *BuildConfiguration* variable as the multiplier. The BuildConfiguration variable typically maps to the Debug and Release configurations. By using this as a multiplier, the build definition will automatically be executed twice, one time for Debug and one time for Release. In addition, you can select to execute this in parallel, so that the debug and release configurations will be process in parallel (assuming that you have more than one available build agent, of course).

---

■ **Note**   Another possibility is to use this functionality to run tests in parallel on different agents. See this MSDN blog post for more details on how to set this up:

```
http://blogs.msdn.com/b/visualstudioalm/archive/2015/07/30/speeding-up-
test-execution-in-tfs.aspx
```

---

## Repository

The Repository tab (Figure 7-13) specifies where the source code for the build is located. You have the following options:

- **Git:** This option lets you select a Git repository and a default branch within that repository in the current team project.

- **Team Foundation Version Control:** When you use TFVC for version control. This option lets you map a workspace definition to include the relevant parts of the source control tree.

- **External Git:** Can be used to build an externally hosted Git repo. Here you need to enter the URL to the Git repository, and also the credentials if required.

- **GitHub:** This is a special version of external Git repositories. The TFS 2015 build integrates with GitHub and allows you to browse your existing GitHub repositories and will even let you trigger a build in TFS when anyone commits to that GitHub repo.

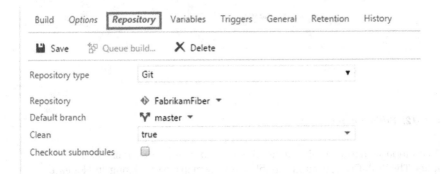

*Figure 7-13. Build repository settings*

The *Clean* option dictates if the build agent will clean the sources from the last build before pulling the code from the server. If you set this to false, you will perform an incremental build which will run faster since the build agent only needs to pull the changes since the last build. The potential downside is that it is not a clean build. There are cases where you might have build results that are different compared to a clean build.

The repository settings when selecting Team Foundation Version Control as repository type are shown in Figure 7-14.

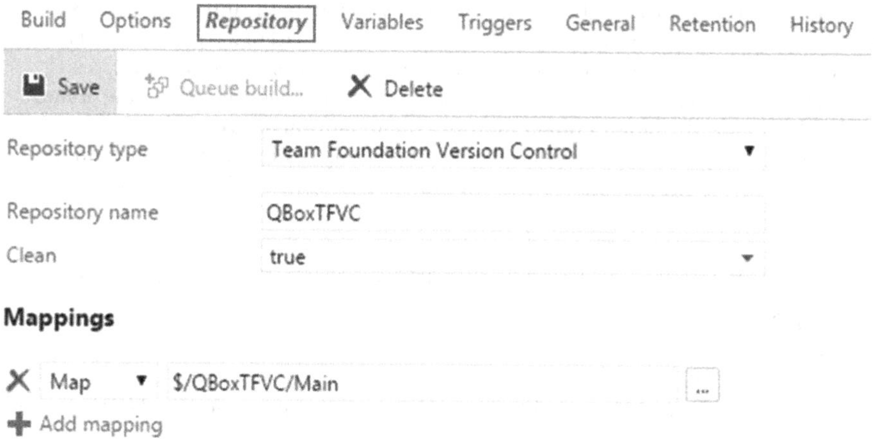

| Build | Options | *Repository* | Variables | Triggers | General | Retention | History |
|-------|---------|--------------|-----------|----------|---------|-----------|---------|

💾 Save       🏗 Queue build...       ✕ Delete

| Repository type | Team Foundation Version Control ▼ |
|-----------------|------------------------------------|
| Repository name | QBoxTFVC |
| Clean | true ▼ |

## Mappings

✕   Map   ▼   $/QBoxTFVC/Main          [...]

➕ Add mapping

*Figure 7-14.  Build repository TFVC settings*

---

■ **Note**    When you use TFVC, be careful to make the workspace as narrow as possible, to avoid pulling down large amounts of code on every build. The default setting here will be the root of the team project, which almost always is a bad choice!

---

## Variables

The Variables tab (shown in Figure 7-15) contains all the variables that are available during the build. This includes predefined variables and custom variables that you add.

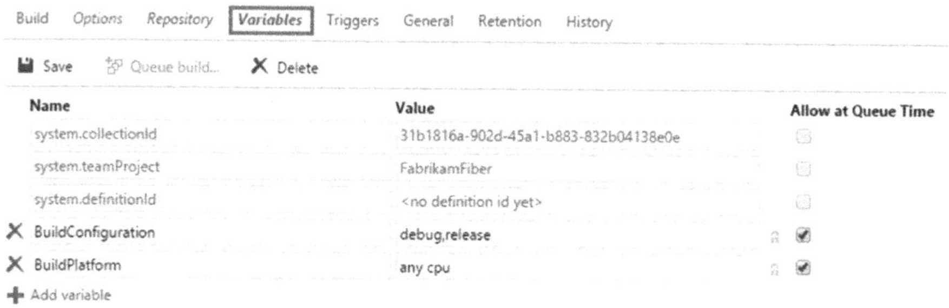

| Build | Options | Repository | *Variables* | Triggers | General | Retention | History |
|-------|---------|------------|-------------|----------|---------|-----------|---------|

💾 Save       🏗 Queue build...       ✕ Delete

| Name | Value | | Allow at Queue Time |
|------|-------|---|---------------------|
| system.collectionId | 31b1816a-902d-45a1-b883-832b04138e0e | | ☐ |
| system.teamProject | FabrikamFiber | | ☐ |
| system.definitionId | <no definition id yet> | | ☐ |
| ✕ BuildConfiguration | debug,release | 🔒 | ☑ |
| ✕ BuildPlatform | any cpu | 🔒 | ☑ |
| ➕ Add variable | | | |

*Figure 7-15.  Build variables*

Build variables are available for all build steps, as part of the input parameters to the build steps and also inside any scripts that you execute as part of the build, such as in PowerShell scripts where the variables are available as environment variables.

Note that you can specify whether variables can be changed at queue time or not. In the above case, the BuildConfiguration and BuildPlatform have default values set, but they can be changed when a build is queued. This is very handy when you want to try something out for one particular build, without modifying the build definition.

---

■ **Note**   There are many more predefined variables available. They are discussed later in this chapter.

---

When you refer to variables within the build definition, you use the $(Build.VAR_NAME) syntax, like this:

$(Build.BuildNumber)

When referring to the variables inside your scripts, you need to refer to them as environment variables, and these take the following naming convention:

$Env:BUILD_BUILDNUMBER

## Triggers

The Triggers tab (Figure 7-16) defines how and when the build definition should be queued. You have two main options, to use a Continuous Integration build that is triggered by commits, or a scheduled build that is triggered at a specific day and time.

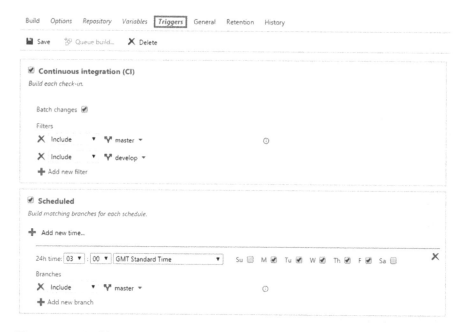

*Figure 7-16.  Build triggers*

For CI builds, you can select to batch changes, which means that while a build is running, any new changes that are committed will be batched and queued in the next build, which will start once the first build has finished. This is sometimes referred to as a *rolling build*.

As you can see, a build definition can be both a CI build and a scheduled build at the same time. Generally, CI and scheduled builds tend to do different things so normally you would select only one of these options.

For a CI build with a Git repository, you must specify which branch, or branches, should trigger a CI build when committed to. For scheduled builds, you also need to specify which branch(es) to build, in addition to when it should be triggered.

# General

The General tab (Figure 7-17) offers some various options for the build definition.

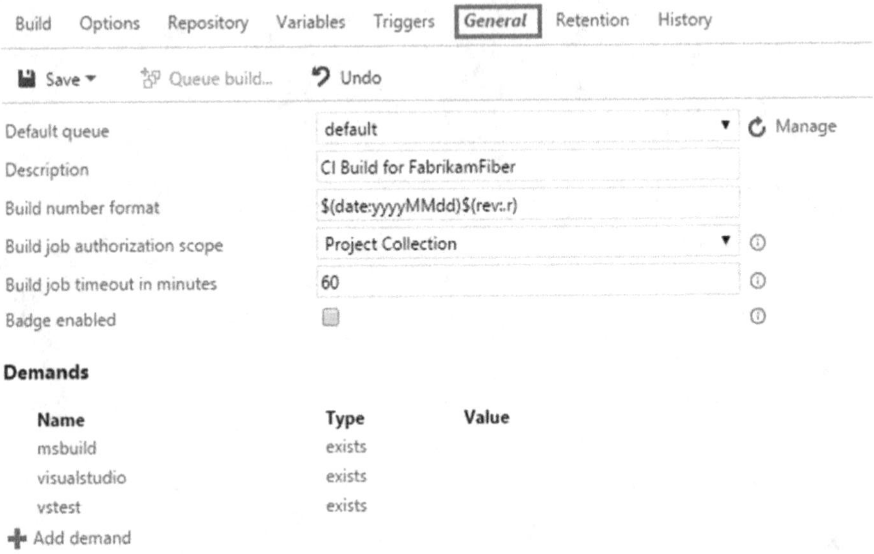

| Build | Options | Repository | Variables | Triggers | General | Retention | History |
|-------|---------|------------|-----------|----------|---------|-----------|---------|

💾 Save ▾     🖳 Queue build...     ↻ Undo

| Default queue | default | ▼ ↻ Manage |
|---|---|---|
| Description | CI Build for FabrikamFiber | |
| Build number format | $(date:yyyyMMdd)$(rev:.r) | |
| Build job authorization scope | Project Collection | ▼ ⓘ |
| Build job timeout in minutes | 60 | ⓘ |
| Badge enabled | ☐ | ⓘ |

**Demands**

| Name | Type | Value |
|------|------|-------|
| msbuild | exists | |
| visualstudio | exists | |
| vstest | exists | |

➕ Add demand

*Figure 7-17.  Build general settings*

The *default queue* assigns the queue that will be used for automatically triggered builds, and as the default when you queue a build manually.

The *build number format* controls what the unique build number for the running builds will look like. We will discuss this parameter in more detail later on when we talk about versioning.

*Build authorization scope* restricts what parts of the source control can be accessed by this build. When set to project collection, this build can download source from any team project in the current project collection. When set to current project, only the source code within the current team project can be accessed.

The *badge enabled* parameter will enable you to link to this build definition from a web page, and it will show a graphical status of the latest completed build. This is very common in open source projects, but is also very nice to put up on internal build monitors to show the current build status.

The badge link will look like this:

```
https://COLLECTION_URL/_apis/public/build/definitions/DEFINITION_GUID/
DEFINITION_ID/badge
```

---

■ **Note** This link allows anonymous access. The intention is for you to publish this image outside TFS, on a wiki page or on a SharePoint site, for example.

---

Lastly, you can add *demands* for the build definition. Demands and capabilities where discussed previously in this chapter; they let you specify the requirements that you have on the build agents that will execute this build definition.

## Retentions

Running builds on multiple build agents, perhaps on every check-in or commit, can quickly take up a lot of space. In particular, this is true of the drop locations where the generated binaries and other artifacts are stored. Retention policies help you cope with this potential problem.

In TFS Build, you can create multiple retention policy rules (Figure 7-18) that dictate how many days that the builds should be kept. By default, the build record will also be deleted, but you can opt out of this.

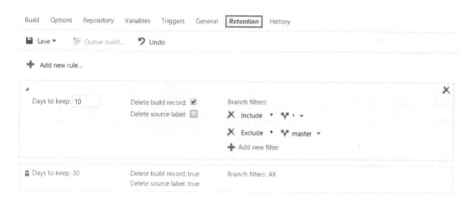

***Figure 7-18.*** *Build retention settings*

Note that for a Git repository you can tie a retention policy rule to a specific branch, or a set of branches. This makes it possible to be more restrictive about what is kept from the master branch than from feature branches, for example.

## History

Finally, the History tab (Figure 7-19) is another nice addition in TFS 2015 compared to previous versions. Every change to a build definition is audited, meaning that you can see all the changes that have been made over time and who did them.

Definitions / QBox.Release | Builds

| Build | Options | Repository | Variables | Triggers | General | Retention | History |

💾 Save ▾          ㌞ Queue build...      ↻ Undo      ◖◗ Diff

| Changed By | Changed Date | Change Type | Comment |
| --- | --- | --- | --- |
| Jakob Ehn | 2015-06-18 10:59:02 | Update | Trying out the MultiConfiguration option |
| Jakob Ehn | 2015-06-18 10:58:45 | Update | Publish installer and web deploy packages as artifacts |
| Jakob Ehn | 2015-06-18 10:58:15 | Update | Added PowerShell script for versioning |
| Jakob Ehn | 2015-06-16 21:49:28 | Update | |

***Figure 7-19.*** *Build history*

To view what has been changed in a particular version, select it and click the *Diff* link. The previous and the selected version will be displayed in the same diff view that is used when comparing code changes. You can also select any two builds, by holding down the CTRL key, to view the difference between them. Figure 7-20 shows the difference between two build definition changes.

***Figure 7-20.*** *Build definition diff*

As you can see, build definitions are stored internally in a JSON format. Currently, it is not possible to undo changes to a build definition.

# Build Definition Drafts

From time to time you may want to make changes to a build definition but you want to make the changes actually work before you make the build definition available for everyone. Previously, this would have meant creating a copy of the build definition, and then manually copying the changes back to the original build definition.

In TFS 2015 Build, you can save drafts of build definitions. These drafts are saved as a copy of the original build definition, but they are linked, meaning that once you are satisfied with your changes you can publish the draft, which will replace the original build definition.

Let's say you want to try the MultiConfiguration option for your build definition. Check this option and then select *Save as a* draft, as shown in Figure 7-21.

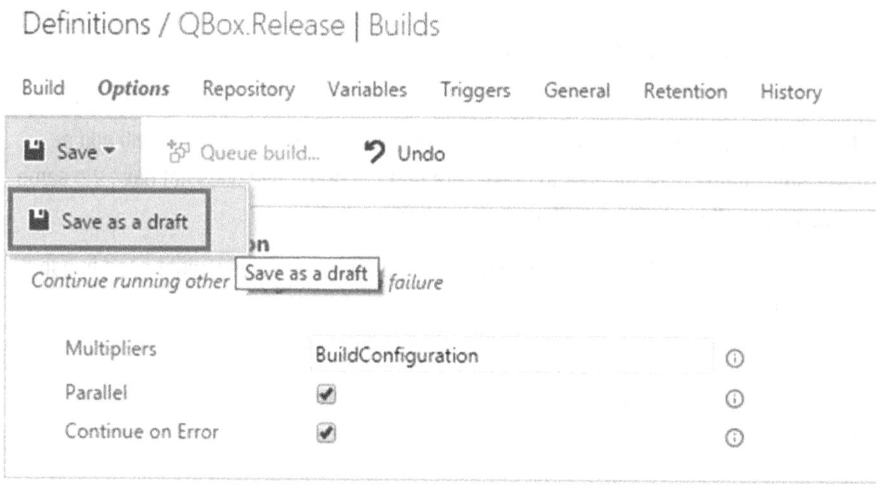

***Figure 7-21.*** *Save build definition draft*

The draft is shown in the Explorer view below the original build definition (Figure 7-22). From here, you can now queue the build, or edit it again until you are done.

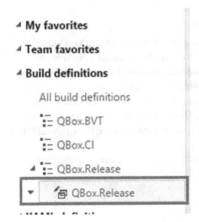

*Figure 7-22. Viewing build definition drafts*

---

■ **Note**  One difference between running a draft build definition is that TFS will add a .DRAFT suffix to the build number to make sure that the draft build does not have the same build number as the original definition.

If you have some kind of dependency on the build number format, you might need to handle this for draft builds.

---

Once you are done and want to update the original build definition, click the *Publish draft* button (Figure 7-23).

*Figure 7-23. Publishing a build definiton draft*

## Build Definition Templates

Even though creating build definitions is much easier than it has been, it can sometimes be useful to extract common build definitions within your organization or community into templates that can be reused by other users.

Start by creating a build definition and configure it the way it should be. When done, right-click the build definition link in the Explorer view and select *Save as a template* (Figure 7-24).

***Figure 7-24.*** *Save build definition as template*

Enter a descriptive name for the template and save it. Now, the next time you create a build definition this template will be available in the Custom tab, as shown in Figure 7-25.

**Figure 7-25.** *Custom build definiton template*

# Securing Sensitive Information

In some circumstances you might be required to store sensitive information in your build parameters. A common example is the user credentials that are necessary in order to communicate with an external resource during the build.

In TFS Build, you can secure information by creating *secret variables*, and then referring to them from different parts of the build definition. You mark a variable as secret by clicking the lock symbol next to the variable definition, as shown in Figure 7-26.

Definitions / QBox.Release | Builds

Build    Options    Repository    *Variables*    Triggers    General    Retention    History

💾 Save ▾    ⚙️ Queue build...    ↩ Undo

List of predefined variables

| Name | Value | | Allow at Queue Time |
|------|-------|---|---------------------|
| system.collectionId | 31b1816a-902d-45a1-b883-832b04138e0e | | ☐ |
| system.teamProject | QBox | | ☐ |
| system.definitionId | 117 | | ☐ |
| ✖ BuildConfiguration | release | 🔒 | ☑ |
| ✖ BuildPlatform | any cpu | 🔒 | ☑ |
| ✖ UserPassword | •••••••• | 🔒 | ☐ |

➕ Add variable

**Figure 7-26.** *Secure build variables*

140

When this is selected, the value is not shown in the UI, and it will not be displayed in any logs or build summaries.

## Showing Build Status on the Homepage

Like many other items in TFS, you can pin build definitions to the home page. You do this by right-clicking the build definition in the Explorer view and select *Pin to homepage*, as shown in Figure 7-27.

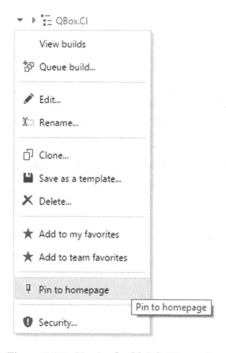

***Figure 7-27.*** *Pinning build definition to homepage*

On the home page, the build widget (Figure 7-28) will show the latest build history of the build definition and the status of the last build.

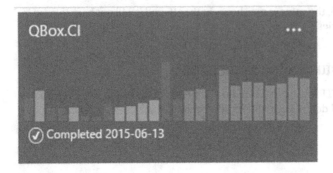

*Figure 7-28. Build status widget*

## Build Tasks Catalog

We won't cover all of the available build steps here, but we will list the most commonly used ones. This will give you a good picture of how build tasks generally are used.

---

■ **Note**   You can find more documentation about the available build steps and the source code at `https://github.com/Microsoft/vso-agent-tasks`.

---

## Common Build Task Options

All build tasks share the following set of options (Figure 7-29). You will see them at the bottom panel of every task option page.

*Figure 7-29. Common build task options*

- **Enabled**: Lets you disable a task that you don't want to execute, but keep around for later use.

- **Continue on Error**: By default, if a build task fails, the build will not continue. This option allows you to override that and let the build continue even if the task fails. If you are running a series of tests using different build steps, you might want to continue with the rest of the test even if one of them fails.

- **Always Run**: This option overrides the previous option in that it lets you always run a particular task, even if any of the previous tasks fails. A common example here is the *Publish Build Artifacts* task that publishes the build artifacts to the drop location. If your tests fail, you might still want to publish the build artifacts.

## Visual Studio Build

This *Build* task (Figure 7-30) is the most common one to use when you are building Visual Studio solutions. Below the surface, it still executes MSBuild to compile the solution, but it first it runs the VSDevCmd.bat file, which is located in the same installation path as Visual Studio. This is the same thing as opening the developer command prompt on your local machine, and makes sure that all paths and other settings are registered. This will make the compilation on the build server identical to what it would be like when you compile locally in Visual Studio.

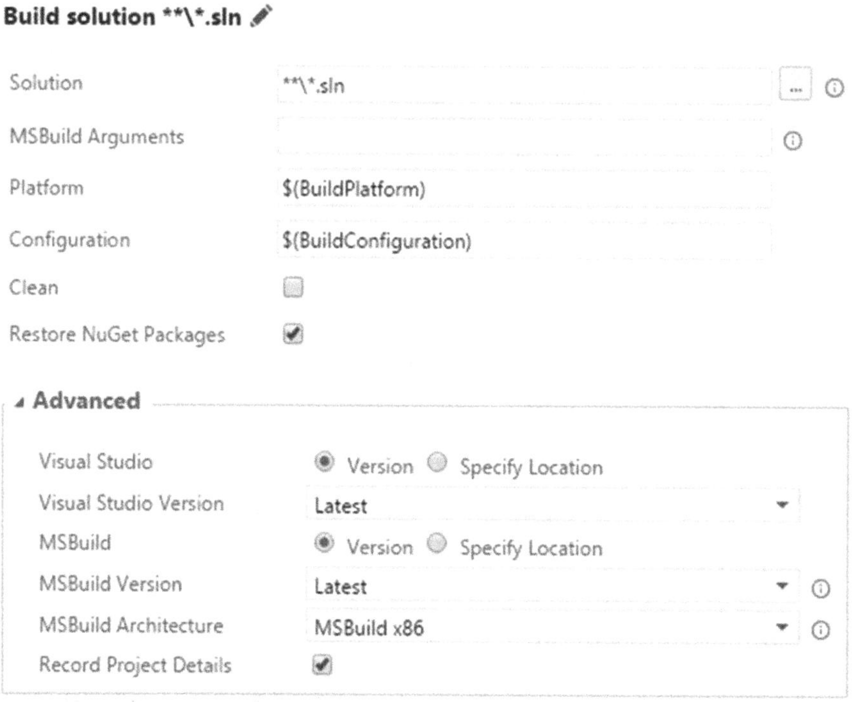

**Build solution \*\*\\\*.sln** 🖉

| | |
|---|---|
| Solution | \*\*\\\*.sln |
| MSBuild Arguments | |
| Platform | $(BuildPlatform) |
| Configuration | $(BuildConfiguration) |
| Clean | ☐ |
| Restore NuGet Packages | ☑ |

◢ **Advanced**

| | |
|---|---|
| Visual Studio | ◉ Version ◯ Specify Location |
| Visual Studio Version | Latest ▼ |
| MSBuild | ◉ Version ◯ Specify Location |
| MSBuild Version | Latest ▼ |
| MSBuild Architecture | MSBuild x86 ▼ |
| Record Project Details | ☑ |

*Figure 7-30.* *Visual Studio Build task*

The main parameter of this task is a list of solution or project files, which can be specified as a pattern as well. For configuration and platform, the predefined variables *$(BuildConfiguration)* and *$(BuildPlatform)* are normally passed in. NuGet Restore is enabled by default, making sure that you do not need to commit your packages to source control. Instead they will be restored prior to the compilation. If you prefer to commit your NuGet packages to source control, you can disable this flag.

In the advanced section of this task, you can specify specific versions of Visual Studio and MSBuild, in case you have a dependency on older versions of these tools.

## Visual Studio Test

This task (Figure 7-31) executes the Visual Studio Test Runner (`vstest.console.exe`), which is the test framework that was introduced with Visual Studio 2012. It supports different test frameworks including MSTest, XUnit, NUnit, and more.

**Test Assemblies \*\*\\\*test\*.dll;-:\*\*\obj\\\*\*** 🖉

| Test Assembly | \*\*\\\*test\*.dll;-:\*\*\obj\\\*\* | ⋯ ⓘ |
| Test Filter criteria | TestCategory!=Integration | ⓘ |
| Platform | | ⓘ |
| Configuration | | ⓘ |
| Run Settings File | | ⋯ ⓘ |
| Override TestRun Parameters | | ⓘ |

⊿ **Advanced**

| Code Coverage Enabled | ☑ | ⓘ |
| VSTest version | Latest ▾ | ⓘ |
| Path to Custom Test Adapters | "$(Build.SourcesDirectory)\packages" | ⓘ |
| Other console options | | ⓘ |

*Figure 7-31. Visual Studio Test task*

The *Test Assembly* parameter specifies which assemblies should be evaluated by TFS Build to locate any unit tests. By default, all assemblies that have the string Test in their name will be evaluated. You can see in this example that everything below the object folders is ignored, using the - character.

The *Test Filter criteria* field is used to narrow the set of tests to run. In this case, you only want to exclude all unit tests that have a test category called Integration.

> ■ **Note** For a description of the test case filter format used by TFS Build, see this blog post on MSDN: http://blogs.msdn.com/b/vikramagrawal/archive/2012/07/23/ running-selective-unit-tests-in-vs-2012-rc-using-testcasefilter.aspx.

The *Run Settings File* and *Override TestRun* parameters are used when you are relying on a .runsettings file for your tests. You *Run Settings File* might have deployment information in here, or where the test results should be placed.

### Running NUnit and XUnit Tests

In order to execute NUnit or XUnit tests on the build server, the build agent must be able to locate the corresponding test adapter. The best way to do this is to add the test adapter as a NuGet package to your test project(s) (the test adapter exists both for NUnit and XUnit at the NuGet gallery). They will be picked up automatically when you run the tests locally in Visual Studio.

In order for TFS build to locate them, you use the *Path to Custom Test Adapters* parameter in the advanced section. Here the value is *$(Build.SourcesDirectory)\packages*, which means that the TFS Build will locate any test adapters that are pulled down from NuGet as part of the solution compilation. This little trick will then handle the solutions that use a mixture of NUnit and XUnit tests.

Later in this chapter you will take a look at how test results are shown.

## Azure Web Site Deployment

This task makes it easy to deploy a web application to an Azure Web App.

> ■ **Note** In general, you shouldn't make a habit of deploying your applications straight from the build, unless you are implementing a deployment pipeline using the build engine. A build server's primary task is to produce artifacts that will later on be picked up by a deployment tool, which will orchestrate the deployment across the target environments.

To use this task, you need to register an Azure subscription to your TFS Server or Visual Studio Online account. You do this on the administration page for the team project, using the Services tab (Figure 7-32). In it you can add a Service Connection to Azure.

***Figure 7-32.** Registering an Azure subscription*

Then you need to enter the subscription Id, a display name for the subscription, and then either add a subscription certificate (available from the publish settings that you can download from the Azure portal), or enter credentials.

When this is done and saved, you can select your subscription in the Azure subscription drop-down in the *Azure Web App Deployment* task (Figure 7-33). Then all you have to do is to select a location, a unique web site name, and which Web Deploy package contains the web application.

**Azure Deployment: QBox** ✎

| | | |
|---|---|---|
| Azure Subscription | MSDN | ▼   Ċ Manage ⓘ |
| Web Site Location | North Europe | ▼   ⓘ |
| Web Site Name | QBox | ▼ |
| Package | $(Build.StagingDirectory)\QBox.WebApp.zip | ⓘ |
| Additional Arguments | -Verbose | |

***Figure 7-33.** Azure Web App Deployment task*

---

■ **Note** This task wraps the *Publish-AzureWebsiteProject* PowerShell Cmdlet. For more information about the additional arguments. take a look at https://msdn.microsoft.com/en-us/library/azure/dn722468.aspx.

---

## Creating Custom Build Tasks

Compared with the previous version of TFS Build, XAML builds, the need for creating custom tasks is not as big anymore. The new build system focuses on making it as easy and transparent as possible to run scripts (as you will see in the next section).

For common scripts or tools that are used in many different build definitions, you can increase the usability by wrapping these in a custom task. Not only can you define default values and descriptive parameter information, you can also package the scripts and tools (and any necessary dependencies) inside the custom build task. This means that you don't have to store these files in every repository that uses them, and you can update them in one place only.

For a nice walkthrough on how to create a custom build task, see Damian Brady's video on Channel9 at `https://channel9.msdn.com/Blogs/MVPANZ/Team-Foundation-Build-Custom-Tasks`.

# Running Scripts

When it comes to build automation, the single most common customization that is done is to run a script at some point in the process. For example, after you have fetched the source code, you might want to add version information to align the version of the compiled binaries and artifacts with the build version. Other common tasks include organizing the build output and running external tools.

In Chapter 6, you took a good look at PowerShell, as it is the de facto standard scripting language for task automation on the Windows platform. As you will see throughout this and subsequent chapters, a lot of the automation that you will perform is done using PowerShell. Also, all of the build tasks that ship with TFS are implemented using PowerShell, even if they often wrap other tools.

---

■ **Note**   Always parameterize your build scripts so that you can test them locally before committing them and adding them to an automated build.

---

## Running PowerShell Scripts

To run a PowerShell script in TFS Build, you use the *PowerShell* task (Figure 7-34) that is available in the Utility category tab.

***Figure 7-34.*** *PowerShell task*

The *PowerShell* task has the following parameters:

- **Script filename:** The path to the PowerShell script file that you want to execute. In a Git repo, this is a relative path from the root of the repo. For TFVC, this is the full source control path. In both cases, you can use the browse functionality to help you locate the file.

- **Arguments:** The is a list of arguments that should be supplied to the script. TFS Build supports named and positional parameters. It does not yet support switch parameters.

    Remember to surround the parameters using quotes in case you have spaces inside, like so:

    *-sourcesDirectory "$(Build.SourcesDirectory)"*

    If you use named parameters, just write them like this:

    *"$(Build.Sourcesdirectory)" "$(Build.BuildNumber)"*

- **Working folder:** Allows you to specify a working folder that should be set before the script is executed. Useful when you have scripts that reference other scripts or files using relative paths.

### Writing to the Output Log

To add informational or debugging messages to the build output log from a PowerShell script, you should use the `Write-Verbose` command with the -Verbose flag, like so:

```
Write-Verbose -Verbose "Message from PowerShell script"
```

If you have a lot of `Write-Verbose` statements in your scripts, you can also set the $VerbosePreference variable in the beginning of the script file:

```
$VerbosePreference = "Continue"
```

## Predefined Build Variables

In all but the simplest scripts you will need to access dynamic information about the build, team project, build server, and other resources. This information is available through the use of build variables that are available both in the build definition itself, where they can be used in arguments for tasks, and inside running scripts as environment variables. There are many predefined variables, and it is possible to add additional user variables in the build definition.

The predefined variables exist at different scopes:

- **Global Build Variables:** These variables are generated on the server and then passed on to the agent during execution. Here you will find variables such as the build number.

- **Agent Variables:** When a build agent is registering itself to a TFS server, a set of variables are collected and sent to the server. These variables contain both machine environment variables, user environment variables, and information from the agent configuration file, plus different tools and framework paths that are typically useful during a build.

- **Agent Build Variables:** Variables that are generated on the agent during a specific build. A typical example is Build. SourcesDirectory that contains the path to where the source code was downloaded to.

Table 7-1 lists a few of the most common variables. Each variable is denoted with S for server variables and A for agent variables.

***Table 7-1.*** *Global Build Variables*

| Variable | Environment Variable | Description | |
| --- | --- | --- | --- |
| System.Team Project | SYSTEM_TEAMPROJECT | The name of the team project that this build belongs to | S |
| System.Team FoundationServerUri | SYSTEM_TEAMFOUNDATION SERVERURI | The URL of the team foundation server | A |
| Build.DefinitionName | BUILD_BUILDDEFINITION NAME | The name of the build definition the current build belongs to | S |
| Build.BuildNumber | BUILD_BUILDNUMBER | The build number assigned to the build by TFS using the build number format specified. | S |
| Build.BuildUri | BUILD_BUILDURI | The Uri for the build | S |

### Agent Variables

| Variable Name | Environment Variable | Description | |
|---|---|---|---|
| Agent.Name | AGENT_NAME | The name of the agent as it is registered with the pool. This is likely different than the machine name. | A |
| Agent.OS | OS | The name of the operating system the agent is installed on. For windows this reports the value of the OS environment variable (Windows_NT). | A |
| Agent.Home Directory | AGENT_HOME DIRECTORY | The directory the agent is installed into. This contains the agent bits. | A |
| Agent.Root Directory | AGENT_ROOT DIRECTORY | The root directory for this agent to sync source. By default it is the same as $(Agent). | A |
| Agent.Working Directory | AGENT_WORKING DIRECTORY | The working directory for this agent. By default $(Agent.RootDirectory)_ work. | A |

### Agent Build Variables

| Variable Name | Environment Variable | Description | |
|---|---|---|---|
| Build.Repository. LocalPath | BUILD_REPOSITORY_ LOCALPATH | The local path on the agent where the sources are synced. Will be $(Agent.BuildDirectory)\$(Build. Repository.Name). | A |
| Build.Sources Directory | BUILD_SOURCES DIRECTORY | The folder where all sources for the build definition are synced to. Will be $(Agent.BuildDirectory)\$(Build. Repository.Name). | A |
| Build.Staging Directory | BUILD_STAGING DIRECTORY | The local path on the agent where any files and artifacts that are expected to be uploaded with the drop need to be placed. It will be cleaned up after the files have been copied to the destination. Will be $(Agent.BuildDirectory)\Staging. | A |
| Agent.Build Directory | AGENT_BUILD DIRECTORY | The local path on the agent where all folders for a given build definition are created. Will be $(Agent. RootDirectory\hash of collection of definitionid and repository URL. | A |

> ■ **Note** For a full list of the available variables, see `https://msdn.microsoft.com/en-us/Library/vs/alm/Build/scripts/variables`.

## Running Builds

As was shown in the previous section, there are a few different ways to trigger a build:

- When a change is committed
- At a scheduled time
- Manually

> ■ **Note** It is also possible to trigger a build by using the different APIs that are available for TFS and Visual Studio Online. We won't be covering this in this book; for more information `www.visualstudio.com/en-us/integrate/default-vsi.aspx`.

When a build is queued, the build system will determine if there are any agents that are online and that match the demands of that particular build definition. If there are, the agent with the least load on it will be selected.

## Queuing a Build Manually

When you queue a build manually, you will be prompted with the dialog shown in Figure 7-35.

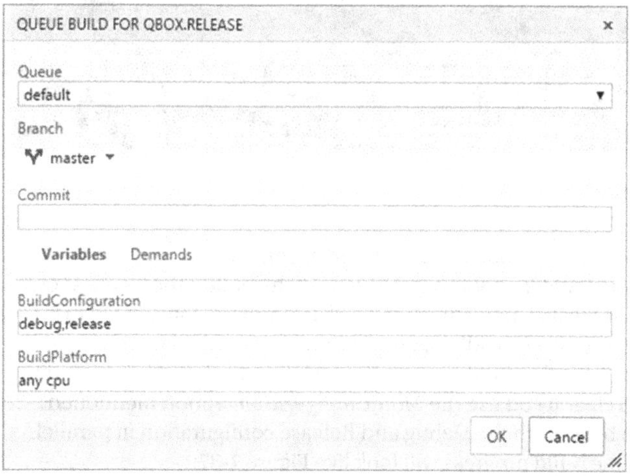

*Figure 7-35. Queue build dialog*

Often you will just select Ok to use the default options, but you have a lot of options here that sometimes can be very handy when you want to change some setting for only this build. You can select a different queue, or in the case of Git, a different branch. You can also build an earlier version of the source code by entering a commit id for Git, or browse to a shelveset for TFVC. This allows you to reproduce an earlier version of your application.

---

■ **Note** Even if you select an earlier version of the source code to build, the latest version of the build definition will be used anyway, since it is not stored in version control.

---

## Viewing Build Progress

When queuing a build manually, the output from the build will immediately be shown in the Console tab, as shown in Figure 7-36.

*Figure 7-36. View build log output*

The console output is sent in real time from the build agent, giving a very good insight into the progress of the build. In addition, the steps of the build process are shown on the left side with a status indicator indicating if the task is running, done, or yet to be executed. Selecting a build step will show all the output from that particular task.

As you can see in Figure 7-36, the build progress to the left is displayed in a hierarchy. The reason for this becomes clear if you use the *MultiConfiguration* option mentioned before. Let's say you want to build both the Debug and Release configuration in parallel. When this build is running, the build progress will look like Figure 7-37.

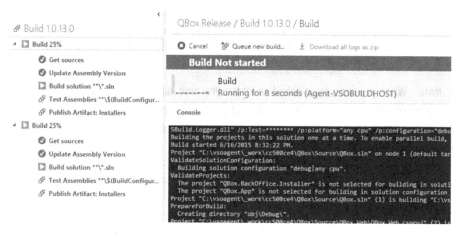

***Figure 7-37.*** *View parallel build output*

Now you can see that both the Debug and Release configurations are being executed at the same time, and you can see the progress of each configuration. Note that you must have two available build agents in order to run these configurations in parallel. Otherwise the build system will build the configurations sequentially.

When the build completes, the build summary will be shown (Figure 7-38). This shows overview information about the compilation and the tests that were executed, including aggregated code coverage information. You can drill down into each of these by using the links.

QBox.CI / Build 1.0.15169.01.DRAFT

    ♘ Queue new build...    ↓ Download all logs as zip

**Build Partially succeeded**

    Build 1.0.15169.01.DRAFT
    Ran for 50 seconds (default), completed 3 minutes ago

Summary    Timeline

**Build details**

| | |
|---|---|
| Definition | QBox.CI (edit) |
| Source branch | refs/heads/master |
| Source version | Commit c4d942 |
| Requested by | Jakob Ehn |
| Queued | Thu Jun 18 2015 15:59:10 GMT+0200 (W. Europe Daylight Time) |
| Started | Thu Jun 18 2015 15:59:18 GMT+0200 (W. Europe Daylight Time) |
| Finished | Thu Jun 18 2015 16:00:08 GMT+0200 (W. Europe Daylight Time) |

**Issues**

Build
❌ VSTest Test Run failed with exit code: 1

**Associated changes**

Commit c4d9422 Authored by Jakob Ehn
minor change

Commit 5fa39cf Authored by Jakob Ehn
Adding category questions

Related Work Items: #545

Commit 8237626 Authored by Jakob Ehn
Adding cateogry questions

**Tags**

Add...

**Test results** ♻
144:VSTest Test Run    ✓ Run completed a minute ago    7 of 9 passed

**Code coverage** ♻
4 modules instrumented - 53.33% of all code blocks covered (Coverage Results)

**Associated work items**
Task 535 Add import UI
Current state is Done. Currently assigned to Jakob Ehn <jakob@ehn.nu>.
Bug 545 All categories does not have questions
Current state is Committed. Currently assigned to Mathias Olausson
<mathias@olausson.net>.
Task 585 Implement it
Current state is Done. Currently assigned to Jakob Ehn <jakob@ehn.nu>.

***Figure 7-38.*** *View build summary*

Also, the list of associated changes and their related work items is shown. TFS Build will aggregate all changes and their related work items since the last successful build of the build definition and list them here.

---

■ **Note** When you run a build definition for the first time, all the changes and work items will be listed, since there is no successful build yet. A good practice is to create a build definition when the project starts and make sure it runs successfully, thereby establishing a baseline for the build.

---

## Viewing Test Results

The displaying of test results has been improved considerably compared to the earlier versions of TFS. If you click on the links in Test results section in the build summary, you will be redirected to the Test hub, where the details of the test run will be shown (Figure 7-39). This page is also used for manual test runs, when you use Microsoft Test Manager to run manual tests.

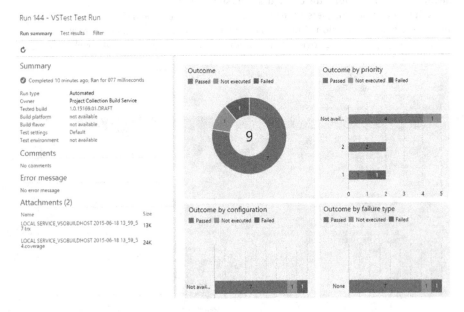

***Figure 7-39.*** *View test run summary*

The test results are presented in several graphs that group the results by outcome, priority, configuration, and failure type.

The Test results tab (Figure 7-40) lets you drill down into the tests to find out why they failed. Here you will see a list of all tests with additional information such as duration, the machine where it was executed, and the error message.

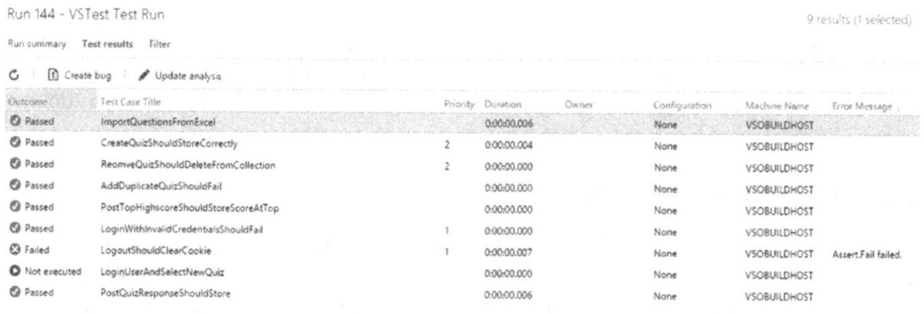

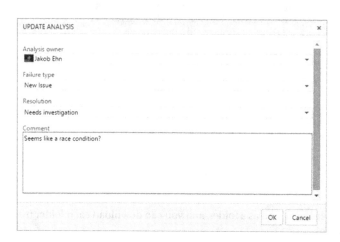

| Outcome | Test Case Title | Priority | Duration | Owner | Configuration | Machine Name | Error Message |
|---|---|---|---|---|---|---|---|
| Passed | ImportQuestionsFromExcel | | 0:00:00.006 | | None | VSOBUILDHOST | |
| Passed | CreateQuizShouldStoreCorrectly | 2 | 0:00:00.004 | | None | VSOBUILDHOST | |
| Passed | ReomveQuizShouldDeleteFromCollection | 2 | 0:00:00.000 | | None | VSOBUILDHOST | |
| Passed | AddDuplicateQuizShouldFail | | 0:00:00.000 | | None | VSOBUILDHOST | |
| Passed | PostTopHighscoreShouldStoreScoreAtTop | | 0:00:00.000 | | None | VSOBUILDHOST | |
| Passed | LoginWithInvalidCredentialsShouldFail | 1 | 0:00:00.000 | | None | VSOBUILDHOST | |
| Failed | LogoutShouldClearCookie | 1 | 0:00:00.007 | | None | VSOBUILDHOST | Assert.Fail failed. |
| Not executed | LoginUserAndSelectNewQuiz | | 0:00:00.000 | | None | VSOBUILDHOST | |
| Passed | PostQuizResponseShouldStore | | 0:00:00.006 | | None | VSOBUILDHOST | |

**Figure 7-40.** *Test results*

If you start analyzing a failing test, you can capture any information that you find by using the *Update analysis* link. This brings up a dialog (Figure 7-41) where you can add extra information about what you found and specify a Failure Type and Resolution for this particular test.

**Figure 7-41.** *Analyzing a test*

Changes to the analysis of a test case will be reflected in the test run summary graphs, where you can see how many tests need to be investigated or if you have too many regression tests.

---

---

If you enabled code coverage in the Visual Studio Test task, you will see the overall
code coverage information in the build summary. To view the details, there are also links
to the generated .coverage files that you can download and view inside Visual Studio.

## Accessing Build Artifacts

Later in this chapter, in the section about packaging, we will walk through in detail
how to configure the output artifacts of your build definition. An artifact in this context
is anything that is useful to the consumers of the build. Often it will include files and
packages that you want to deploy, such as Web Deploy packages, Windows Installer files,
PowerShell scripts, and ZIP packages.

The artifacts can be viewed on the build summary page by selecting the *Artifacts* link
at the top right, shown in Figure 7-42.

*Figure 7-42.  Accessing build artifacts*

Here you will see each artifact listed as a folder, and you can download each folder by
clicking on the Download link.

You can also peek inside each artifact using the Explore link (Figure 7-43). This will
show a tree view where you can drill down and see what is inside that particular artifact.
Here you can also download individual files by using the context menu.

***Figure 7-43.*** *Exploring artifact contents*

# Analyzing Builds

Sometimes a build doesn't work the way you intended. You might get compilation errors or failed tests, or perhaps the build is taking much longer than you expected. Here is how you can troubleshoot problematic builds.

## Accessing Build Logs

As you saw previously, you can view the output of each build step by clicking it in the tree view on the left in the build summary page. You can also download all the logs by using the *Download all logs as zip* link (shown in Figure 7-44) at the top of the build summary page.

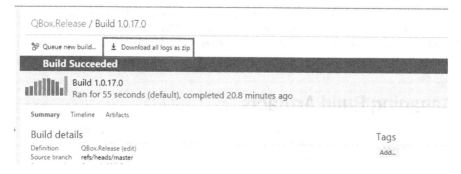

***Figure 7-44.*** *Download all build logs*

The downloaded ZIP package will contain a folder with one log file for every build step. At the root is a concatenated log file with all the log output, which makes it easier to quickly search for something without having to open all of the log files.

## Viewing Build Task Duration

Also in the build summary is a *Timeline* link (Figure 7-45). This page shows all the build steps and the duration for each step. This is very useful when you want to understand what is slowing down the build.

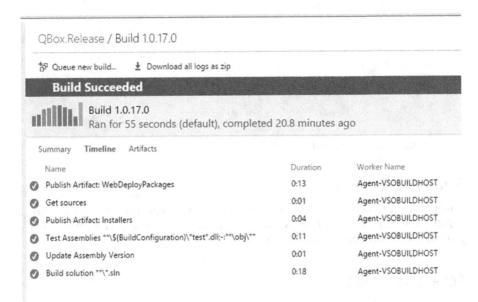

**Figure 7-45.** *Build timeline*

## Building Agent Logs

If you need even more information to understand why a build failed, you can get it by accessing the diagnostic output from the agents. These files are located below the installation path of the agent, in a folder called _diag. Every build that is started will generate a log file here.

# Managing Build Artifacts

The purpose of the commit stage, in which the automated build resides, is to produce a set of artifacts that will be used in the later stages in the release pipeline. These artifacts include Web Deploy packages, Windows installers (MSI), NuGet packages, and PowerShell scripts for deployment.

These artifacts should be versioned in a way so that they can be traced back to the build that produced them, and then copied or published to a shared repository from which the different steps in the release pipeline can access them later when needed.

A common way to store build output in TFS is to either use a shared drop folder or to use the built-in server storage, which can be accessed using HTTP. Another option is to publish the output to an external artifact repository, such as Artifactory or Nexus.

The option you should choose often depends on your choice of tools in the release pipeline.

# Configuring Artifacts for a Build

Organizing the output from the build is important. You want to make sure that you only output what you actually need from the build, and that you create a folder structure that makes sense. There are often several consumers of the build output. The deployment pipeline is one such client, of course, but developers will from time to time need to download the build output to, for example, do a test installation on their own machines.

In TFS Build, the functionality of defining the artifacts is encapsulated in a separate build task called, appropriately, *Publish Build Artifacts*. For each artifact that you want to output, add this task and specify the file pattern to include the desired files into the artifact. An artifact can be a single file, multiple files, or a hierarchy of files.

Figure 7-46 shows an example from the QBox sample application that defines an artifact called *Installers* that contains all MSI files that can be located anywhere below the source root directory of the build.

***Figure 7-46.** Publish build artifacts*

The parameters of this task are the following:

- **Copy Root:** This is the root folder from where TFSBuild will match the paths and patterns defined. The default is the root of the repository, but you can specify any path here. As always, you can use build variables here.

- **Contents:** Defines which files should be included in the artifact. This is a multiline field so you can add several paths or patterns here. The patterns are defined using *minimatch*, which is a library that is used by the Node.js package manager (npm).

This means it supports expressions such as

```
**/bin/**
out/package.zip
out/**/*.zip
$(agent.builddirectory)/out/pkg?(2|1).zip
```

- **Artifact name:** Specifies the name of the published artifact. Must be unique within this build definition.

- **Artifact Type:** Can be either Server or File share.

- **Server:** The default type, which will publish the build output back to TFS and stored it in the TFS database. The artifact can then be downloaded through the web access or using a REST API.

- **File share:** A network share path. Make sure that the build service account has write permissions to this path.

Make sure that you place the Publish Build Artifacts at the end of the build, after compilation and any other scripts that produce the artifacts in question.

## Versioning

We talked about different version strategies in Chapter 4, such as semantic versioning. Being able to easily tell which version a running application has is crucial for achieving Continuous Delivery. You should also be able to trace these version numbers back to the build that produced them. This means that you should align the build number with the version number.

In TFS 2015 Build, the build number is defined on the General tab of the build definition, as shown in Figure.

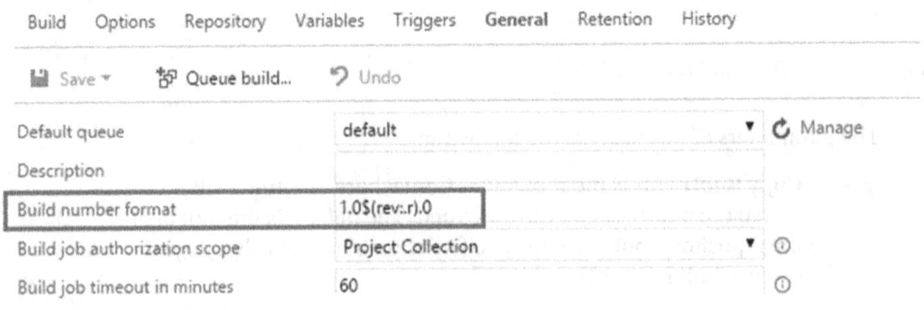

| Build | Options | Repository | Variables | Triggers | **General** | Retention | History |
|---|---|---|---|---|---|---|---|

| | |
|---|---|
| 💾 Save ▾     🗗 Queue build...     ↺ Undo | |
| Default queue | default                                            ▾  ↻ Manage |
| Description | |
| Build number format | 1.0$(rev:.r).0 |
| Build job authorization scope | Project Collection                                          ▾  ⓘ |
| Build job timeout in minutes | 60                                                             ⓘ |

*Figure 7-47.  Build number format*

The *$(rev.r)* is a macro that expands to an integer value that is incremented for each build of this particular version. In this case, you have set the build number to *1.3.0$(Rev)* which results in build numbers like 1.3.0.0, 1.3.0.1 and so on.

Use the generated build number to stamp each artifact with a version number, so that they are aligned to the build that produced them. The build number is available to use through the *$(build.BuildNumber)* variable, so you will pass this in to your scripts that perform the versioning.

## Versioning .NET Assemblies

Whenever a new .NET assembly project is created in Visual Studio, a file named AssemblyInfo is created that contains attributes used to define the version of the assembly during compilation.

Using assembly versions effectively enables various team members to identify deployed assemblies and help troubleshoot problems that may occur in a particular environment (e.g. Development, Test, or Production).

When building the solution, there are two version numbers that need to be considered: the file version number and the .NET assembly version number.

- **File Version:** This is controlled by the AssemblyFileVersion attribute. This attribute should be incremented on every build.

- **Assembly Version:** The AssemblyVersion attribute is the version that .NET uses when linking assemblies. You might not always want to update this attribute on every build, since any dependent client of this code will have to be recompiled or adding binding redirects. For applications, this might not be a problem, but if you are building a library where the public interface does not change, the clients of this library should not have to be recompiled.

To update the assembly version attribute, you will use a PowerShell script that you run in your automated build that will accept the build version as a parameter and then update the AssemblyFileVersion and AssemblyVersion attributes. Here is the script:

```
[CmdletBinding()]

param(
        [Parameter(Mandatory=$True, Position=1)]
        [string]$sourcesDirectory,
        [Parameter(Mandatory=$True, Position=2)]
        [string]$buildNumber
)

# Regular expression pattern to find the version in the build number
# and then apply it to the assemblies
$versionRegex = "\d+\.\d+\.\d+\.\d+"
```

```
# Get and validate the version data
$versionData = [regex]::matches($buildNumber,$versionRegex)
switch($versionData.Count)
{
   0
     {
         Write-Error "Could not find version number data in $buildNumber."
         exit 1
     }
   1 {}
   default
     {
         Write-Warning "Found more than instance of version data in
         buildNumber."
         Write-Warning "Will assume first instance is version."
     }
}
$newVersion = $versionData[0]
Write-Verbose -Verbose "Version: $newVersion"

# Apply the version to the assembly property files
$files = gci $sourcesDirectory -recurse -include "*Properties*" |
    ?{ $_.PSIsContainer } |
    foreach { gci -Path $_.FullName -Recurse -include AssemblyInfo.* }
if($files)
{
    Write-Verbose -Verbose "Will apply $newVersion to $($files.count)
files."

    foreach ($file in $files) {
        $filecontent = Get-Content($file)
        attrib $file -r
        $filecontent -replace $versionRegex, $newVersion | Out-File $file
        Write-Verbose -Verbose "$file.FullName - version applied"
    }
}
else
{
    Write-Warning -Verbose "Found no files."
}
```

This script accepts the build number and the root folder from where it should look for AssemblyInfo.* files. You pass these parameters from the build definition. The script then extracts the four-part version number from the build number, and then applies this to all files that match the AssemblyInfo.* pattern.

When calling this script using a PowerShell task, you send in the necessary parameters, as shown in Figure 7-48.

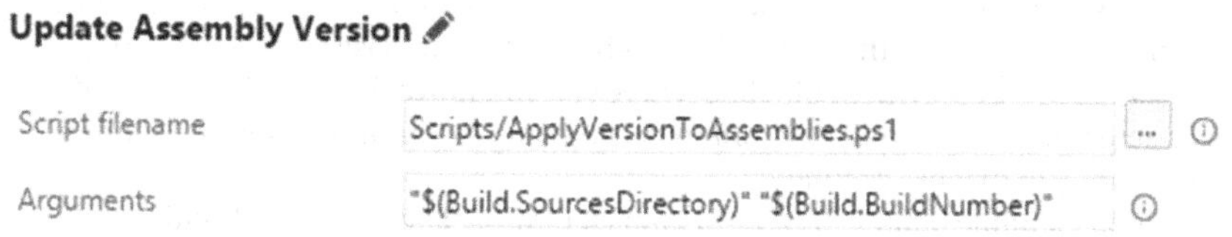

**Update Assembly Version** ✎

| | |
|---|---|
| Script filename | Scripts/ApplyVersionToAssemblies.ps1    ... ⓘ |
| Arguments | "$(Build.SourcesDirectory)" "$(Build.BuildNumber)"   ⓘ |

*Figure 7-48.  Update assembly version script*

Running this script before the compilation starts ensures that all assemblies that are compiled will end up with the same version as the build itself.

# Common Package Formats

One of the main goals for using build automation in the delivery pipeline is to produce something that can be deployed to the target environments. In all but the simplest cases you need to package all the files that are needed to deploy the application. Doing XCopy deployment with a large bunch of files is seldom a good idea. Instead, you should be using the most appropriate package mechanism that exists for the technology and platforms that you are using.

This section will list the most common options for packaging and how you can build and version these packages with TFS 2015 Build. The scope of this book does not allow us to cover all details of the different formats, but we will go through the common scenarios and setups, and then link to more information about each format.

## Web Deploy

Web Deploy is one of the most popular ways to deploy web applications that run on IIS (including Azure Web Apps). It is built on top of MSDeploy and has a rich set of commands and options to deploy and sync web sites, as well as related resources such as registry settings and GAC assemblies.

---

■ **Note**   You can read more about Web Deploy at www.iis.net/downloads/microsoft/web-deploy.

---

## Web Deploy Overview

Web Deploy is built on top of MSDeploy and it integrates with MSBuild using something called the *Web Publishing Pipeline (WPP)*. This is a set of MSBuild targets that extend the functionality of MSBuild and enable it to integrate with Web Deploy. This means that it is easy to trigger Web Deploy during an automated build, since you are already using MSBuild for compilation. All options that configure the creation process are passed in using MSBuild arguments.

A key feature of Web Deploy is the ability to assign environment-specific variables at deployment time, such as the name of the web site or a database connection string. This is essential in a deployment pipeline where you will move the same binaries and packages across all the different environments, applying environment-specific settings when you deploy to that environment.

Here is an example of how to create a Web Deploy package using MSBuild:

```
msbuild.exe /p:Configuration=Release /p:DeployOnBuild=true
/p:DeployTarget=Package /p:PackageLocation="./packageoutput"
```

The following MSDeploy-specific properties were used here:

- DeployOnBuild: Triggers the Web Deploy MSBuild targets that are triggered after the compilation part of the build completes successfully.

- DeployTarget: Specifies which Web Deploy target should be called. For release management scenarios, you are most often interested in the Package target, which will create a Web Deploy package but not deploy it.

- PackageLocation: Defines a relative or absolute output path of the Web Deploy package and the related files.

These are just a few of all the available parameters that Web Deploy can use. Instead of specifying all these settings as parameters to MSBuild like this, you can group them together in a *publish profile*. Publish profiles were introduced with Visual Studio 2012; they are a MSBuild file that you add to each web project, and they contain the necessary information to create a Web Deploy package.

Visual Studio has built-in support for creating and managing publish profiles. To see this, open a web project in Visual Studio, right-click the project, and select Publish. This will show the *Publish Web* dialog (Figure 7-49), from where you can create and manage the publish profiles for this project.

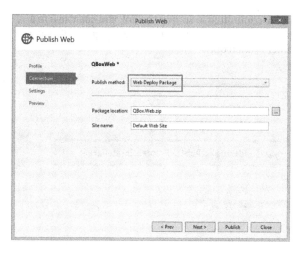

*Figure 7-49.* Create Web Deploy Package profile

Make sure that you select *Web Deploy Package* as the publish method, since you just want to create the package, not deploy it.

The publish profile will be stored below the Properties folder in the web project, as shown in Figure 7-50.

*Figure 7-50.* Publish profile

---

■ **Note**   It is quite common to create different publish profiles for different environments (Dev, Test, Prod, etc.), but this is not something that we recommend for the same reasons that we have mentioned a few times already. You should not have to rebuild the application every time you want to deploy it to a new environment. In addition, you want to avoid storing environment-specific settings, such as logins and password, in source control. This information should instead be authored using a release management tool, where it can be secured and used at deployment time.

---

When you have the publish profile committed to source control, you can use it in a build, by using the MSBuild arguments of the *Visual Studio Build* task. Figure 7-51 shows an example with the MSBuild arguments filled out.

**Build solution \*\*\\\*.sln** 🖊

| | | |
|---|---|---|
| Solution | \*\*\\\*.sln | ... ⓘ |
| MSBuild Arguments | /p:DeployOnBuild=true /p:PublishProfile=CreatePackaç ⓘ | |
| Platform | $(BuildPlatform) | |
| Configuration | $(BuildConfiguration) | |
| Clean | ☐ | |
| Restore NuGet Packages | ☑ | |

***Figure 7-51.*** *Generating a Web Deploy package*

The full argument string is

```
/p:DeployOnBuild=true /p:PublishProfile=CreatePackage
/p:PackageLocation="$(build.stagingDirectory)"
```

Here you have referenced a publish profile called *CreatePackage* and you configured MSDeploy to place the output in the staging directory of the build. You can then easily grab the generated packages and publish them to the drop location.

## Web Deploy Output

When you are using the MSBuild arguments specified above, you will get the following files in the build output (the name *project* will be replaced with the name of the web project):

- *project*.zip: This is the Web Deploy package that you will deploy.

- *project*.deploy.cmd: This is a command file that contains a set of parameterized MSDeploy commands for deploying the package to a IIS web server. It serves as a simple way to deploy the package without knowing all of the MSDeploy commands.

- *project*.SetParameters.xml: This file contains a set of parameter values, such as the name of the IIS web application where you want to deploy the package, and any connection strings or service endpoints that are defined in the web.config file. You can also add custom properties here, by adding a Parameters.xml file to your project. You will see an example of this in the sample application later in this chapter.

- *project*.SourceManifest.xml: This file is created during the compilation phase and is used by Web Deploy to determine what files should be included in the Web Deploy package. This file is not used afterwards, but will by default end up in the output directory.

So the important files here are *.zip and *.SetParameters.xml. When you implement the deployment pipeline, you will be applying the settings for that particular environment and updating the *.SetParameters.xml file and then deploying the ZIP package using MSDeploy.

## Handling Multiple Web Projects

The above solution works fine if you have only one web application in the solution. If you have multiple web applications projects in the same solution, MSDeploy will try to find a publish profile in every web project with the name that you pass in using the PublishProfile property.

To solve this, you have a couple of options. One is to make sure that all web projects have a publish profile with the same name. This will work as expected, but is a rather fragile solution.

A better solution is to inject the name of the publish profile into each web project by adding an MSBuild property to the .csproj file (or .vbproj), like so:

```
<PropertyGroup>
    <PublishProfile>MyWebAppProfile</PublishProfile>
</PropertyGroup>
```

Using this approach, you don't specify the publish profile in the MSBuild arguments, since this will be picked up automatically by Web Deploy.

## NuGet

NuGet is the premier package management system for .NET. It is used to reference and install application dependencies (referred to as packages), such as jQuery or Json.NET. NuGet also handles dependencies between packages, and makes sure that when you install or update a package the necessary dependencies are also downloaded and installed.

NuGet integrates with Visual Studio and makes it easy to locate and install packages from the public NuGet gallery.

The NuGet gallery is the most obvious choice when it comes to publishing a NuGet package and making it public to everyone. There are other available NuGet repositories such as MyGet, which also supports private NuGet feeds that can be used for internal NuGet packages, for example.

It is also possible to host your own NuGet repository within your company network. This is often the best option if you need to distribute shared dependencies between different applications.

## NuGet and Build Automation

When it comes to the automatic creation of NuGet packages from an automated build, you need to perform the following steps:

- Stamp the NuGet manifest file with a version number.
- Create a NuGet package using the nuget.exe command line tool.
- Optionally, publish the package to a NuGet repository.

We recommend that you implement the creation of the NuGet package as part of the MSBuild pipeline. This means that the package creation becomes part of the normal compilation phase, and any errors here will be notified locally. Versioning and publishing of the package should be performed only on the build server.

---

■ **Note**   With ASP.NET 5 comes new project types for class libraries and console applications that automatically create a NuGet package as output. These are built upon the new build system in ASP.NET 5, and therefore support cross-compiling to multiple targets. This project type was still in preview at the time of writing. Read more about this at
`http://docs.asp.net/en/latest/conceptual-overview/aspnet.html`.

---

Implementing automatic creation of NuGet packages by extending the MSBuild project is not very complicated. But there are some available open source tools that make it even easier.

One of these is the *MsBuild.NuGet.Pack* NuGet package (available at `https://github.com/roryprimrose/MsBuild.NuGet.Pack`). This NuGet package implements the packaging process by adding custom MSBuild targets to the project that are automatically trigged on compilation. It also defines some MSBuild properties that control some functionality around creating and publishing the package.

You install this package by opening the Package Manager Console in Visual Studio and running

```
Install-Package MsBuild.NuGet.Pack
```

This will add a sample `.nuspec` file to the project and import the custom MSBuild targets into your project. Figure 7-52 shows a simple class library project with the NuGet package installed.

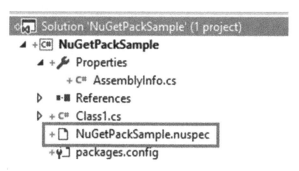

*Figure 7-52. NuGet sample project*

Here are some of the MSBuild properties that are available when using this NuGet package:

- RunNuGetPack: Enables/disables creating a NuGet package when the project is compiled.

- IncludeBuildVersion: If true, the fourth part of the version number will be included in the package version.

- FileExclusionPattern: Controls which file paths are excluded from the automatic bundling of files into the package. Defaults to *.CodeAnalysisLog.xml;*.lastcodeanalysissucceeded;*Test*.*.

- RunNuGetPublish: If true, the package will be published.

- NuGetServer: Which NuGet server to publish the package to.

- NuGetApiKey: The ApiKey for publishing to the NuGet server.

Since you always want to create a NuGet package when you compile, you will set the RunNuGetPack property to true for your project. You do this by opening the .csproj file in a text editor and adding the following at the top of the file, as shown in Figure 7-53.

```
<PropertyGroup>
  <RunNuGetPack>true</RunNuGetPack>
</PropertyGroup>
```

*Figure 7-53. Trigger NuGet creation on build*

Now when you compile the project, a NuGet package will be created in the output directory of the project. Notice in Figure 7-54 that the NuGet package gets the same version as the project.

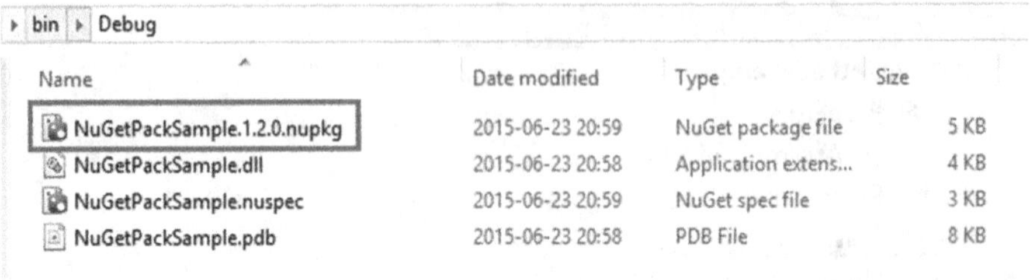

*Figure 7-54. NuGet project output*

So this package handles both versioning and packaging the NuGet package for use. Since you will be updating the AssemblyInfo attributes as part of your automated build, this solution will pick up the correct version number for the package as well.

If you want to publish the package, you could add the NuGet server and ApiKey properties to the project file. This is not recommended, since it would try to publish every time you build locally; also, you don't want to store API keys in source control. Instead, you specify this information using the MSBuild arguments in your build definition, as shown in Figure 7-55.

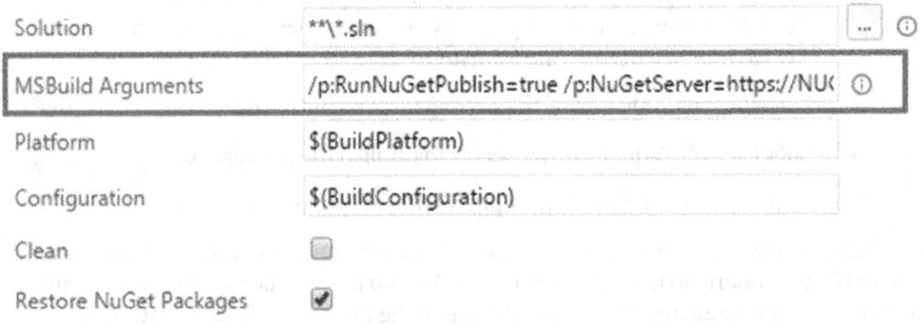

*Figure 7-55. Trigger NuGet packaging on build*

Here you set the RunNuGetPublish, NuGetServer, and the NuGetApiKey properties using the MSBuild Arguments property.

This will also publish the NuGet package after it has been created.

■ **Note** One could argue that in the spirit of release management you should not publish (deploy) the packages from the build, but instead do it using a deployment pipeline, like you will do with the rest of the applications.

However, the workflow for deploying internal libraries and dependencies differs from applications. Publishing a new version of a NuGet package does not mean that all dependent applications automatically start using it. Instead, these applications must manually update their dependencies to the latest version when suitable.

You must, of course, make sure that your NuGet package passes any validation steps before you publish it, so make sure you have good unit test coverage for these projects, and only publish the package if all tests pass.

# Windows Installer (MSI)

Microsoft Windows Installer is an installation and configuration service provided with Windows. Applications and services that should be installed using Windows Installer are packaged into a known format called MSI (based on the file extension .msi). The files that make up the application, together with the installation instructions, are packaged into an installation package commonly known as "MSI files," from their default file extension.

There are several tools available that can generate valid MSI files. Here are the most common ones:

- **Windows Installer XML (WiX):** A free toolset that was originally built and used internally at Microsoft, but was released in 2004 as Microsoft's first release under an open-source license. WiX uses XML for authoring Windows Installer packages and has a set of command line tools for creating the MSI packages. WiX is very mature and has been used to package applications such as Microsoft Office, SQL Server, and Visual Studio.

- **InstallShield:** A commercial product from Flexera that comes with a UI for design installer projects. Since Visual Studio 2012, Microsoft has partnered with Flexera to ship a limited version of InstallShield together with Visual Studio.

- **Visual Studio Setup Projects:** A separate project type that has shipped with Visual Studio since 2002. In the 2012 version, Visual Studio Setup Projects were discontinued and Microsoft recommended either moving to WiX or using the shipped version of InstallShield. On popular demand, though, in 2014, Microsoft re-shipped the setup project as a separate extension that is downloadable from the Visual Studio Gallery.

- **NSIS:** The Nullsoft Scriptable Install System is a script-based, open source system for creating Window installers.

WiX is generally considered to be the most powerful option, and since it is based on command line tools, it lends itself very well to be executed on continuous integration server. You will use WiX for your sample application; in this section, you will take a brief look at how to create a simple setup project using WiX and how to apply versioning to it.

---

■ **Note** There is a great tutorial on WiX available at `www.firegiant.com/wix/tutorial`.

---

## Getting Started with WiX

To get started, you need to download and install the latest version of the WiX toolset. You can find it at `http://wixtoolset.org/`; when this was written, the latest version was v3.9 R2.

This will install the necessary command line tools plus a set of Visual Studio templates that makes it easier to get started.

Once installed, you can find the project templates in the *Windows Installer XML* section (Figure 7-56).

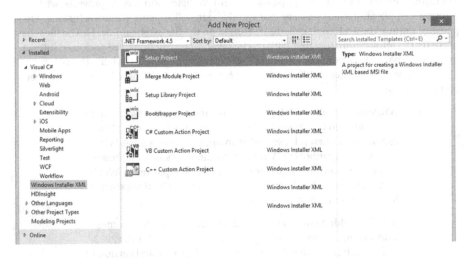

***Figure 7-56.** Create WiX Setup project*

Select the Setup Project template and give it a name. In this case, you will add an installer for the Quizbox BackOffice WPF application, so you'll call it *QBox.BackOffice. Installer*. This will create a .wixproj project file that contains one file called Product.wxs. By convention, this is where you define the metadata (such as version number) and the features of the installer.

The first thing you want to do is to add a reference to the project containing the project that you want to install, in this case QBox.Backoffice (Figure 7-57).

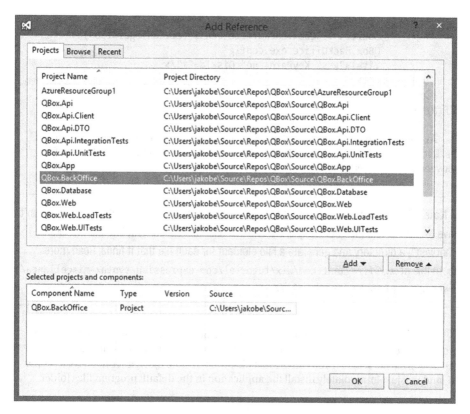

***Figure 7-57.*** *WiX project reference*

This project reference will make sure that the application project is always built before the installer. But it will also create a set of variables that you can use; you will see an example of this when it comes to versioning later on.

Now, to actually install something, you must add some information to your Products.wxs file. The default setup file contains a ComponentGroup element called ProductsComponents, with a Directory attribute with the value INSTALLDIR. This component group is referenced from your only feature, defined inside the Product element, and it is where you should include all files that you want to have installed. To start with, you want to install the executable and the configuration file, as shown in the following code:

```
<Fragment>
    <ComponentGroup Id="ProductComponents" Directory="INSTALLFOLDER">
        <Component Id="ProductComponent" Guid="{AD83D0BB-B16B-4E0A-9069-
        50D55BD19F10}">
            <File Id="QBoxBackOfficeExe"
                    Source="..\QBox.BackOffice\bin\$(var.Configuration)\
                    QBox.BackOffice.exe"
                    Vital="yes" KeyPath="no" DiskId="1"/>
```

```
    <File Id="QBoxBackOfficeExeConfig"
        Source="..\QBox.BackOffice\bin\$(var.Configuration)\
        QBox.BackOffice.exe.config"
        Vital="yes" KeyPath="no" DiskId="1"/>
    </Component>
  </ComponentGroup>
</Fragment>
```

As you can see, you have added two File elements, each referencing a specific file. Each file much have a unique Id within the installer project that identifies the file between installations.

---

■ **Note**   There are ways of automatically generating these WiX fragments so that you don't have to refer to each file manually like this. There is a tool called *Heat* that can traverse ("harvest") a directory and generate a File element for each file that it finds. Read more about this at www.firegiant.com/wix/tutorial/com-expression-syntax-miscellanea/components-of-a-different-color/.

---

Update the Name and Manufacturer attributes of the Product element to reflect your product. If you compile the project now, it should product a MSI file located in the bin\debug\en-us folder. If you run the installer, you will note that it does not have a proper UI, and will just immediately install the application in the default program files folder.

## Versioning

All artifacts that you produce in your commit stage must be versioned. This is also valid for the Windows installer MSI. The version of a Windows Installer is visible in the *Programs and Features* control panel. Incrementing the version also makes it possible to upgrade the application without uninstalling it first. This is a requirement of Windows Installer itself; it is not possible to install a new version of an application with the same version number as one that is already installed.

In WiX, you can achieve this quite easy. You will use a feature called binder variables, which are generated by the WiX linker called Light. Light generates several variables for each managed and native assembly that it processes, such as variables, which lets you refer to a dynamically generated variable. When adding a project reference from a WiX project, this will dynamically generate a set of preprocessor variables during the compilation that can be used inside the WiX source files. Table 7-2 lists the binder variables that are related to file versioning.

*Table 7-2. Binder Variables*

| Variable | Example Usage | Example Value |
|---|---|---|
| bind.fileVersion.FileID | !(bind.fileVersion.MyFile) | 1.0.0.0 |
| bind.assemblyFile Version.FileID | !(bind.assemblyFileVersion.MyAssembly) | 1.0.0.0 |
| bind.assembly Name.FileID | !(bind.assemblyName.MyAssembly) | MyAssembly |

So, since you already added versioning to your assemblies, you can now use either the bind.fileVersion or the bind.assemblyFileVersion variables, as shown in the following code:

```
<Product Id="*"
  Name="QBox.BackOffice.Installer"
  Language="1033"
  Version="$(var.VERSION)"
  Manufacturer="QuizBox International"
  UpgradeCode="6ef49cb0-e881-4a97-bc20-2cf9b1e7b361">
```

Now every time you compile the WiX project, it will have the same version as the application that you are installing, which is what you want.

# WiX and Build Automation

WiX project files (*.wixproj) are standard MSBuild project types, meaning that integrating them with TFS Build (or any continuous integration server, really) is easy: just install the WiX toolset on the build server(s) and the WiX projects will be built along with the rest of the projects in the solution.

There is a very common issue that occur when build WiX projects on a build server, which is related to ICE validation. The error message often looks like this:

*light.exe : error LGHT0217: Error executing ICE action 'ICE01'. The most common cause of this kind of ICE failure is an incorrectly registered scripting engine. See http://wixtoolset.org/documentation/error217/ for details and how to solve this problem. The following string format was not expected by the external UI message logger: "The Windows Installer Service could not be accessed. This can occur if the Windows Installer is not correctly installed. Contact your support personnel for assistance.".*

This error is caused by the fact the light.exe, the WiX linker application, runs a validation, *Windows Installer Internal Consistency Evaluators (ICEs)*, after every successful build. Unfortunately, it can often cause the error shown above, and there are two ways around it:

- Disable ICE validation by setting the SuppressValidation property to true in the .wixproj file:

```
<PropertyGroup>
    <SuppressValidation>true</SuppressValidation>
</PropertyGroup>
```

- Add the build agent account into the local administrator group.

Neither of these solutions are perfect. Running ICE validations can catch common authoring errors. Adding the build agent account to the local administrators groups is not recommended, following the principle of least privileges.

---

■ **Note** Since WiX projects can take a long time to compile, it is common to exclude this project in the Debug solution configuration to avoid building it all the time during development. When building on the server, you are always building the Release configuration, which will include the WiX project as well.

---

## SQL Databases

Databases in general have always been one of the hardest parts of deployment automation, the main reason being that they are stateful, which means that you must upgrade them properly so that you don't lose any data.

When it comes to tracking and deploying the changes to a database, there are two main approaches.

## Model-driven

In a model-driven approach, you keep artifacts in source control that represents the desired state of your database. This is done by having a set of SQL scripts that contain CREATE statements for all the database objects. To create the database from scratch, you run these scripts in the correct order. However, to upgrade a running database to the latest version, you must create a change script that will apply all the changes in the correct order until the target database is identical.

There are several tools available for generating change scripts, such as SQL Server Data Tools and RedGate SQL Compare. They will usually work very well and create change scripts that can be executed against a target database without any problems. There are some cases, however, where the changes done can confuse the compare tool. One common example is when a SQL column is renamed; most compare tools will record this as a column drop and add, which will in effect lose all existing data.

# Migration-Driven

In a migration-driven model, instead of storing the entire database model in source control, you track each incremental change that is done and store it in a separate SQL script, often referred to as a *migration* script. There also code-driven approaches like Entity Framework Code First, where every migration is implemented in a separate C# class that will take care of upgrading (or rollbacking in the case of an error).

This approach is preferred when it comes to implementing Continuous Delivery, since it is much more explicit and removes the need of "guessing" what changes have been done.

There are several tools available that help out with implementing this approach. Entity Framework Code First from Microsoft contains support for tracking and running migrations using a code-based approach. DbUp (available at http://dbup.github.io/) is another popular .NET library that assists with change tracking and running the change scripts in the correct order.

# Versioning

When it comes to versioning databases, migration-based approaches typically handle this by adding a table in which the current state and version of the database are stored. This table is checked during deployment to analyze which of the migrations must be executed. After the migration, the version table is updated to reflect the new version.

Entity Framework Code First adds a table called _MigrationHistory, which contains the list of scripts that have been executed. Figure 7-58 shows an example of the contents of such a table.

| | MigrationId | ContextKey | Model | ProductVersion |
|---|---|---|---|---|
| 1 | 201502091343195_Initial | Platform.Data.Context.ApplicationDbContext | 0x1F8B0800000000000400ED1DDB6EDCB8F5BD40FF61304F6... | 6.1.1-30610 |
| 2 | 201502100939402_School... | Platform.Data.Context.ApplicationDbContext | 0x1F8B0800000000000400ED1DDB6EDCBAF1BD40FF41D8A7... | 6.1.1-30610 |
| 3 | 201502102051041_AddCla... | Platform.Data.Context.ApplicationDbContext | 0x1F8B0800000000000400ED1DDB6EDDB8F1BD40FF41384F6... | 6.1.1-30610 |
| 4 | 201502102101317_Update... | Platform.Data.Context.ApplicationDbContext | 0x1F8B0800000000000400ED1DD96EE4B8F13D40FEA1D14F4... | 6.1.1-30610 |
| 5 | 201502120731515_SetCas... | Platform.Data.Context.ApplicationDbContext | 0x1F8B0800000000000400ED1DD96EE4B8F13D40FEA1D14F4... | 6.1.1-30610 |
| 6 | 201502170944020_AddAp... | Platform.Data.Context.ApplicationDbContext | 0x1F8B0800000000000400ED1D6B6FDCB8F17B81FE87C57E6... | 6.1.1-30610 |
| 7 | 201502201358496_AddSc... | Platform.Data.Context.ApplicationDbContext | 0x1F8B0800000000000400ED1D6B6FDCB8F17B81FE87C57E6... | 6.1.1-30610 |
| 8 | 201502201554288_Nullabl... | Platform.Data.Context.ApplicationDbContext | 0x1F8B0800000000000400ED1D6B6FDCB8F17B81FE87C57E6... | 6.1.1-30610 |
| 9 | 201505070430545_Produc... | Platform.Data.Context.ApplicationDbContext | 0x1F8B0800000000000400ED1D6B6FDCB8F17B81FE87C57E6... | 6.1.1-30610 |
| 10 | 201505201125475_TinCan... | Platform.Data.Context.ApplicationDbContext | 0x1F8B0800000000000400ED1D6B6FDCB8F17B81FE87C57E6... | 6.1.1-30610 |

*Figure 7-58. Migration history table*

Entity Framework analyzes the content of this table and runs any migrations that might need a correct target database. DbUp has a similar solution with a table called SchemaVersion.

If you are using SQL Server Data Tools (SSDT) for a model-driven approach, there is support for versioning and drift analysis if you register the database as a *data-tier application (DAC)*. A DAC provides a single unit for authoring, deploying, and managing the data-tier objects instead of having to manage them separately.

---

■ **Note**   Read more about Data-tier Applications at `https://technet.microsoft.com/`
`en-us/library/ee240739(v=sql.110).aspx`.

---

One feature that is available when using DAC is versioning. The version number is
applied in the project settings, as shown in Figure 7-59.

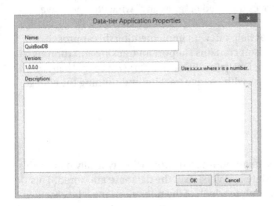

***Figure 7-59.***  *Data-tier Application properties*

When deploying this database, SQL Server will record the version and you can fetch
it by running the following query:

```
SELECT * FROM [msdb].[dbo].[sysdac_instances]
```

Figure 7-60 shows a sample output that shows the QuizBoxDB database with a
version number.

| instance_id | instance_name | type_name | type_version | description | type_stream | date_created | created_by | database_name |
|---|---|---|---|---|---|---|---|---|
| 1 EEE5AD90-3972-47... | QuizBox | QuizBoxDB | 1.0.0.0 | Local build | 0x504B030414000000... | 2015-06-25 15:1... | ACTIVE\jakobe | QuizBox |

***Figure 7-60.***  *Database version*

In an automated build scenario, you want to update this version number during the
build together with the rest of the applications. The version number is stored inside the
project file (`.sqlproj`) in an element called `DacVersion`.

Here is a PowerShell script that can be used to update the `DACVersion` element in all
`.sqlproj` files with a new version number:

```
function Set-XmlElementsTextValue(
    [xml]$XmlDocument,
    [string]$ElementPath,
    [string]$TextValue)
```

```
{
    $node = Get-XmlNode -XmlDocument $XmlDocument -NodePath $ElementPath
    # If the node exists, update its value.
    if ($node)
    {
        $node.InnerText = $TextValue
    }
}


# Apply the version to the .sqlproj property files
$files = gci $sourcesDirectory -recurse |
        ?{ $_.Extension -eq ".sqlproj" } |
        foreach { gci -Path $_.FullName -Recurse -include *.sqlproj }
if($files)
{
    Write-Verbose -Verbose "Will apply $newVersion to $($files.count)
.sqlproj files."

    foreach ($file in $files) {
        if(-not $Disable)
        {
        $sqlProject = Get-Content $file
        $sqlProject = $sqlProject -replace
                            "\<DacVersion\>(\d+)\.(\d+)\.(\d+)\.(\d+)\
                            <\/DacVersion\>",
                            "<DacVersion>$newVersion</DacVersion>"
        Set-Content $file -Value $sqlProject
        Write-Verbose -Verbose "$file.FullName - version applied"
        }
    }
}
else
{
        The version numbersWrite-Warning -Verbose "Found no .sqlproj files."
}
```

You will into how you can deploy data-tier applications in Chapter 10 when you learn about deployment of databases.

# QuizBox Sample Application

For your sample application, you will implement three different builds: a CI build that runs on every commit and runs your unit tests, a QA build that performs different types of analysis on the codebase, and a release build that performs versioning and creates the necessary package that will be used by your deployment pipeline later.

The CI build compiles the solution and runs the unit tests. You have already looked at how to do this. In the next chapter, you will look at technical debt and how you can use TFS Build to automate the analysis that will help you keep the technical debt to a minimum.

The release build (QuixBox.Release) performs versioning using the PowerShell script that you looked at before, and also produces the MSI, SQL DacPac file, and the Web Deploy package. Figure 7-61 shows the build tasks that are used for the release build.

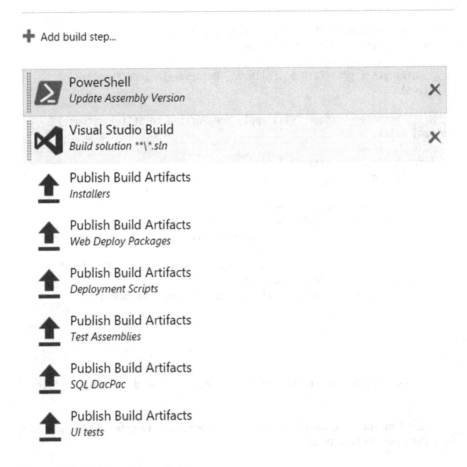

*Figure 7-61. QuizBox Release build*

As you can see, there are multiple instances of the *Publish Build Artifacts* task. The reason for this is that you want to generate a well-structured output from your release build that is easy to consume later from the deployment pipeline. Figure 7-62 shows the artifacts page of a finished release build. As you can see, you generate a folder for each type of artifact. This will make it easier later to copy and deploy these artifacts to the different environments.

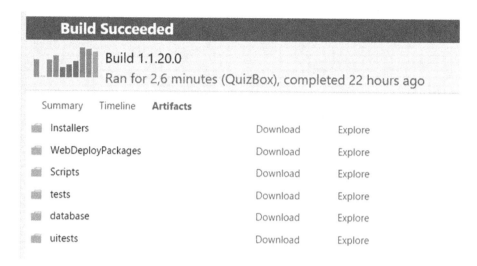

**Figure 7-62.** *QuizBox Release build artifacts*

As mentioned, this task accepts multiple lines for configuring which files to publish. So you could generate all your output using one of these tasks. This would not allow you to structure the output, though, by having each type of artifact in a separate folder.

# Summary

In this chapter you learned about build automation in general and about the TFS Build in particular. This brand new build system is much more powerful and flexible than the previous build system (XAML builds). You also walked through a few of the most common ways of packaging your .NET applications and libraries, and how to implement this using TFS Build.

In the next chapter, you will dive into quality management and different ways to manage the technical debt that tends to occur in most development projects over time.

# CHAPTER 8

# Managing Code Quality

As developers, we want to create high quality code. But high quality often means a lower development pace because we need to go through more checks on our code. But does it need to be a slow and burdensome process? In this chapter, you will examine several powerful tools you can use to get control of your code quality while developing at full speed.

Visual Studio 2015 offers several tools to help you along here. There are unit tests with code coverage, great tools to automatically check your application logic, and ways to get feedback on how well your automated tests are covering the code.

There is also the static code analysis framework to check your code for code-level correctness, over and above the syntactical checks performed by the compiler. Static code analysis helps you enforce coding conventions and automate parts of the code review process.

You can also use code metrics to get feedback on the quality of your code and identify areas that need attention; often this is driven from a maintainability perspective. A common problem with maintainability is code duplication. To mitigate that problem, you can use the new clone detection tool in Visual Studio that will analyze code for similarities, which you then can refactor to get a better structure.

The tools are all good on their own but when you integrate them into your development process, or better yet, automate them into your delivery pipeline, they become great instruments to ensure that the quality stays high as you continuously add new features to your product. When you add metrics into your development process, you can use them to enforce code quality, for instance by setting up a rule to fail a build if the technical debt increases above a certain threshold.

But before you dive into the tools, let's look at why you want to use them.

## What Is Good Code?

Building great software is a challenging process. It usually involves work by different people and over a long time. Most commonly you've not sure what to build from the start so the product evolves incrementally. There is a big chance the codebase changes so many times during the development that once a feature is working, the code behind is hard to understand (at best).

Think of good code as code that is easy to understand and maintain. To avoid eroding codebases, you need a way to evaluate what is good code and what is not. There are many ways to define these characteristics but here is a good set to get started:

- **Clean**: The code is easy to read and understand. You have shared coding convention (indentation, naming conventions, etc.).

- **Consistent**: It is easy to understand what the code does. You use design patterns so you can make assumptions about the code without reading every line.

- **Extensible**: The code is written for general purposes use rather than specific ones so that it is easy to reuse and make modifications.

- **Correct**: You design the code to be correct and you use good patterns for error handling. You use unit testing to have a safety net around the code. If you know the code works, you can focus on adding new features instead of fixing broken code.

As good these practices are, you are still but human and you may forget some of the rules at times. To help you stay on track, you should use tools to enforce your coding conventions. You will look at several different tools to manage code quality in this chapter. But tools are just tools, so you should use your teammates to review your code. In Chapter 5, we discussed how to do code reviews.

# What Is Technical Debt and Why Should I Care?

Technical debt is a term first coined by Ward Cunningham in 1992. It is the debt that comes from making bad technical decisions (or prioritizations).

It is easy to think of technical debt in economic terms. If a person takes a loan, he starts building a debt. If he makes regular payments on the loan, then the debt will become manageable and will eventually be cleared. If he does not make payments on the loan for some time, there will be some penalties such as an interest fee, which makes the debt increase (without any additional value to the person). If things get even worse and the person is unable to pay back the debt, the person may become bankrupt.

The same reasoning can easily be applied to software, and we've all seen it happening. If you develop code without thinking about good code practices, the software will slowly start to decay and you will build a technical debt that becomes harder and harder to control. You can only make money by delivering software, and the bigger the debt, the more difficult it will become to actually deliver something. You end up with customers moving away from your product.

There are more dimensions to technical debt than implementation debt caused by poor code quality. Other aspects include the following:

- **Architecture debt**: Bad architectural principles, design rule violations, lacking design patterns

- **Test debt**: Missing test cases, lack of test coverage, lack of test automation

- **Documentation debt**: Missing documentation, poorly updated documentation, low traceability between documentation and implementation

Technical debt doesn't happen by itself (or at least that's not the only reason). Many times a temporary debt can be the right decision as long as you are aware of it and make sure you start making down payments. Here are some common classifications of technical debt:

- **Strategic debt**: Debt caused to gain strategic benefits (such as time to market)

- **Tactical debt**: Short-time gains, for instance cutting some corners to make an extra release for increased customer satisfaction

- **Inadvertent debt**: This is typically caused by lack of awareness or knowledge

- **Incremental debt**: Caused by repeating the above without any work to reduce the debt

The practices we are going to discuss in the following sections are all good candidates to use for controlling technical debt. You will also look at a great solution that gathers metrics from different sources and gives you a number on your technical debt; it's called SonarQube.

# Unit Testing

Unit testing has been around for a while and is generally considered a best practice for modern development. Let's start by defining what we mean by unit tests: unit tests are automatic tests that operate very closely to the actual business logic. The focus here is to test individual rules in isolation to certify that the intended result is achieved and maintained over the lifetime of an application. Each test typically sends a method a known request and verifies that it returns a predicted answer. In practical terms, this means that you write programs that test the public interfaces of all of the classes in your application. This is not the same as requirements testing or acceptance testing, which you will explore in Chapter 10. Rather, it is testing to ensure the methods you write are doing what you expect them to do.

The goal with unit tests is to increase the overall quality of the system and reduce the number of bugs that are created, since all changes are guarded by the existing suite of unit test, which certify that changes made to the code do not break the existing system.

The feedback from a unit test should be instant since they can be triggered and run automatically each time the code is built (manually or by a CI server).

A true unit test should adhere to basic rules such as these:

- A unit test must be able to run without user interaction. Use asserts to automatically validate the test outcome.

- A unit test must be repeatable. Use initialize and cleanup methods to prepare and clean up the tests.

- A unit test must be fast. Use fakes to remove external dependencies during testing.

Unit tests are programs written to run in batches to test other code.

## What Is Test-Driven Development?

Test-driven development (TDD) is one of the core practices in Extreme Programming (XP). Even if you do not practice XP, you can still use this practice as a way to help developers write better code. In TDD, you write the tests before you write the code. When all your tests are working, you know that your code is functioning correctly. As you add new features, these tests continue to verify that you haven't broken anything.

Instead of designing a module, then coding and testing it, you turn the process around and do the testing first. To put it another way, you don't write a single line of production code until you have a test that fails.

By working this way, you are using a process called *coding by intention*. When practicing coding by intention you write your code top-down instead of bottom-up. Instead of thinking, "I'm going to need this class with these methods," you just write the code that you expect to be there before the class actually exists.

In traditional software development, tests were thought to verify that an existing bit of code was written correctly. When you do TDD, however, your tests are used to define the behavior of a class before you write it.

## Elements of a Unit Test

Unit tests are just code with some test-specific context added to it. To declare code as unit test code, you need to reference the `Microsoft.VisualStudio.QualityTools.UnitTestFramework.dll`, which will import the unit test framework into your project. Next, you annotate the code with the following attributes:

- `TestClass`: Indicates that the given class contains test methods

- `TestMethod`: Indicates a method as a test method

A core Visual Studio unit test is therefore declared like the following:

```
[TestClass]
public class QuizTest
{
    [TestMethod]
    public void CreateQuizShouldStoreCorrectly ()
    {
    }
}
```

Sometimes you will want to set up an initial state before a test run or clean up state after it is complete. The test attributes [TestInitialize] and [TestCleanup] can be applied to a method in order to control the initialization and cleanup of the tests. There are several others, so check the documentation for your unit test framework of choice.

A unit test is more than just running a method under test; you also need to verify that the tested functionality behaves as expected. To help, a testing framework can contain a number of test attributes that you can use to check various types of expectations, for instance Assert.AreEqual() to test expected result against the actual result.

You may also need to control various aspects of how a test is run. To support this, in MSTest, you have a context class in the framework, TestContext, which allows you to control the test run and test environment when the test is running.

The TestContext contains static information that can be read from the test when run, including attributes like a DataConnection for data-driven tests or Properties to get context-specific variables.

---

■ **Tip**　You will see examples of the use of the test context in Chapter 10 when you look at how to manage the environment-related configuration in your automated acceptance tests.

---

To access the TestContext in a unit test, you need to declare a property called TestContext wrapping a TestContext instance:

```
private TestContext testContextInstance;
public TestContext TestContext
{
    get { return testContextInstance; }
    set { testContextInstance = value; }
}
```

The test framework will automatically set the property for you. You can then use the property in your test code to interact with the TestContext. The following example writes to the test output:

```
TestContext.WriteLine("Quiz {0} updated to {1}.", quizId, quizStatus);
```

The result will be written to the output for the test run, as shown in Figure 8-1.

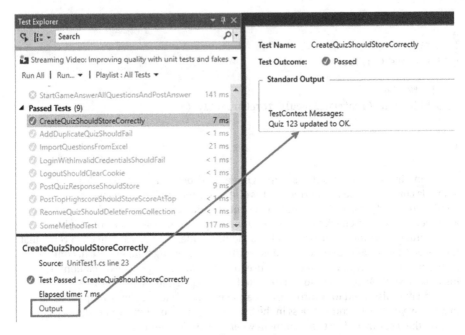

***Figure 8-1.*** *Using TestContext to write to the test result output*

# Data-Driven Automated Tests

Visual Studio unit tests contain the concept of data-driven tests. This is not to be confused with database testing; instead data-driven tests are used to map parameterized values in an external resource to a unit test (also known as data pools). There are several uses for data-driven tests; the most common is to use data pools for functions that will require many test permutations.

Visual Studio unit tests support a number of data sources, such as CSV files, XML files, Excel files, and database tables.

Some tests can be run multiple times with different data sets. Instead of implementing a number of different tests permutations, you can bind the test to a data source and then access the current data row from the unit test.

You connect a unit test with a data source by adding the DataSource attribute to the test method. The DataSource attribute lets you specify the following arguments:

- ProviderName: The provider for the data source to use. See Table 8-1 for examples of provider names.

*Table 8-1. Data Sources for Data-Driven Tests*

| Data Source | Data Source Attribute |
| --- | --- |
| CSV | DataSource("Microsoft.VisualStudio.TestTools.DataSource.CSV", "\|DataDirectory\|\\data.csv", "data#csv", DataAccessMethod. Sequential) |
| Excel | DataSource("System.Data.Odbc", "Dsn = Excel Files;Driver = {Microsoft Excel Driver (*.xls)};dbq = \|DataDirectory\| \\Data.xls;defaultdir = .;driverid = 790;maxbuffersize =2048;pagetimeout = 5;readonly = true", "Sheet1$", DataAccessMethod.Sequential) |
| Test Case | DataSource("Microsoft.VisualStudio.TestTools.DataSource. TestCase", "http://tfs:8080/tfs/DefaultCollection;Agile", "30", DataAccessMethod.Sequential) This data source will create a strong dependency to TFS and may not be suitable for pure unit tests. But for other automated test it can be a good alternative since it allows you to edit the test data from the test case parameters. |
| XML | [DataSource("Microsoft.VisualStudio.TestTools.DataSource.XML", "\|DataDirectory\|\\data.xml", "Iterations", DataAccessMethod. Sequential) |
| SQL Express | [DataSource("System.Data.SqlClient", "Data Source = .\\sqlexpress;Initial Catalog = tempdb;Integrated Security = True", "Data", DataAccessMethod.Sequential) |

- ConnectionString: The connection string to the data source (database, data file, etc.).

- TableName: The name of the data table in the data source.

- DataAccessMethod: Specifies how the test data is drawn from the data pool. Can be either Sequential or Random.

To access the data row, you use the TestContext class discussed earlier in the chapter. It gets called by the test framework one time for each set of data in the DataSource so you only need to think about the current row when accessing data from the store. The code sample below shows a complete example of a data-driven unit test. The dependency to the data source should be handled using a DeploymentItem attribute so that the unit test can be run anywhere as long as the dependent item is deployed when the test is run.

```
[DeploymentItem("QuizSampleData.csv")]
[DataSource("Microsoft.VisualStudio.TestTools.DataSource.CSV",
    "|DataDirectory|\\QuizSampleData.csv",
    "QuizSampleData#csv",
    DataAccessMethod.Sequential)]
[TestMethod]
```

```
public void CreateQuizShouldStoreCorrectly()
{
    var question = (string)TestContext.DataRow["question"];
    var answers = (string)TestContext.DataRow["answers"];
    var correctAnswer = (string)TestContext.DataRow["correct_answer"];

    var quizService = new QuizService();
    var quiz = quizService.AddQuiz(question, answers, correctAnswer)

    Assert.AreEqual("OK", quiz.Status);
}
```

## Running Tests

In Visual Studio, unit test are managed from the Test Explorer window. The Test Explorer will run tests from any test framework as long as they provide a test adapter for the Visual Studio framework.

When you build your solution and its test project, the unit tests will be displayed in the Test Explorer. If the Test Explorer is not visible, you can open it from the Test ➤ Windows ➤ Test Explorer menu.

The tests are group into four categories; Failed Tests, Skipped Tests, Passed Tests, and Not Run Tests. You can run tests from the menus in Test Explorer or by selecting one or more tests in the list. You can also start a debug session from the tests the same way.

The Test Explorer will show the status of the last run and only for the tests that ran (Figure 8-2). The color bar at the top of the window is shown in the color of the last test run and gives direct feedback on the test status in a nice way.

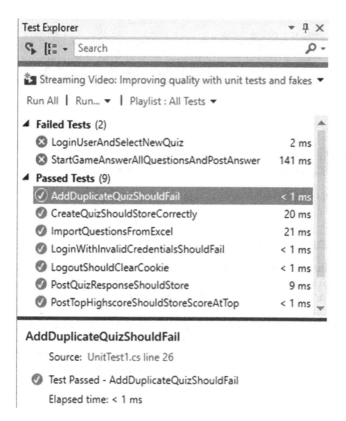

*Figure 8-2. The Test Explorer*

In true test-driven spirit, you can also select to run all tests after you build in Visual Studio. You can configure this behavior by clicking the Run Tests After Build option in the Test Explorer or from the Test ➤ Test Settings ➤ Run Tests After Build menu (Figure 8-3).

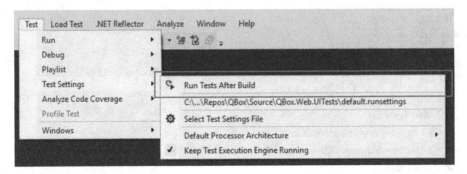

*Figure 8-3.* *Configure to run test after build*

## Working with Other Test Frameworks

A nice feature in Visual Studio is that it is possible to mix unit test frameworks, so if you prefer the semantics of nUnit or xUnit over MSTest, you can just install the third-party framework and use it instead. You can even have multiple test frameworks in the same unit test project!

To add additional third-party test frameworks, you can do this in Visual Studio using the Extension Manager (Tools ➤ Extensions and Updates) or by adding the framework as a NuGet package. If you want to integrate unit testing with the CI process (and you do) when you add the adapter as a NuGet package, this will save you some pain since the build process will automatically download the NuGet package on the build server so the tests can run.

---

■ **Note**  In order for the Test Runner to find third-party test frameworks, you need both the unit test framework and a test adapter. In your case, you want to add nUnit so you use the NuGet package that contains both, nUnitTestAdapter.WithFramework.

---

Figure 8-4 shows how to add the nUnit framework using NuGet.

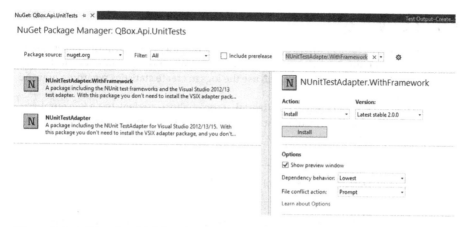

**Figure 8-4.** *Adding the nUnit Test frameworks to Visual Studio using NuGet*

# Integrating Unit Tests with CI builds

You've seen how to run the tests in Visual Studio. Now let's take a look at the integration with TFS build. In Chapter 7, you went through the Test step in detail, so let's configure the QubeBox CI build to run both VS and nUnit tests. The trick to get the nUnit tests to run is to add the path to the NuGet package under the advanced section of the test task, as shown in Figure 8-5.

### Test Assemblies **\\*.UnitTests.dll;-:**\obj\\** 🖉

| | | |
|---|---|---|
| Test Assembly | **\\*.UnitTests.dll;-:**\obj\\** | ... ⓘ |
| Test Filter criteria | | ⓘ |
| Platform | | ⓘ |
| Configuration | | ⓘ |
| Run Settings File | | ... ⓘ |
| Override TestRun Parameters | | ⓘ |

**▲ Advanced**

| | | |
|---|---|---|
| Code Coverage Enabled | ☐ | ⓘ |
| VSTest version | Latest | ▼ ⓘ |
| Path to Custom Test Adapters | $(Build.SourcesDirectory)\Source\packages | ⓘ |
| Other console options | | ⓘ |

**Figure 8-5.** *Adding unit tests to the CI build*

# Code Coverage

Code coverage is a concept where components are instrumented with additional logging information. When the components are executed (typically through automated tests), the execution paths are tracked and you can use the logs to create statistics regarding how the components are used.

Note that 100% coverage will not assert that the quality is perfect, but a low number will tell you to that you have insufficient testing. Code coverage somewhere in the range of 85% is a good number.

---

■ **Note**    Code coverage requires Visual Studio 2015 Enterprise.

---

In Visual Studio 2015, unit tests can create code coverage data for all assemblies without any explicit configuration. All solution binaries that get loaded during unit test runs are analyzed by default. Figure 8-6 shows how to run code coverage analysis inside Visual Studio.

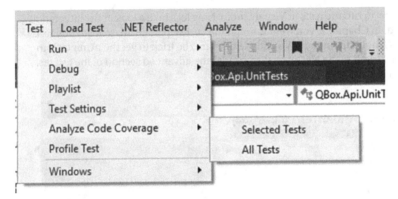

*Figure 8-6.  Running code analysis in Visual Studio 2015*

## Analyzing Code Coverage Results

Regardless of how you gather the code coverage data, you can analyze the result using the Code Coverage Result window in Visual Studio. The result view shows the assemblies analyzed and you can drill down into namespaces, classes, and methods (Figure 8-7). You can also export and import results for analysis (for instance, you can import the result from a build).

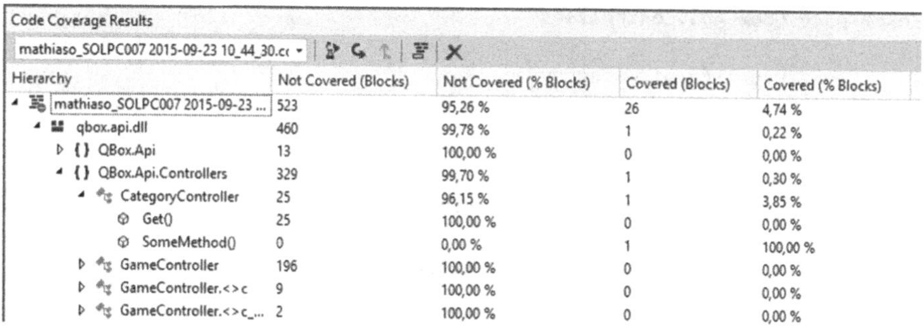

**Code Coverage Results**

mathiaso_SOLPC007 2015-09-23 10_44_30.c(  ▾

| Hierarchy | Not Covered (Blocks) | Not Covered (% Blocks) | Covered (Blocks) | Covered (% Blocks) |
|---|---|---|---|---|
| ▲ ▓ mathiaso_SOLPC007 2015-09-23 … | 523 | 95,26 % | 26 | 4,74 % |
| ▲ ▦ qbox.api.dll | 460 | 99,78 % | 1 | 0,22 % |
| ▷ {} QBox.Api | 13 | 100,00 % | 0 | 0,00 % |
| ▲ {} QBox.Api.Controllers | 329 | 99,70 % | 1 | 0,30 % |
| ▲ ♦ CategoryController | 25 | 96,15 % | 1 | 3,85 % |
| ⊕ Get() | 25 | 100,00 % | 0 | 0,00 % |
| ⊕ SomeMethod() | 0 | 0,00 % | 1 | 100,00 % |
| ▷ ♦ GameController | 196 | 100,00 % | 0 | 0,00 % |
| ▷ ♦ GameController.<>c | 9 | 100,00 % | 0 | 0,00 % |
| ▷ ♦ GameController.<>c_… | 2 | 100,00 % | 0 | 0,00 % |

*Figure 8-7. Code coverage results in Visual Studio 2015*

The coverage data is shown by default as % blocks measured. If you prefer % lines covered instead, this can be shown by adding the additional columns to the result view.

Finally, if you want to understand why a section of code has a particular coverage number, the best way is to show the coverage data in line with the code. The Show Code Coverage Coloring button enables coloring, so when you click on a code item the coverage information is shown in different shades of blue and red (Figure 8-8). This is great feedback in many ways; it show which paths you missed testing, something that can be a result of missing tests as well as unused code.

```
namespace QBox.Api.Controllers
{
    [RoutePrefix("api/category")]
    1 reference | Jakob Ehn, 37 days ago | 1 author, 4 changes
    public class CategoryController : ApiController
    {
        0 references | Jakob Ehn, 126 days ago | 1 author, 2 changes
        public IEnumerable<CategoryDTO> Get()
        {
            using (var ctx = new QuizBoxContext())
            {
                return ctx.Category.Select(
                    c => new CategoryDTO()
                    {
                        Id = c.Id,
                        Name = c.Name,
                        Description = c.Description
                    }).ToList();
            }
        }

        1 reference | 1/1 passing | Jakob Ehn, 37 days ago | 1 author, 1 change
        public string SomeMethod()
        {
            return "42";
        }
    }
}
```

***Figure 8-8.*** *Code coverage result shown in source code*

## Integrating Code Coverage with CI Builds

Code coverage is an important metric to track over time if you are interested in how the ratio of automated tests compares to the amount of code being written. A good way to get the code coverage measured regularly is to include automated tests and code coverage in your automated build process. In the new build system, it's almost as transparent to gather code coverage in Visual Studio; you only need to select the Code Coverage Enabled checkbox in the test task (Figure 8-9).

**Test Assemblies \*\*\\\*.UnitTests.dll;-:\*\*\obj\\\*\*** ✎

| | |
|---|---|
| Test Assembly | \*\*\\\*.UnitTests.dll;-:\*\*\obj\\\*\* |
| Test Filter criteria | |
| Platform | |
| Configuration | |
| Run Settings File | |
| Override TestRun Parameters | |

▲ **Advanced**

| | |
|---|---|
| Code Coverage Enabled | ☑ |
| VSTest version | Latest |
| Path to Custom Test Adapters | $(Build.SourcesDirectory)\Source\packages |
| Other console options | |

*Figure 8-9.* *Configuring code coverage for build*

In the build summary, you can now see the code coverage data and, if you want, you can also download the coverage file for analysis in Visual Studio (Figure 8-10).

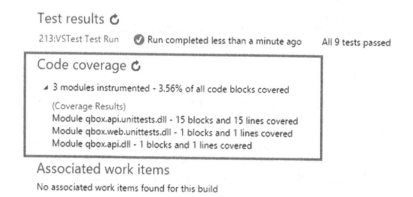

## Test results ↻

213:VSTest Test Run  ✅ Run completed less than a minute ago   All 9 tests passed

### Code coverage ↻

▲ 3 modules instrumented - 3.56% of all code blocks covered

(Coverage Results)
Module qbox.api.unittests.dll - 15 blocks and 15 lines covered
Module qbox.web.unittests.dll - 1 blocks and 1 lines covered
Module qbox.api.dll - 1 blocks and 1 lines covered

## Associated work items

No associated work items found for this build

*Figure 8-10.* *Code coverage result shown in build result*

Later in this chapter you will look at how to use SonarQube to monitor various metrics, including the code coverage trend.

# Customizing How Code Coverage Is Collected

By default, all files touched by the unit tests will be included in the code coverage analysis. This is not always what you want; you may have projects with lots of generated code that you want to exclude, or perhaps you want to exclude the test assemblies from the code coverage statistics. Fortunately, you can create a profile for your test session and specify what should be included or excluded in the code coverage analysis.

At this point, there is no designer for the .runsettings file, so it needs to be edited as XML in Visual Studio. To create a custom coverage setting, simply create a new XML file and use the extension .runsettings. The following is an example of a .runsettings file that excludes all test assemblies from code coverage:

```xml
<?xml version="1.0" encoding="utf-8"?>
<!-- File name extension must be .runsettings -->
<RunSettings>
  <DataCollectionRunSettings>
    <DataCollectors>
      <DataCollector friendlyName="Code Coverage" uri="datacollector:
      //Microsoft/CodeCoverage/2.0" assemblyQualifiedName="Microsoft.
      VisualStudio.Coverage.DynamicCoverageDataCollector, Microsoft.
      VisualStudio.TraceCollector, Version=11.0.0.0, Culture=neutral,
      PublicKeyToken=b03f5f7f11d50a3a">
        <Configuration>
          <CodeCoverage>
            <ModulePaths>

              <Exclude>
                <ModulePath>.*UnitTest.*</ModulePath>
                <ModulePath>.*IntegrationTest.*</ModulePath>
                <ModulePath>.*UITest.*</ModulePath>
              </Exclude>
            </ModulePaths>

            <!-- You recommend you do not change the following values: -->
            <UseVerifiableInstrumentation>True</
            UseVerifiableInstrumentation>
            <AllowLowIntegrityProcesses>True</AllowLowIntegrityProcesses>
            <CollectFromChildProcesses>True</CollectFromChildProcesses>
            <CollectAspDotNet>False</CollectAspDotNet>

          </CodeCoverage>
        </Configuration>
      </DataCollector>
    </DataCollectors>
  </DataCollectionRunSettings>
</RunSettings>
```

To use the custom settings file in Visual Studio, select the runsettings file from Test ➤ Test Settings ➤ Select Test Settings File, as shown in Figure 8-11. The next time you analyze code coverage, the runsettings will be used.

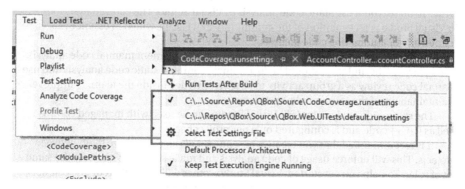

***Figure 8-11.*** *Selecting the runsettings in Visual Studio*

If you want to use the custom settings in TFS build, you do something very similar: you select the runsettings from the Test build task (Figure 8-12).

## Test Assemblies **\*.UnitTests.dll;-:**\obj\** ✎

| | | | |
|---|---|---|---|
| Test Assembly | **\*.UnitTests.dll;-:**\obj\** | ... | ⓘ |
| Test Filter criteria | | | ⓘ |
| Platform | | | ⓘ |
| Configuration | | | ⓘ |
| Run Settings File | Source/CodeCoverage.runsettings | ... | ⓘ |
| Override TestRun Parameters | | | ⓘ |

**◢ Advanced**

| | | |
|---|---|---|
| Code Coverage Enabled | ☑ | ⓘ |
| VSTest version | Latest ▾ | ⓘ |
| Path to Custom Test Adapters | $(Build.SourcesDirectory)\Source\packages | ⓘ |
| Other console options | | ⓘ |

***Figure 8-12.*** *Selecting the runsettings in TFS build*

# Static Code Analysis

Now that you have seen how unit testing and code coverage can help you validate your code, let's shift focus and look at how to enforce coding best practices in the code you write. To do so, you'll use static code analysis in Visual Studio. The code analysis tool in Visual Studio is an evolution of the community tool FxCop, which in essence is a framework for automating code analysis.

The code analysis tool is intended to be used to complement manual code analysis, not replace it. The ambition should be to automate common static code analysis and use manual code review as a group activity to share knowledge inside the team, to improve maintainability of the source code, and so on.

The static code analysis tools in Visual Studio can be used with managed code as well as C/C++ code and is configured on a per project basis.

It is recommended that you create a baseline set of rules and share them between projects. This will enforce usage of code analysis and make sure everyone uses the same set of rules. To help you get started, Visual Studio comes with a set of predefine rule sets, so make sure to go through them to determine a good baseline for your project.

After you have decided which rules apply to your code, you need to configure each project in the solution with the proper settings. You can assign the rule set on each project's properties or on the solution level.

Static code analysis is executed similar to a standard compilation of the code. When code analysis is enabled on the project, it will be analyzed after it has been compiled (Figure 8-13). To enable code analysis as part of the build process, you set the Enable Code Analysis on Build flag on each project. You can always run the code analysis manually from the Analyze menu in Visual Studio.

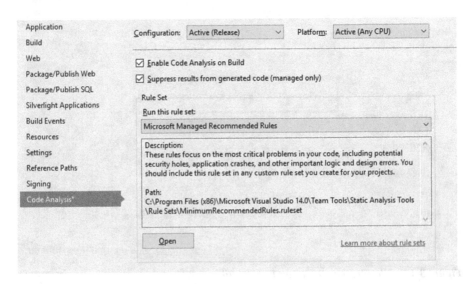

***Figure 8-13.*** *Enable Code Analysis on Build*

> **Note** Running code analysis as part of the local build will slow down the development experience. As a compromise, we recommend manually running code analysis while developing and then integrating it with the server build processes to ensure code analysis is run.

After the code analysis has been run, any errors found are shown in the Code Analysis window (Figure 8-14). From the list, you can select an item, which will show the documentation of the analysis rule, examples of why it happened, and suggestions of what to do to resolve the issue.

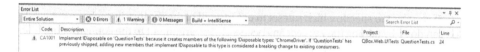

*Figure 8-14. Working with the code analysis results*

## Integrating Code Analysis with CI builds

Running code analysis as part of the local build can slow down the development experience. As a compromise, you can use TFS server-side builds to validate the code. Enabling this in a default TFS build workflow is as easy as adding a MS Build argument, as shown in Figure 8-15. The following are our choices:

- `/p:RunCodeAnalysis=True`: Always run code analysis.

- `/p:RunCodeAnalysis=False`: Never run code analysis as part of the build.

- Omitted. Run code analysis according to each project's setting.

Figure 8-15 shows how to enable code analysis in the build process.

*Figure 8-15. Integrating code analysis with TFS Build*

After running a build, issues from code analysis are shown in the build report (Figure 8-16).

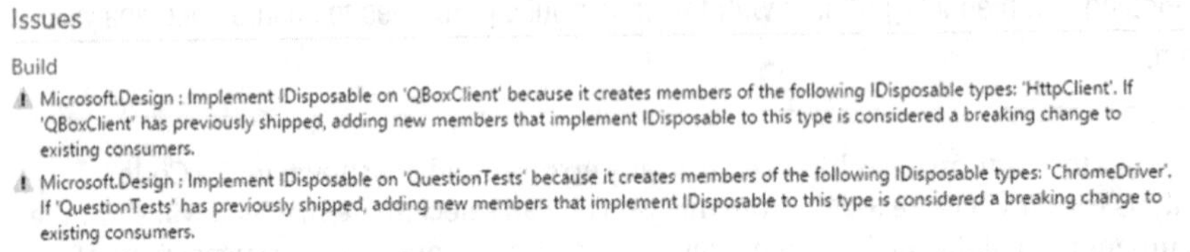
Issues
Build
Microsoft.Design : Implement IDisposable on 'QBoxClient' because it creates members of the following IDisposable types: 'HttpClient'. If 'QBoxClient' has previously shipped, adding new members that implement IDisposable to this type is considered a breaking change to existing consumers.
Microsoft.Design : Implement IDisposable on 'QuestionTests' because it creates members of the following IDisposable types: 'ChromeDriver'. If 'QuestionTests' has previously shipped, adding new members that implement IDisposable to this type is considered a breaking change to existing consumers.

***Figure 8-16.*** *Code analysis result in Build*

If you want to specify which ruleset to use instead of the settings in each project, you can do so by adding the `/p:CodeAnalysisRuleSet` argument to the configuration, for instance `/p:CodeAnalysisRuleSet=GlobalizationRules.ruleset` to use the `GlobalizationRules` set.

## Creating Custom Rule Sets

You have seen how to use the predefined rule sets to quickly get started with code analysis. Sometimes you may want to exclude certain rules or use rules from multiple standard rule sets. If this is the case, you can create a custom rule set, save it as a `.ruleset` file, and reference it from the projects to which it applies.

To create a new rule set from scratch, create a new Code Analysis Rule Set from the General file templates. Next, select the rule groups that apply, and drill down and customize which rules should be applied, as well as if the rule should be treated as a warning or an error (Figure 8-17).

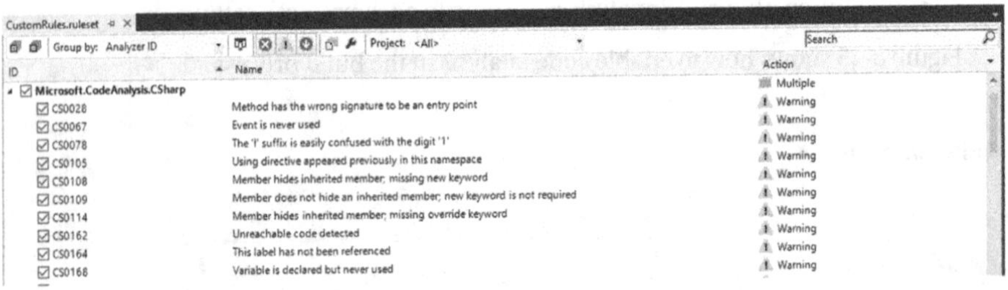
CustomRules.ruleset
Group by: Analyzer ID
Project: <All>
Search
ID
Name
Action
Microsoft.CodeAnalysis.CSharp
Multiple
CS0028
Method has the wrong signature to be an entry point
Warning
CS0067
Event is never used
Warning
CS0078
The 'l' suffix is easily confused with the digit '1'
Warning
CS0105
Using directive appeared previously in this namespace
Warning
CS0108
Member hides inherited member; missing new keyword
Warning
CS0109
Member does not hide an inherited member; new keyword is not required
Warning
CS0114
Member hides inherited member; missing override keyword
Warning
CS0162
Unreachable code detected
Warning
CS0164
This label has not been referenced
Warning
CS0168
Variable is declared but never used
Warning

***Figure 8-17.*** *Adding a custom code analysis rule set*

Having defined the rule set, you can now apply it to the projects (Figure 8-18).

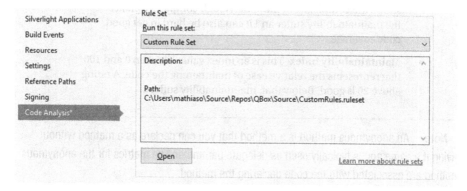

**Figure 8-18.** *Using a custom code analysis rule set*

You can also create a custom rule set from an existing set by opening the code analysis properties in a project and saving the resulting changes as a new `.ruleset` file.

# Code Metrics

As your software evolves, it is important to understand the complexity of the code. A common situation is that the older the code is, the harder it is to maintain. Often the reason for this is that it is easy to just add new features to existing code rather than refactor and re-design the solution. To avoid degraded code quality, you can analyze the code and get a report on the code metrics. The code metrics you get from Visual Studio are the following:

- **Lines of code**: This is an approximate number based on IL code. A high count might indicate that a type or method is doing too much work and should be split up. This might also be a warning that code will be hard to maintain.

- **Class coupling**: Measures the coupling to unique classes through parameters, local variables, return types, method calls, generic or template instantiations, base classes, interface implementations, fields defined on external types, and attribute decoration. Low coupling is better to strive for because high coupling indicates a design that is difficult to reuse and maintain because of its many interdependencies on other types

- **Depth of inheritance**: Indicates the number of class definitions that extend to the root of the class hierarchy. The deeper the hierarchy, the more difficult it might be to understand where particular methods and fields are defined or/and redefined.

- **Cyclomatic complexity**: This is created by calculating the number of different code paths in the flow of the program and shows the complexity of the code. A high complexity makes the maintainability suffer and it can also be hard to get good code coverage.

- **Maintainability index**: This is an index value between 0 and 100 that represents the relative ease of maintaining the code. A rating above 20 is good. Below that, maintainability suffers.

---

■ **Note**    An anonymous method is a method that you can declare as a method without giving it a name and is typically used as delegate parameter. The metrics for the anonymous method are associated with the code declaring the method.

Generated code is generally excluded from code metrics.

---

To calculate the code metrics for your code, you can do so on all or individual projects by selecting the solution or project. Next, you run the analysis from the Analyze menu in Visual Studio and then Calculate Code Metrics for Solution or project. When the analysis is complete, the result is shown in the Code Metrics Results window (Figure 8-19). You can analyze the result by filtering for behaviors you are interested in as well as do a drill-down into the code you want to understand better.

| Hierarchy ▲ | Maintainability Index | Cyclomatic Complexity | Depth of Inheritance | Class Coupling | Lines of Code |
|---|---|---|---|---|---|
| ▲ One or more projects were skipped. Code metrics are available only for C#, Vi... | | | | | |
| ▷ QBox.Api (Release) | 86 | 142 | 2 | 61 | 254 |
| ▷ QBox.Api.Client (Release) | 86 | 18 | 1 | 27 | 43 |
| ▷ QBox.Api.DTO (Release) | 93 | 68 | 1 | 3 | 80 |
| ▷ QBox.Api.IntegrationTests (Release) | 100 | 2 | 1 | 2 | 1 |
| ▷ QBox.Api.UnitTests (Release) | 96 | 12 | 1 | 8 | 9 |
| ▷ QBox.BackOffice (Release) | 96 | 2 | 9 | 3 | 3 |
| ▷ QBox.Logging (Release) | 88 | 8 | 1 | 8 | 10 |
| ▷ QBox.Web (Release) | 89 | 311 | 4 | 203 | 477 |
| QBox.Web.LoadTests (Release) | 100 | 0 | 0 | 0 | 0 |
| ▷ QBox.Web.UITests (Release) | 81 | 16 | 1 | 21 | 37 |
| ▷ QBox.Web.UnitTests (Release) | 100 | 2 | 1 | 2 | 1 |

*Figure 8-19. Code metrics summary*

You can also export the results to Excel to do further analysis or just to save the result from the run as a way of documenting your code quality. If you find issues you want to address later, you can also create a work item from the result view.

# Integrating with CI Builds

There is no built-in support for running the code metrics as part of the CI process. But you can roll your own solution by using the Visual Studio Code Metrics PowerTool for Visual Studio 2015 (www.microsoft.com/en-sg/download/details.aspx?id=48213). It lets you run the code metrics analysis from the command line, producing an XML result file. Here's an example that calculates code metrics for all QuizBox web assemblies:

```
metrics.exe /f:qbox.web\bin\qbox*.dll /o:metrics.xml
```

You can easily create a PowerShell script that runs the tool if you want to integrate it into the build process.

The resulting file contains an easy-to-understand structure of the metrics information (Figure 8-20) but unfortunately there's no support for generating, for instance, an HTML table from it.

```xml
<?xml version="1.0" encoding="UTF-8"?>
<CodeMetricsReport Version="14.0">
  <Targets>
    <Target Name="C:\Users\mathiaso\Source\Repos\QBox\Source\qbox.web\bin\QBox.Api.Client.dll">
      <Modules>
        <Module Name="QBox.Api.Client.dll" FileVersion="1.0.0.0" AssemblyVersion="1.0.0.0">
          <Metrics>
            <Metric Name="MaintainabilityIndex" Value="66"/>
            <Metric Name="CyclomaticComplexity" Value="65"/>
            <Metric Name="ClassCoupling" Value="37"/>
            <Metric Name="DepthOfInheritance" Value="1"/>
            <Metric Name="LinesOfCode" Value="206"/>
          </Metrics>
          <Namespaces>
            <Namespace Name="QBox.Api.Client">
              <Metrics>
                <Metric Name="MaintainabilityIndex" Value="66"/>
                <Metric Name="CyclomaticComplexity" Value="65"/>
                <Metric Name="ClassCoupling" Value="37"/>
                <Metric Name="DepthOfInheritance" Value="1"/>
                <Metric Name="LinesOfCode" Value="206"/>
              </Metrics>
              <Types>
                <Type Name="IQBoxClient">
                  <Metrics>
                    <Metric Name="MaintainabilityIndex" Value="100"/>
                    <Metric Name="CyclomaticComplexity" Value="7"/>
                    <Metric Name="ClassCoupling" Value="8"/>
                    <Metric Name="DepthOfInheritance" Value="0"/>
                    <Metric Name="LinesOfCode" Value="0"/>
                  </Metrics>
                  <Members>
                    <Member Name="GetCategories() : Task<List<CategoryDTO>>">
                      <Metrics>
                        <Metric Name="MaintainabilityIndex" Value="100"/>
                        <Metric Name="CyclomaticComplexity" Value="1"/>
                        <Metric Name="ClassCoupling" Value="3"/>
                        <Metric Name="LinesOfCode" Value="0"/>
                      </Metrics>
                    </Member>
```

***Figure 8-20.*** *Code Metrics PowerTool results XML*

Later in this chapter, you will look at SonarQube, where you can get similar metrics calculated for you.

# Code Clones

Have you ever worked on a piece of code and thought you've seen it before? Have you wished for a tool that would show you where the same or similar code exists in your code base? Copy-paste is probably the most common (anti) design pattern used by programmers and, though quick to use to solve a problem, it will likely degrade your product in the long run.

Visual Studio has a code analysis tool for detecting code with similar structure. You can search for code clones in a couple of ways. You can choose to analyze the entire solution for clones by selecting Analyze Solution for Code Clones from the Analyze menu (Figure 8-21).

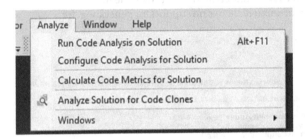

***Figure 8-21.*** *Detecting a cloned code section from selected code*

You can also select a section of code and have the tool find matching code. Select a code snippet you want to analyze for clones and choose Find Matching Clones in solution from the context menu.

---

■ **Note**   The code clones options require Visual Studio 2015 Enterprise.

---

The code clone analysis will find direct copies of code but also fragments that are similar but may differ in naming of variables or parameters.

The results will be shown in the Code Clone Analysis Results window, where you can analyze the detected clones. If you want to compare the differences, you can select the original and the clone to compare. In Figure 8-22, you can see how a Save method has been copied and the entity to save has been changed. The code structure is semantically the same but the details are too different to find with a simple "find-in-files" match.

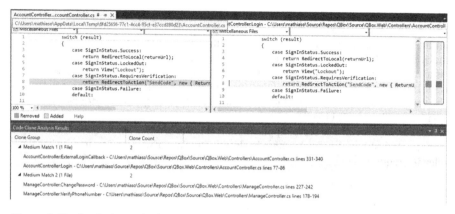

**Figure 8-22.** *Analyzing code clones*

It is recommended to run the code clone analysis whenever you change existing code. When you modify code, you can first run the analysis to learn if the code you are about to change exists in other areas. You can also use the results from the analysis to consider if you should refactor the code to make it more maintainable.

## Integrating Code Clones with CI Build

Unfortunately, there is no out-of-the-box support for running the code clone analysis as part of the build. In the next section, you will look at SonarQube, which also has a feature for code clone analysis.

# SonarQube

So far in this chapter you've looked at different tools to help you track and understand code quality. Each of the tools is great on its own, but if you could aggregate all the different metrics, it would be even better. SonarQube is an open-source product just for that.

SonarQube helps you manage technical debt by collecting code-related data into a data hub. Different data sources can send data to SonarQube, which has tools to help you analyze and visualize the metrics so you can see trends and patterns in how your code quality changes over time. With support for more than 20 different languages, SonarQube is a great solution for the entire team, independent of platform.

SonarQube has worked with Microsoft to improve the integration between Visual Studio, TFS build, and SonarQube, and it can now be used locally, on a TFS 2013/2015 server, or in Visual Studio Online.

All you need to do is to install the SonarQube server and configure the build process to capture and send data to SonarQube. Let's walk through how to get this up and running!

# Setting up SonarQube

Setting up the SonarQube server is a pretty lengthy procedure but fortunately quite straightforward and well documented. The ALM Rangers have authored a great installation guide that will help you set up a server; go to http://blogs.msdn.com/b/visualstudioalmrangers/archive/2015/04/22/understanding-the-visual-studio-alm-rangers.aspx. You can also find information at https://github.com/SonarSource/sonar-.net-documentation.

SonarQube is run as a server application. It consists of a web server front end for the analysis dashboard and a database back end. The time of writing, SonarQube has the following requirements:

- Java (7 or greater)

- SQL Server, MySQL, Oracle or ProgresSQL

- More than 1GB RAM

After setting up the server, you need to add a service endpoint in VSO to enable the communication between the servers. Go to the Services hub for your TFS collection (Figure 8-23) and add a new generic endpoint.

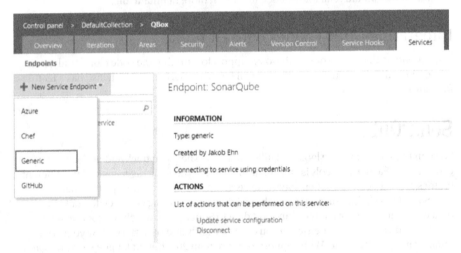

***Figure 8-23.*** *Adding a generic service endpoint for SonarQube*

Fill in the details for the SonarQube connection (machine, username/password), as shown in Figure 8-24.

*Figure 8-24. SonarQube endpoint configuration*

# Working with SonarQube

SonarQube is a very configurable application. When you first start working with your analysis, the starting point will likely be your project dashboard (Figure 8-25).

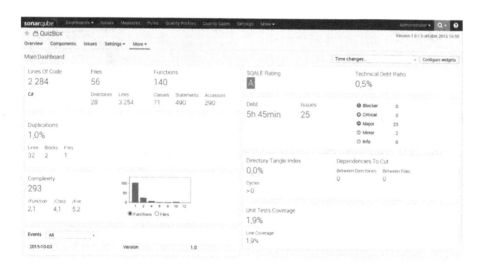

*Figure 8-25. The SonarQube dashboard*

The dashboard will show a number of widgets with various metrics about your product, such as lines of code, duplications, complexity, code coverage, and technical debt. All of the good things we've talked about in this chapter in one place! The dashboard is nice, but you can get a lot more information from it, so let's look at some of the core widgets.

## Lines of Code

The Lines of Code widget works like many of the other widgets: you get a summary tile with links to detailed content. It's a nice summary of all analyzed code with semantics for the programming language used (Figure 8-26).

| Lines Of Code | Files | | Functions | | |
|---|---|---|---|---|---|
| 2 284 | 56 | | 140 | | |
| C# | Directories | Lines | Classes | Statements | Accessors |
| | 28 | 3 254 | 71 | 490 | 290 |

*Figure 8-26.* *SonarQube LoC widget*

If you select a file, you get to the file content and you also get metrics clearly visible on top of the file (Figure 8-27).

*Figure 8-27.* *SonarQube LoC details view*

If you scroll the code, you will get analysis information shown inline in the code (Figure 8-28).

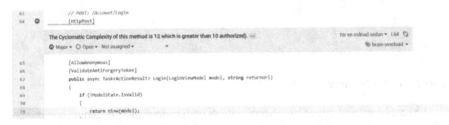

*Figure 8-28.* *SonarQube analysis inline in code*

You can also click the Issues button to see all issues in the file and start working through them (Figure 8-29). It's nice to get an estimate on how long it would take to fix the issue. This is, of course, configurable for your own estimates.

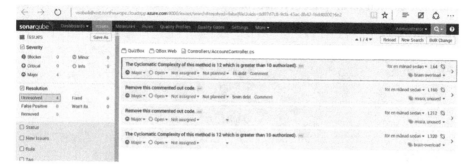

***Figure 8-29.** SonarQube code issues*

# Code Duplication

The code duplication analysis is similar to the code clones in Visual Studio but now you have the nice integration with the build system. Figure 8-30 shows an example of a file with code duplications, and it's pretty clear what you can do to improve the code here, isn't it?

```
        QuizBox
Overview   Components   Issues   Settings ▾   More ▾
    64
    65          public class RegisterViewModel
    66          {
    67              [Required]
    68              [EmailAddress]
    69              [Display(Name = "Email")]
    70              public string Email { get; set; }
    71
    72              [Required]
    73              [StringLength(100, ErrorMessage = "The {0} must be at least {2} characters long.", MinimumLength = 6)]
    74              [DataType(DataType.Password)]
    75              [Display(Name = "Password")]
    76
    77    Duplicated By
    78    Lines 85 - 100
    79
    80              [Compare("Password", ErrorMessage = "The password and confirmation password do not match.")]
    81              public string ConfirmPassword { get; set; }
    82          }
    83
    84          public class ResetPasswordViewModel
    85          {
    86              [Required]
    87              [EmailAddress]
    88              [Display(Name = "Email")]
    89              public string Email { get; set; }
    90
    91              [Required]
    92              [StringLength(100, ErrorMessage = "The {0} must be at least {2} characters long.", MinimumLength = 6)]
    93              [DataType(DataType.Password)]
```

***Figure 8-30.** SonarQube code duplications*

## Technical Debt

The Technical Debt widget is really interesting. It gives a summary of all code issues found and also gives you a number for your debt in hours (Figure 8-31). Multiply by your hourly rate and you get the price of your debt!

*Figure 8-31. SonarQube debt widget*

## Issues

If you drill into the details from the debt widget or go to Issues from the menu, you get a list of all issues found (Figure 8-32).

*Figure 8-32. SonarQube analysis issues*

## Differentials

When you do your analysis, it's very powerful to be able to compare two sets of data. SonarQube lets you analyze results and compare them. Figure 8-33 shows how you can select a time change delta, for instance over the last 30 days.

***Figure 8-33.*** *SonarQube differentials filter*

When the interval is selected, the view is changed to show the differentials (Figure 8-34). Note how nicely all metrics are shown with an increase or decrease. This really makes it easy to see trends and figure out when things started to improve (or get worse).

***Figure 8-34.*** *SonarQube differentials view*

# Customize

Finally, let's take a quick look at how you can customize the dashboard. When you are logged on to SonarQube, you get a Configure button in the top right corner (Figure 8-35).

***Figure 8-35.*** *SonarQube dashboard customization*

From the dashboard configuration pane you get to add any of the installed widgets (Figure 8-36).

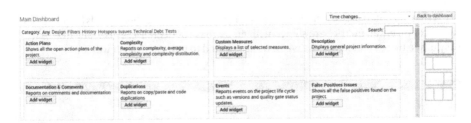

***Figure 8-36.*** *SonarQube dashboard customization, adding widgets*

Save the changes and the dashboard is updated (Figure 8-37)!

***Figure 8-37.*** *SonarQube dashboard customized*

# Integrating SonarQube with Build

One of the greatest things about SonarQube is the ability to monitor code quality over time. And what better way to feed the system than with data produced from one of your regularly running builds?

You should choose a build type that runs at an appropriate frequency to get as relevant a metric to the system as possible. A nightly build is ideal here since it gives you day-by-day feedback about your code. Let's call this build definition *the QA build* since its goal is to capture additional code metrics above what the quicker CI build would do.

To integrate SonarQube in the build, you're going to use two build steps, one to start capturing data and one to end the analysis and publish the result. These steps are available as custom build steps from SonarQube and are available by default in VSO. For an on-premise TFS, you must add them manually by following the steps below. From TFS 2015 Update 1, these will be included in the boxed product as well.

1.  Download the SonarQube build tasks by cloning the official repository at `https://github.com/Microsoft/vso-agent-tasks`.

2.  Upload the tasks to TFS using the `tfx` command. See Chapter 6 for details on how to work with custom build tasks. Run the following commands from the root of where you cloned the tasks in step one:

    a.  `tfx login --authtype basic`

    b.  `tfx build tasks upload .\Tasks\SonarQubePreBuild`

    c.  `tfx build tasks upload .\Tasks\SonarQubePostTest`

Figure 8-38 shows how to add the begin and end analysis steps to your build process.

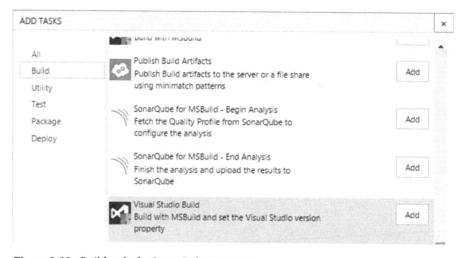

***Figure 8-38.*** *Build tasks for SonarQube integration*

First is the SonarQube for MS Build - Begin Analysis step. This step starts the SonarQube session and must be run before any other build step that will generate analysis data is run. The begin analysis step will contact the SonarQube server and fetch the quality profile, create rulesets for code analysis, and prepare so that the following MS Build steps produce data.

This task requires some configuration. First, you need to point to the SonarQube server. This is done by selecting the service endpoint configured in Figure 8-23.

Next, you provide the project settings, a project key, a name, and a project version. The project key must be unique and is used as the key to the project on the SonarQube server. The version number should be a relevant granularity to analyze for your product. Let's use major.minor.

The third group you provide is settings for the SonarQube database. This will go away in a later version of the product but for now you need to provide the connection string, a username, and a password. Since this is sensitive information, it should be managed as variables in the build process (Figure 8-39).

| Build | Options | Repository | *Variables* | Triggers | General | Retention | History |

💾 Save ▾   ⚙ Queue build...   ↩ Undo

List of predefined variables

| Name | Value | | | Allow at Queue Time |
| --- | --- | --- | --- | --- |
| system.collectionId | 31b1816a-902d-45a1-b883-832b04138e0e | | | ☐ |
| system.teamProject | QBox | | | ☐ |
| system.definitionId | 125 | | | ☐ |
| ✗ BuildConfiguration | debug | | 🔒 | ☑ |
| ✗ BuildPlatform | any cpu | | 🔒 | ☑ |
| ✗ $(SonarConnectionString) | •••••••••••••••••••••••••••••••••••••••••••••••••••••••• | | 🔒 | ☐ |
| ✗ $(SonarUser) | sonar | | 🔒 | ☐ |
| ✗ $(SonarPassword) | ••••• | | 🔒 | ☐ |
| ➕ Add variable | | | | |

*Figure 8-39.* *Variables for the SonarQube database*

Figure 8-40 shows the completed build step.

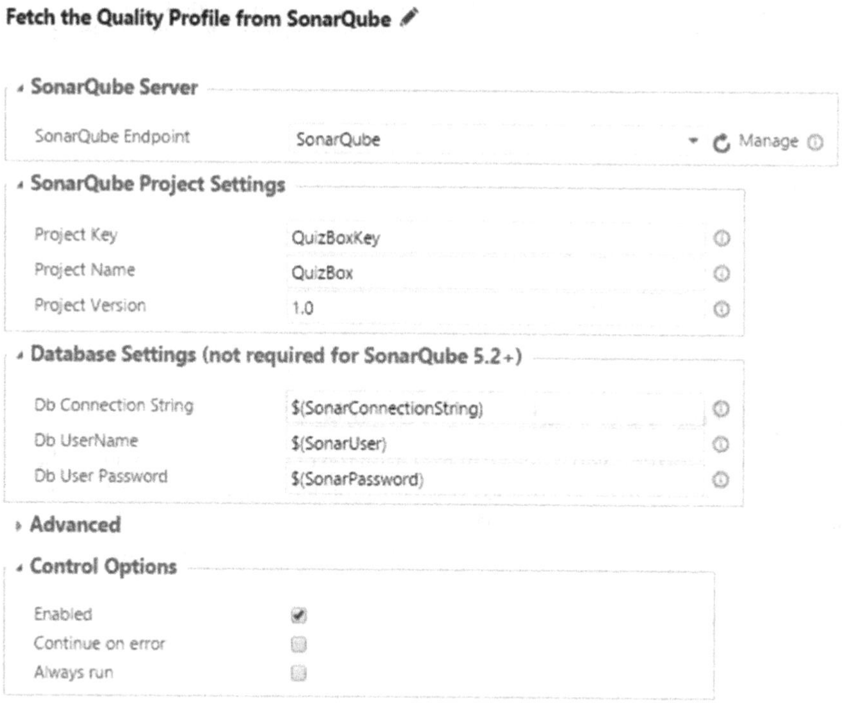

**Fetch the Quality Profile from SonarQube** ✏

**⊿ SonarQube Server** ─────────────────────────────

SonarQube Endpoint      SonarQube          ▾ ↻ Manage ⓘ

**⊿ SonarQube Project Settings** ──────────────

Project Key      QuizBoxKey        ⓘ

Project Name      QuizBox        ⓘ

Project Version      1.0        ⓘ

**⊿ Database Settings (not required for SonarQube 5.2+)** ─────────

Db Connection String      $(SonarConnectionString)        ⓘ

Db UserName      $(SonarUser)        ⓘ

Db User Password      $(SonarPassword)        ⓘ

▸ **Advanced**

**⊿ Control Options** ─────────────────────────────

Enabled      ☑

Continue on error      ☐

Always run      ☐

*Figure 8-40.* *SonarQube for MSBuild - Begin Analysis step*

Then after the build step, or after the test step if you want to capture test coverage data, you add the end analysis step. The end analysis step completes the analysis by computing code clones, metrics, and other analysis, and then sends the result to the server (Figure 8-41).

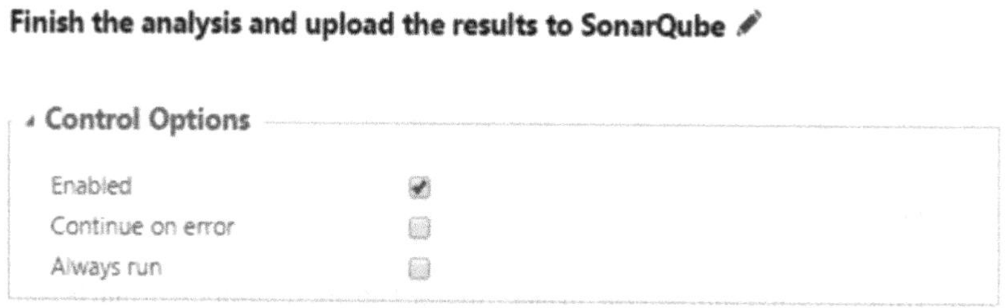

**Finish the analysis and upload the results to SonarQube** ✏

**⊿ Control Options** ─────────────────────────────

Enabled      ☑

Continue on error      ☐

Always run      ☐

*Figure 8-41.* *SonarQube for MSBuild - End Analysis step*

When the build completes, you get a summary section for the SonarQube analysis (Figure 8-42) with a link to the project dashboard where you can look at the results of the analysis.

Summary

#SonarQube Analysis Report _Analysis succeeded for SonarQube project "QuizBox", version 1.0_ Analysis results

- Product projects: 7, test projects: 5
- Invalid projects: 0, skipped projects: 0, excluded projects: 0

*Figure 8-42.  SonarQube section in build summary*

# Configuring Code Quality for QuizBox

When developing QuizBox, you really want to stay on top of code quality so you can be sure it's going to be easy to maintain and evolve the product. You want to take advantage of the full set of code quality solutions discussed in this chapter. Use SonarQube for the code quality metrics so the QA build definition is really clean, as shown in Figure 8-43.

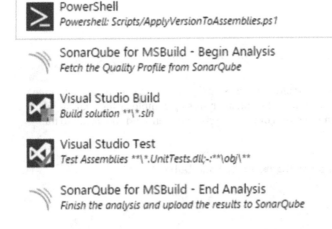

*Figure 8-43.  SonarQube for MSBuild - End Analysis step*

You're applying a version number for all assemblies. The build number format is set in the General settings (Figure 8-44), and you're manually controlling the major, minor, and revision numbers by using automatic revision numbers.

**Figure 8-44.** *Configuring the QuizBox build number format*

The Visual Studio build task compiles the project without code analysis; you will use SonarQube for that. Just to make it clear, you set the MS Build property /p:RunCodeAnalysis=false to disable native code analysis (Figure 8-45).

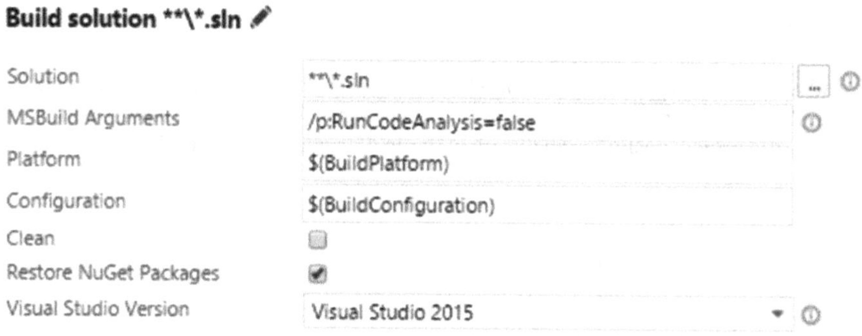

**Build solution **\*.sln** ✎

| | |
|---|---|
| Solution | **\*.sln |
| MSBuild Arguments | /p:RunCodeAnalysis=false |
| Platform | $(BuildPlatform) |
| Configuration | $(BuildConfiguration) |
| Clean | ☐ |
| Restore NuGet Packages | ☑ |
| Visual Studio Version | Visual Studio 2015 |

**Figure 8-45.** *Configuring the QuizBox Visual Studio build settings*

Next, the test step will run unit tests and have code coverage enabled (Figure 8-46).

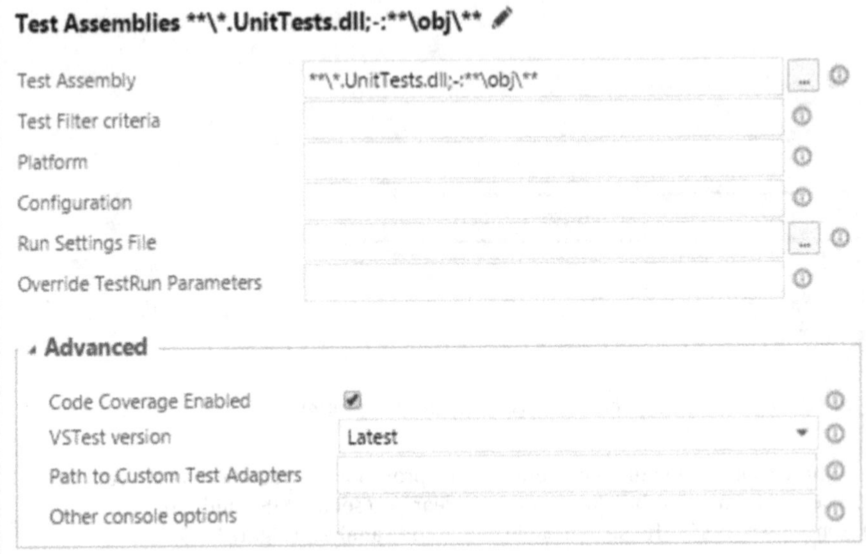

## Test Assemblies **\*.UnitTests.dll;-:**\obj\** ✎

| | |
|---|---|
| Test Assembly | **\*.UnitTests.dll;-:**\obj\** |
| Test Filter criteria | |
| Platform | |
| Configuration | |
| Run Settings File | |
| Override TestRun Parameters | |

### ▲ Advanced

| | |
|---|---|
| Code Coverage Enabled | ☑ |
| VSTest version | Latest |
| Path to Custom Test Adapters | |
| Other console options | |

*Figure 8-46.  QuizBox unit test step*

And after that you just end the SonarQube analysis and let SonarQube do the rest. Figure 8-47 shows a completed build with the SonarQube summary, and Figure 8-48 shows how the project dashboard lights up with the data generated from the build.

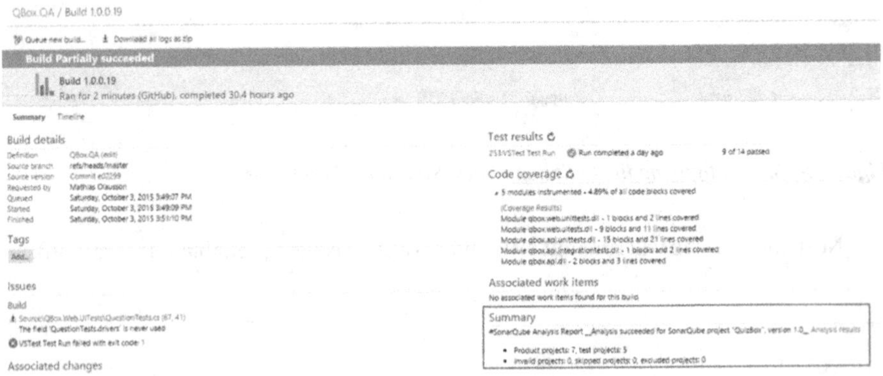

*Figure 8-47.  SonarQube build summary*

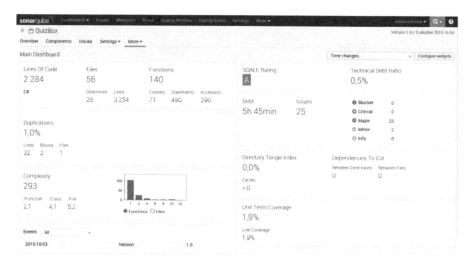

*Figure 8-48.* *QuizBox SonarQube dashboard*

# Summary

In this chapter, you learned about code quality and technical debt. You first looked at unit testing as a development practice. Whether you choose to follow a test-driven approach or not, unit tests should be the foundation for keeping on top of code quality. Unit tests are the driver of many of the other tools you can use to capture important quality metrics.

You can use code analysis and code metrics to understand how well your code is written. Together with code clone detection, you have several ways to detect deficiencies in your code, which you can then refactor to make the code base more maintainable.

By using a platform like SonarQube you get a way to collect various quality metrics and evaluate them in a quality dashboard. You can manage technical debt by looking at analysis data over time to see if you are improving or not. This can be an invaluable tool to help understand where your pain points are and find where and when they were introduced. It even gives you the price of your technical debt, something that's really useful in the discussion on what good code quality is allowed to cost.

# CHAPTER 9

# Continuous Testing

Testing in an agile project with a Continuous Delivery process on top can be challenging. With a common mindset in which you embrace change and want to work incrementally and iteratively, you have good conditions to deliver what your customer asks for on time.

To get testing to work in an agile environment, you need to rethink the testing approach you use. Working with incremental development typically means you need to do lots of regression testing to make sure the features you have developed and tested still continue to work as the product evolves. Iterative development with short cycles often means you must have an efficient test process or you will spend lots of time in the cycle preparing for testing rather than actually running the tests.

You can solve these problems by carefully designing your tests; this helps you maintain only the tests that actually give value to the product. As the product evolves through increments, so should the tests, and you can choose to add only relevant tests to your regression test suite. To make the testing more efficient, you should automate the tests and include them in your Continuous Integration scheme to get the most value from the tests.

In this chapter, you will start by looking at tools to manage your test process and learn how you can first run the tests manually. When a feature is stable enough, you can evolve some of your manual (regression) tests to automated tests; you will explore the types of tests you have at hand to do that. Finally, you will look at how to provision and configure your test and production environments and then run your automated tests on a distributed test environment. But first let's take a look at what agile testing means.

## Agile Testing

You will now look at ideas to help you design your tests. In the coming sections, you will look at how you can improve your testing process to help you perform testing in an agile context.

### Defining Tests

To define tests you need to think about what you want to achieve with the tests. Are you testing requirement coverage? Are you testing to make sure the software performs according to your service level agreement? Are you testing new code or retesting working software? These and other aspects affect the way you think about tests.

Brian Marick created the model shown in Figure 9-1, which is excellent source when reasoning about what kind of tests you should create, when, and for what purpose. Let's take a look at the model and how it can be used to help you define your tests in a suitable way.

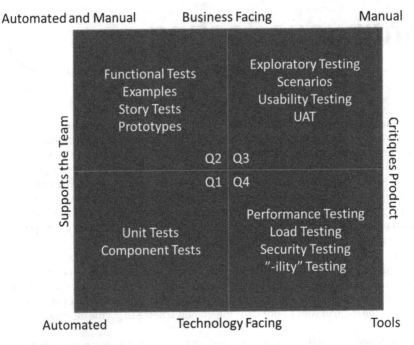

**Figure 9-1.** *Testing quadrants*

## Q1 – Unit and Component Tests

Unit and component tests are automated tests written to help the team develop software effectively. With good suites of unit and component level tests, you have a safety net that helps you develop software incrementally in short iterations without breaking existing functionality. The Q1 tests are also invaluable when refactoring code. With good test coverage, a developer should feel confident about making a change without knowing about every dependency. The tests should tell you if you did wrong!

## Q2 – Functional Tests

Functional tests are mainly your traditional scripted system tests in different flavors. It is hard to avoid running these tests manually at first, but you should try to find ways to automate them as you learn more about your product and how it needs to be tested. Many functional tests can be automated and then you can focus on early testing for the manual tester.

## Q3 – Exploratory Testing

Exploratory testing is a form of software testing in which the individual tester can design and run tests in a freer form. Instead of following detailed test scripts, the tester explores the system under tests based on the user stories. As the tester learns how the system behaves, the tester can optimize the testing work and focus more on testing than documenting the test process.

You should leave this category of tests as manual tests. The focus should be to catch bugs that would fall through the net of automated tests. A key motivation for automated testing is to let it do more of exploratory and usability testing because these tests validate how the end user feels when using the product.

## Q4 – Capability Testing

Lastly are the capability tests. These tests are run against the behavior of the system; you test non-functional requirements, performance, and security. These tests are generally automated and run using special purpose tools, such as load test frameworks and security analyzers.

# Test Management

Regardless of how you structure your projects, you need a good way to plan, document, run, and analyze your test efforts. Visual Studio comes with great tools for test management that can be used with both very formal processes and the agile ones. You can use them for manual testing as well as automated testing so let's look at how they work.

## Clients for Test Planning and Manual Testing

Visual Studio and TFS come two options for managing tests, the desktop application Microsoft Test Manager and the web-based Microsoft Web Test Manager.

## Microsoft Test Manager

The Microsoft Test Manager, MTM, is a stand-alone desktop application added to the product family when Visual Studio and TFS 2010 were released. MTM can be seen as the Visual Studio for testers, the one-stop shop for the entire test process. A tester can do all the testing activities within a single application (not entirely true, but pretty close actually).

At a high level, MTM provides functionality for

- Test planning
- Test design
- Test execution and test run analysis
- Rich bug reporting with data collection from the machines under test

- Work item tracking (including bug tracking, of course)

- Test environment management

MTM comes with Visual Studio 2015 Enterprise and Microsoft Test Professional 2015, as shown in Figure 9-2.

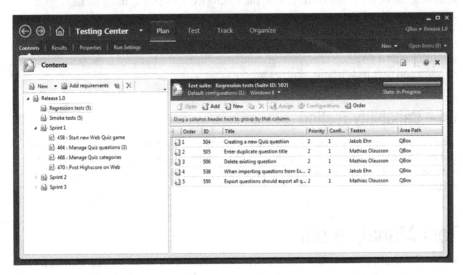

***Figure 9-2.*** *Microsoft Test Manager 2015*

## Microsoft Web Test Case Manager

The second client for working with test cases is the Microsoft Web Test Case Manager, also known as WTM or the Test Hub. This is a new addition to the Team Web Access, introduced in TFS 2012. WTM is a lightweight solution for when you want the integrated testing experience with TFS but don't want to (or cannot) install the MTM client. Figure 9-3 shows the Web Test Manager client.

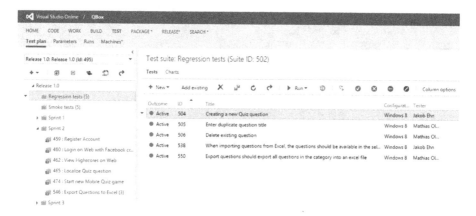

*Figure 9-3.* *Microsoft Web Test Manager*

Currently WTM offers a subset of the functionality in MTM and may also require someone in the team to work with MTM to manage part of the testing configuration. The scenarios WTM enables are

- Test design

- Test execution

- Basic bug reporting

- Environment management

# Planning the Tests

In this first section, you will use the planning features in the testing tools to create a plan for your testing. You can use either the Web Test Case Manager from the Team Web Access Test Hub or the Microsoft Test Manager desktop application. (I will use the WTM as the default application in the examples and show MTM for the features currently only available in the desktop client.)

# Creating a Test Plan

To start testing you must create a test plan to organize your tests. A team project can contain multiple test plans, but a test plan can't contain other test plans. Depending on how you organize your team project, a test plan will typically be associated with an application, a release, or a specific sprint/iteration.

I recommend keeping test plans small; I prefer one test plan per sprint over one for the entire the release. Small plans are more to the point and map well into the test process. If you look at the status of a test plan, you can grasp what it means. If the plan covers the entire project, it is much harder to understand whether you are progressing as planned. Figure 9-4 shows a typical test plan with different types of test suites.

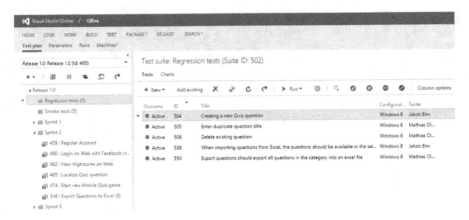

***Figure 9-4.*** *QuizBox test plan*

## Test Suites

Test suites group together the tests you want to run and track in this plan. You can choose from three types of suites:

- **Static suite:** The content of this suite is manually added test cases.

- **Query-based suite:** A query-based suite lists all test cases matching a given work item filter.

- **Requirements-based suite:** This suite shows the test cases associated with a selected TFS requirement.

The query-based suite is great for any situation where you want to make sure you have an up-to-date list of tests based on some criteria (Figure 9-5). Typical usages are suites of tests for a specific application area or all automated tests.

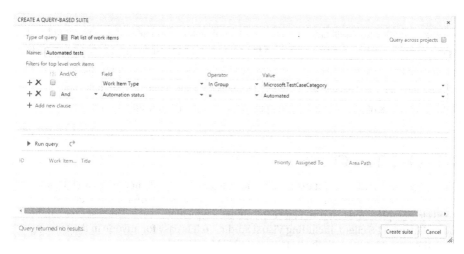

***Figure 9-5.*** *Query-based suite for all automated test cases*

The requirement suite is a little different. Here you use a work item category called RequirementCategory that maps to the configured work item type(s) representing a requirement. In your scenario using Scrum, this would map to a product backlog item and bug.

You would typically add all requirements in the sprint to the test plan to associate the acceptance tests with the corresponding requirement. Figure 9-6 shows how to use a work item query matching the requirement category to find the requirements that you now can add to your plan.

---

■ **Note**    Removing a test case from a requirement deletes the link to the requirement and therefore affects other test plans that use the same test case/requirement association. Adding a test case has a similar effect; the test case will be added to all existing test plans where the requirement is used. This will affect the test statistics for the test plans, so make sure to think through how this behavior affects testing so you don't get any unwanted surprises.

---

## What Is a Test Case?

A test case represents the test instructions for a tester. It is implemented as a TFS work item, which means you can customize it so that it contains the information the tester needs to complete the test run. Figure 9-7 shows a typical test case. The test case can be viewed in any TFS client, including Visual Studio, so it is easy for anyone in the team to work the tests. You can edit the tests steps in MTM or WTM.

***Figure 9-7.***  *Test case for QuizBox*

Let's now walk through the core elements of a test case.

## Test Steps

The steps section is, of course, the central part of the test case, as shown in Figure 9-8. You add steps for the test instructions and provide expected results. It is important to spend time thinking about the expected result because these are the validation points that you use to assert that the test case is testing the right thing. If the expected result is well formulated, you can use it to validate the test step in a manual test as well as if you automate it, saving time and making the test runs more repeatable.

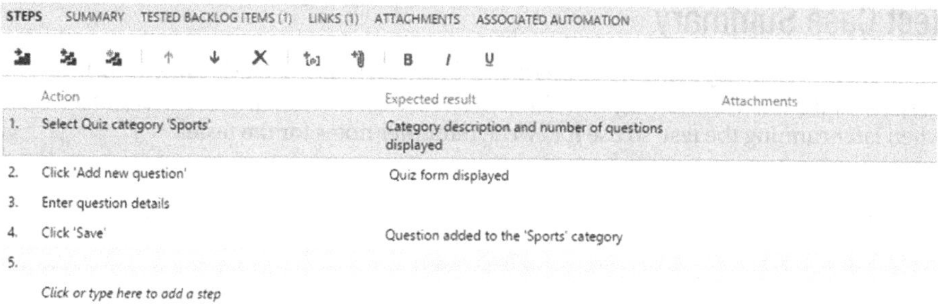

*Figure 9-8.* *Test case with formatted steps*

Use formatting to highlight important sections of the test steps. It's worth mentioning that the test step is selectable when the test is being run, so if you provide a URL in the test step, the tester can copy the URL and paste it into the browser instead of having to type it.

For recurring steps you can create shared steps. Shared steps are stored as a separate work item and can be shared between test cases, for example to encapsulate the login steps, which might be the first sequence in many test cases.

If you want to test multiple combinations of a test, say to test how the application behaves for users of different roles, you can add parameters to the test case. Figure 9-9 shows the previous test case which now uses parameters for different datasets.

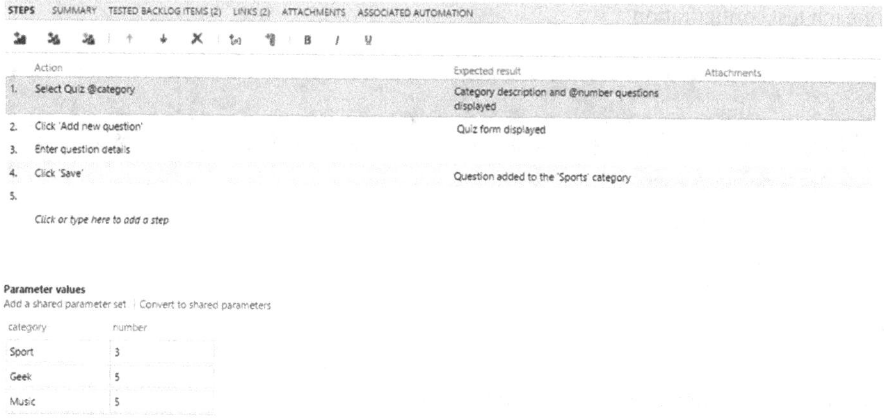

*Figure 9-9.* *Test case with parameters*

Each set of parameters shows as test iterations when the test case is run. Each data value is copied into the Windows clipboard so you can paste it into the target UI element, something that also makes it possible to fast-forward the rest of the test iterations.

231

## Test Case Summary

The test case summary contains a description field that is useful for documenting the purpose of the test case (see Figure 9-10). This field is also shown in the Test Runner when later running the test, so use it to write reminder notes for the tester.

STEPS    **SUMMARY**    TESTED BACKLOG ITEMS (1)    LINKS (1)    ATTACHMENTS    ASSOCIATED AUTOMATION

Description

This test should focus on finding problems when adding new quiz questions.

If you have time run negative flows as well.

*Figure 9-10.  Test case summary*

## Test Configurations

The test configurations allow you to define the test matrix for your tests. A common example is that you need to test your web application on both Internet Explorer and Chrome. To do so, create matching configurations, as shown in Figure 9-11. This is done from the Organize tab in MTM by managing configuration variables. By creating multiple configurations like this, you don't have to write and maintain a test case for every configuration; instead the tester will be able to run the same test multiple times, one time for each test configuration.

Testing Center ▼    Plan    Test    Track    **Organize**    QBox ▶ Release 1.0

Test Plan Manager | **Test Configuration Manager** | Test Case Manager | Shared Steps Manager    New ▼    Open Items (0) ▼

**Test Configuration Manager**

New   Open   ✕   Manage configuration variables

| ID | Name | Default | State | Configuration variables | Description |
|----|------|---------|-------|------------------------|-------------|
| 40 | chrome | No | Active | | |
| 41 | firefox | No | Active | | |
| 42 | ie | No | Active | | |
| 32 | Windows 8 | Yes | Active | Operating System: Windows 8 | Default operating system for testing |

*Figure 9-11.  Managing test configurations in MTM*

Later in this chapter you will learn how to use configurations to group automated tests.

# Setting Up Environments

To be able to run both manual and automated tests in your deployment pipeline, you need to provision and configure the different environments for the application. You can break up the different activities that are part of deploying an application onto an environment and verify it into different stages, as shown in Figure 9-12.

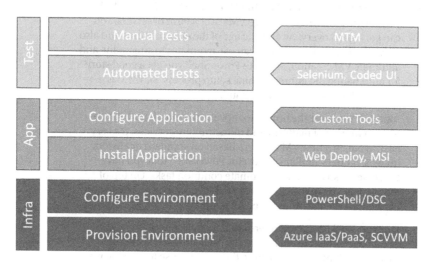

***Figure 9-12.*** *The stage stack*

Figure 9-12 shows the different stages (infrastructure, application, and test) and what activities typically go into each of these stages. For every stage, there is a related set of tools and techniques that can be used for implementation. You looked at some of these tools in Chapter 7 when I discussed different ways of packaging an application for deployment. In the next chapter, where you will implement a deployment pipeline, you will see how to leverage these techniques for carrying out the deployment of the different application components. Here you will focus on the infrastructure part, namely provisioning and configuring the environments.

There are many options available for you to create environments. Before you dive into the details on provisioning and configuring an environment, let's first take a look at some of the options.

- **Physical machines**: There are still scenarios where you want or need to use a physical machine, for instance when you have dependencies on the hardware or you need exclusive access to the hardware. But performance may not be the case anymore; you can get excellent performance from a virtual machine, and in a hosted environment, the VMs may offer better specs than the physical machine you could get your hands on.

- **Hyper-V**: On premise you can use Hyper-V to create and manage virtual machines. It's a great system that's easy to use, but for large scale deployments it does not offer a management solution that spans multiple machines. There is good support for PowerShell to automate the configuration of a machine but the provisioning is often manual.

- **System Center Virtual Machine Manager, SCVMM**: With SCVMM you get the platform to manage VMs over a farm of servers. You can get a good overview of the usage of the environments and also provision new machines. You can use templates to streamline and automate VM creation, and with PowerShell you get a good story for automating the entire machine setup process. SCVMM is a good platform for your private cloud.

- **Azure**: If you have the option to move to the cloud, then Azure offers a rich set of platform and infrastructure services. It's very easy to create a new VM in Azure based on standard or custom images. It offers similar support for PowerShell that you have for Hyper-V, so it's easy to automate common tasks. On top of that, it offers the Azure Resource Manager, which can create and configure new machines based on templates.

- **Docker**: Docker, or container-based models, offers a new way to manage and scale environments. You can view a container as a lightweight virtual machine that you can use to create your environments. A big difference between a container and a VM is that the container will share the OS with the host, preserving resources so you can run many more containers on the host than you can using VMs.

In this chapter, you will look at the Azure Resource Manager to provision new environments because it is a good example of how to use templates to automate the environment creation. SCVMM and containers are other interesting options I recommend looking into since they also give you a platform to automate the environment management process.

## Getting Your Environment Ready for Deployment

To use your machines from TFS Build or Visual Studio Release Management they must be accessible using *Windows Remote Management* (WinRM).

WinRM is a SOAP-based protocol that implements the *WS-Management* standard protocol, which allows for operating systems and hardware from different vendors to communicate with each other. One common usage of WinRM is to use *PowerShell Remoting*, which is built on top of WinRM, to perform administrative tasks against a remote server. By default, WS-Management and PowerShell Remoting use port 5985 and 5986 for connections over HTTP and HTTPS, which makes it a friendly protocol when it comes to firewall. The default option is to enable WinRM over HTTPS, using port 5986. This was used in the example above.

# WinRM for Azure Virtual Machines

If you create a Windows Server 2012 virtual machine in Azure, PowerShell Remoting will be enabled and port 5986 will be opened in the endpoint configuration for the virtual machine, as shown in Figure 9-13.

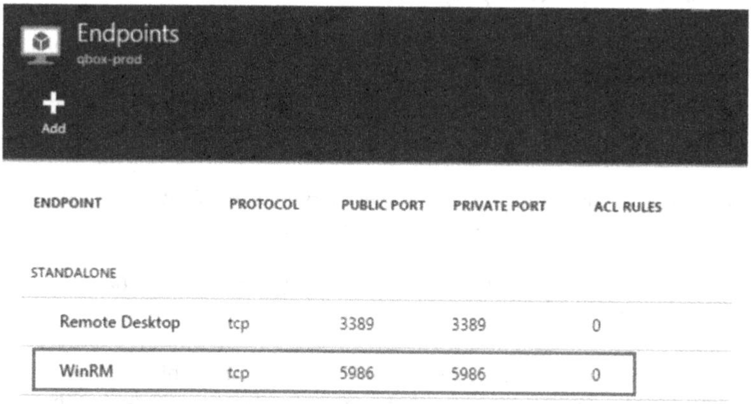

| ENDPOINT | PROTOCOL | PUBLIC PORT | PRIVATE PORT | ACL RULES |
|---|---|---|---|---|
| STANDALONE | | | | |
| Remote Desktop | tcp | 3389 | 3389 | 0 |
| WinRM | tcp | 5986 | 5986 | 0 |

*Figure 9-13. WinRM endpoint definition*

# Enabling WinRM for On-Premise Servers

For on-premise servers, you might need to explicitly enable PowerShell Remoting on the target. This is done by opening a PowerShell console window in administrative mode, and then running

```
Enable-PSRemoting
```

Figure 9-14 shows an example of how to enable PowerShell Remoting.

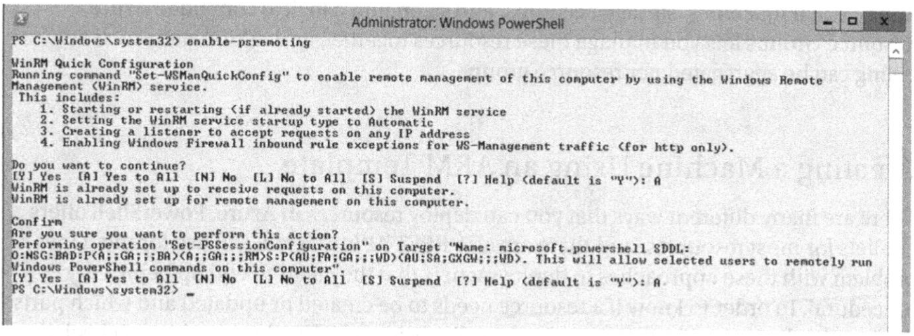

*Figure 9-14. Enabeling PowerShell Remoting*

Running the Enable-PSremoting cmdlet makes the following changes to the computer:

- Sets the WinRM service to start automatically and restart it
- Registers the default endpoints (session configurations) for use by Windows PowerShell
- Creates an HTTP listener on port 5985 for all local IP addresses
- Creates an exception in the Windows Firewall for incoming TCP traffic on port 5985

## Verifying WinRM Access

To verify that it is possible to communicate with a target server using WinRM, you can try this out from a client machine by executing a remote command:

```
Invoke-Command -ComputerName qbox-dev.cloudapp.net -ScriptBlock { Get-
ChildItem C:\ } -credential jakob -UseSSL
```

This will, if WinRM is set up properly, execute the PowerShell script block Get-ChildItem c:\ on the remote server named qbox-dev.cloudapp.net. Note that the account credentials that are passed must have administrative rights on the target server to be able to run a remote command.

## Azure Resource Groups

From the beginning, all resources in Microsoft Azure (web sites, SQL databases, virtual machines) were created on the subscription level, meaning that there was no way to group these resources. Typically every application consists of a set of resource that belongs logically, but there was no way to handle this in the Azure management portal.

This changed with the introduction the Azure Resource Manager (ARM) and Azure Resource Groups, which were introduced with the new Azure Portal.

Azure Resource Group is a container that groups a set of resources, such as Web Apps, virtual machines, storage accounts, and so on into a logical container. Azure Resource Groups lets you manage these resources together, and information such as billing can be aggregated per resource group.

### Creating a Machine Using an ARM Template

There are many different ways that you can deploy resources in Azure. PowerShell offers cmdlets for most resources, and there are also REST APIs that you can use for this. One problem with these approaches to deployment is that they tend to end up being very procedural. In order to know if a resource needs to be created or updated and which parts that need to be updated, you must check explicitly in code. In other words, you check if an Azure Web App exists, and if it does, you only update it, and so on.

The two technologies that you will look at in this section, Azure Resource Manager (ARM) templates and PowerShell DSC, are idempotent, meaning that you can run them multiple times and are guaranteed to get the same results.

In this section, you will learn how to create and update an Azure Resource Group that contains a Windows Server 2012 R2 virtual machine, and you will configure it at the same time using a PowerShell DSC script. You will look at how to trigger the deployment manually using PowerShell and how to automate it using an automated build.

## Azure Resource Groups in Visual Studio 2015

Azure Resource Groups are defined using JSON template files that define which resources should be deployed in the resource group. At deployment time, the template files are uploaded to Azure and deployed using Azure Resource Manager.

Although these files can be created manually, there is a specific Visual Studio project template that installs with the Azure SDK.

---

■ **Note**    You can download the Azure SDK and other resources at
`https://azure.microsoft.com/en-you/downloads/`.

---

When you have installed the Azure SDK, you will find a new project template called *Azure Resource Group* located in the Cloud category, as shown in Figure 9-15.

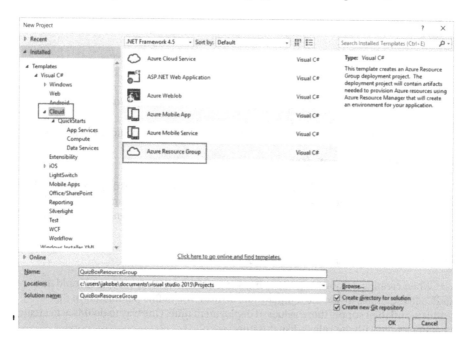

*Figure 9-15.  Create a new Azure Resource Group project*

When creating a project using this project template, you can start off by selecting from a variety of different Azure templates, as shown in Figure 9-16. What you select here is just the start of the template; you will be able to add more resources to your resource group template afterwards. In this case, select the Windows Virtual Machine template.

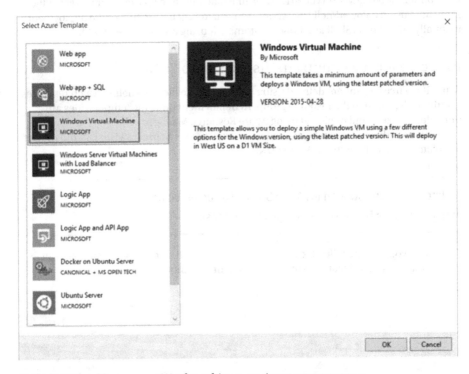

*Figure 9-16.* *Adding a new virtual machine to an Azure resource group*

All Azure Resource Group projects contain the following set of files from the start:

### Templates\<ResourceType>.json

This is the template file that defines all resources that should be deployed with this resource group. It also defines parameters that can be passed in dynamically, as well as variables that can be used inside the template. You will look at this template file in more detail soon.

### Templates\<ResourceType>.param.dev.json

When creating a resource group using a resource group template, you should not hardcode the values inside the template file. Instead, you define parameters in the template and then supply these values at deployment time. One way to do this is to create a parameter file with the values, like this one.

### Scripts\Deploy-AzureResourceGroup.ps1

238

This is a PowerShell script that can deploy the resource group. You will soon look at how it works.

### Tools\AzCopy.exe

AzCopy is a standalone tool that is used for uploading files to Azure blob storage. The PowerShell script uses AzCopy to upload the generated output of the project so that these files are available when the ARM service deploys the resource group template.

Figure 9-17 shows the contents of the newly created Azure Resource Group project.

***Figure 9-17.*** *Structure of a new Azure Resource Group project*

The template file, which is a JSON file, can often become quite large and hard to work with. To help you out, the Azure SDK also installs a nifty JSON explorer that shows a graphical tree structure of the JSON file, and is also aware of Azure Resource Group templates so it will let you create new resources right from the view (Figure 9-18).

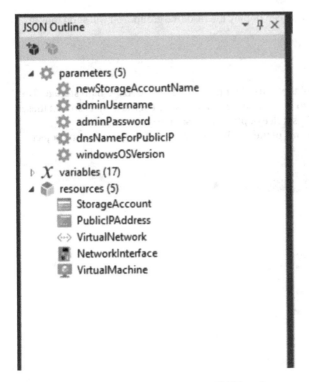

*Figure 9-18. The Azure Resource Group JSON explorer*

Here you can see the JSON Outline view of the template file that you just created. It contains five input parameters, a set of variables used inside the template, and then five resources that are the result of selecting the Windows Virtual Machine template. For every virtual machine in Azure, there is also a storage account, a public IP address, a virtual network, and a network interface. All these different artifacts are different resources in Azure Resource Manager.

Now, you do not just want to create a virtual machine when deploying this resource group; you also want to configure it so that it contains the prerequisites of the application that will be deployed. To do this, you will run a PowerShell DSC script after the virtual machine has been created. DSC scripts can also be defined as a resource in an ARM template, so let's create one.

Click the Add Resource button at the top left in the JSON Outline view. This will bring up the Azure Template window again. Select the *PowerShell DSC Extension* template and call it *ConfigureServer* (Figure 9-19).

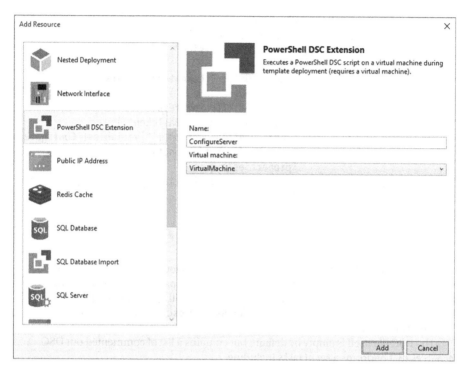

***Figure 9-19.*** *Adding a DSC script resource to ARM template*

This template will, since you named in *ConfigureServer*, add a DSC script called ConfigureServerConfiguration.ps1 and a resource inside the template file that refers to this script. Note that this DSC resource is placed inside the VirtualMachine resource; this is how ARM manages dependencies. By nesting resources like this, ARM can provision or execute them in the correct order.

Here is the JSON resource that was added, inside the VirtualMachine resource:

```
{

                "name": "ConfigureServer",
                "type": "extensions",
                "location": "[variables('location')]",
                "apiVersion": "2015-05-01-preview",
                "dependsOn": [
                    "[concat('Microsoft.Compute/virtualMachines/',
                    variables('vmName'))]"
                ],
                "tags": {
                    "displayName": "ConfigureServer"
                },
                "properties": {
                    "publisher": "Microsoft.Powershell",
```

```
                    "type": "DSC",
                    "typeHandlerVersion": "2.1",
                    "autoUpgradeMinorVersion": true,
                    "settings": {
                        "modulesUrl": "[concat(parameters
                        ('_artifactsLocation'), '/', 'dsc.zip')]",
                        "sasToken": "[parameters
                        ('_artifactsLocationSasToken')]",
                        "configurationFunction": "[variables('Configure
                        ServerConfigurationFunction')]",
                        "properties": {
                            "nodeName": "[variables('vmName')]"
                        }
                    }
                }
            }
        }
```

The modulesUrl setting points to where the script is located. As you can see, it creates a URL by concatenating the _artifactsLocation parameter with the string dsc.zip. The _artifactsLocation is set by the PowerShell script and will point to the Azure Blob storage where these files will uploaded. The dsc.zip file is created when compiling this project.

The DSC file itself is empty by default, but contains a list of commented out DSC resources that performs a set of tasks including

- Installing the web server role, including the IIS management tools

- Installing ASP.NET 4.5 with a lot of related options, such as logging, authentication, and so on

- Downloading and installing Web Deploy

Here is a shorter version of this DSC file that shows the main configuration resources, leaving out some of the ASP.NET and IIS settings that are also included:

```
Configuration Main
{

Param ( [string] $nodeName )

Import-DscResource -ModuleName PSDesiredStateConfiguration

Node $nodeName
  {
    WindowsFeature WebServerRole
    {
      Name = "Web-Server"
      Ensure = "Present"
    }
```

```
WindowsFeature WebManagementConsole
{
  Name = "Web-Mgmt-Console"
  Ensure = "Present"
}
WindowsFeature WebManagementService
{
  Name = "Web-Mgmt-Service"
  Ensure = "Present"
}
WindowsFeature ASPNet45
{
  Name = "Web-Asp-Net45"
  Ensure = "Present"
}
WindowsFeature HTTPRedirection
{
  Name = "Web-Http-Redirect"
  Ensure = "Present"
}
Script DownloadWebDeploy
{
    TestScript = {
        Test-Path "C:\WindowsAzure\WebDeploy_amd64_en-US.msi"
    }
    SetScript ={
        $source = "http://download.microsoft.com/download/A/5/0/
        A502BE57-7848-42B8-97D5-DEB2069E2B05/WebDeploy_amd64_en-US.msi"
        $dest = "C:\WindowsAzure\WebDeploy_amd64_en-US.msi"
        Invoke-WebRequest $source -OutFile $dest
    }
    GetScript = {@{Result = "DownloadWebDeploy"}}
    DependsOn = "[WindowsFeature]WebServerRole"
}
Package InstallWebDeploy
{
    Ensure = "Present"
    Path  = "C:\WindowsAzure\WebDeploy_amd64_en-US.msi"
    Name = "Microsoft Web Deploy 3.6 Beta"
    ProductId = "{50638DB8-30CE-4713-8EA0-6AA405740391}"
    Arguments = "ADDLOCAL=ALL"
    DependsOn = "[Script]DownloadWebDeploy"
}
```

```
Service StartWebDeploy
{
    Name = "WMSVC"
    StartupType = "Automatic"
    State = "Running"
    DependsOn = "[Package]InstallWebDeploy"
}
}
}
```

With this all set up, it is time to deploy the resource group. It is possible to do this by right-clicking the project in Visual Studio and selecting Deploy. As shown in Figure 9-20, this will let you select subscription, storage, and a few other things. You can also set the parameter values and then start the deployment process.

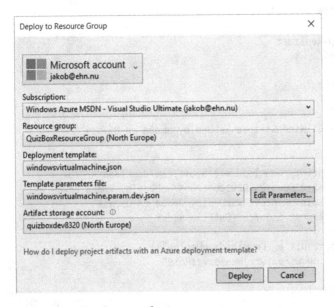

*Figure 9-20.* *Deploying to the Azure resource group*

But since you are interested in automating things, let's look at how you can use the PowerShell script directly. The script takes a number of parameters, the most important ones being the name of the resource group and storage account, and the path to the template and parameters files.

Here is an example of executing the script:

```
.\Deploy-AzureResourceGroup.ps1 -ResourceGroupLocation NorthEurope
-ResourceGroupName QuizBoxResourceGroup -UploadArtifacts -StorageAccountName
quizboxdev8320 -StorageAccountResourceGroupName quizbox-dev -TemplateFile
..\Templates\WindowsVirtualMachine.json -TemplateParametersFile
..\Templates\WindowsVirtualMachine.param.dev.json


WARNING: The Switch-AzureMode cmdlet is deprecated and will be removed in a
future release.
Finished 4 of total 4 file(s).

Transfer summary:
-----------------
Total files transferred: 4
Transfer successfully:    4
Transfer failed:          0
Elapsed time:             00.00:00:01
WARNING: The Switch-AzureMode cmdlet is deprecated and will be removed in a
future release.

cmdlet New-AzureResourceGroup at command pipeline position 1
Supply values for the following parameters:
(Type !? for Help.)
adminPassword: ********
WARNING: The deployment parameters in New-AzureResourceGroup cmdlet is being
deprecated and will be removed in a future release. Please use
New-AzureResourceGroupDeployment to submit deployments.
WARNING: The output object of this cmdlet will be modified in a future
release.
VERBOSE: 22:28:55 - Created resource group 'QuizBoxResourceGroup' in
location 'northeurope'
VERBOSE: 22:28:56 - Template is valid.
VERBOSE: 22:28:57 - Create template deployment 'WindowsVirtualMachine'.
VERBOSE: 22:28:59 - Resource Microsoft.Storage/storageAccounts
'quizboxstorage' provisioning status is succeeded
VERBOSE: 22:29:01 - Resource Microsoft.Network/networkInterfaces 'myVMNic'
provisioning status is succeeded
VERBOSE: 22:29:01 - Resource Microsoft.Network/publicIPAddresses
'myPublicIP' provisioning status is succeeded
VERBOSE: 22:29:01 - Resource Microsoft.Network/virtualNetworks 'MyVNET'
provisioning status is succeeded
```

```
VERBOSE: 22:29:06 - Resource Microsoft.Compute/virtualMachines 'MyWindowsVM'
provisioning status is running
VERBOSE: 22:32:43 - Resource Microsoft.Compute/virtualMachines 'MyWindowsVM'
provisioning status is succeeded
VERBOSE: 22:32:45 - Resource Microsoft.Compute/virtualMachines/extensions
'MyWindowsVM/ConfigureServer' provisioning status is running
VERBOSE: 22:41:56 - Resource Microsoft.Compute/virtualMachines/extensions
'MyWindowsVM/ConfigureServer' provisioning status is succeeded


ResourceGroupName : QuizBoxResourceGroup
Location          : northeurope
ProvisioningState : Succeeded
Resources         :
Name                 Type                                          Location
===============      =========================================     ========
MyWindowsVM          Microsoft.Compute/virtualMachines             westus
ConfigureServer      Microsoft.Compute/virtualMachines/extensions  westus
myVMNic              Microsoft.Network/networkInterfaces           westus
myPublicIP           Microsoft.Network/publicIPAddresses           westus
MyVNET               Microsoft.Network/virtualNetworks             westus
quizboxstorage       Microsoft.Storage/storageAccounts             westus

ResourceId          : /subscriptions/da5ebe2e-3657-4249-a296-e00abdf4180c/
resourceGroups/QuizBoxResourceGroup
```

From the output, you can see that it uploaded four files (the two PowerShell scripts, the template file, and the generated dsc.zip file), used the New-AzureResourceGroup PowerShell cmdlet to start the creation of the resource group and, at the end, executed the ConfigureServer DSC resource. Figure 9-21 shows the created resource group in the Azure portal.

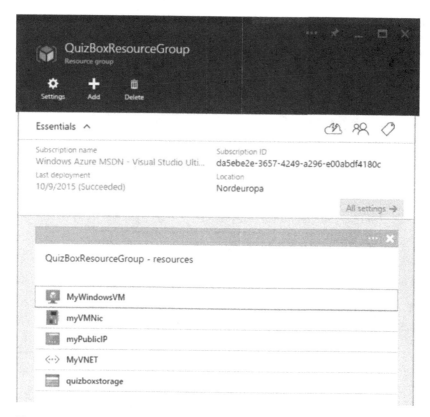

*Figure 9-21.  Resource group in Azure portal*

One of the most powerful attributes of the Azure Resource Manager is that all deployments are idempotent, meaning that you can safely run the same deployment multiple times without affecting anything that is already configured.

## Automating ARM Deployments

Provisioning and configuring machines using an ARM template fits nicely into the concept of a deployment pipeline, where you want to make sure you can automate the whole process of deploying your application, including the environment it runs on.

There are two options for deploying ARM templates from a build definition:

- Run the PowerShell script showed above, using the Azure PowerShell task.

- Use the built-in Azure Resource Group Deployment task.

The first option gives you more flexibility, since you can customize the script the way you want it, and potentially add other features to it.

Since you already know how to run PowerShell scripts as part of a build, let's look at the second option here. It uses the *Azure Resource Group Deployment* task, which is available in the *Deploy* category, as shown in Figure 9-22.

*Figure 9-22. Adding an Azure Resource Group Deployment task*

When using this task you need to supply the following information:

- **Azure Subscription:** Here you select to which subscription you should deploy the resource group. The subscriptions are managed in the administration of the TFS server or Visual Studio account level. You looked at this back in Chapter 7.

  There is a little caveat here in that the task requires an Azure subscription that is registered using either credentials or a service principal, since the Azure Resource Manager does not support certificates. Also, when using credentials, you must use a work account, you can't use a Microsoft account here.

- **Name of Resource Group and Location:** The name of the resource group and its location. If this is an existing resource group, the task will update the resource group with the resources specified in the Azure template. If no resource group with the name exists in the subscription, a new one will be created.

- **Template:** *QuizBoxResourceGroup/Templates/ WindowsVirtualMachine.json*

  This is the path to the JSON template files to use for deployment. When using this task from a build definition you can browse the source control repository, and when using it from a Release definition you can browse the output of the linked build definition (these concepts are explained in detail in Chapter 10).

- **Template Parameters:** *QuizBoxResourceGroup/Templates/ WindowsVirtualMachine.param.dev.json*

  The path to the parameters file that contains the default values for the template parameters.

- **Override Template Parameters:**
  *-vmName QuizBoxServer -newStorageAccountName qbstorage -vmSize Standard_A2*

  This field is used to override any default values that are defined in the template parameter file. Typically you will apply all the environment specific information here.

Figure 9-23 shows an example of the *Azure Resource Group Deployment* task.

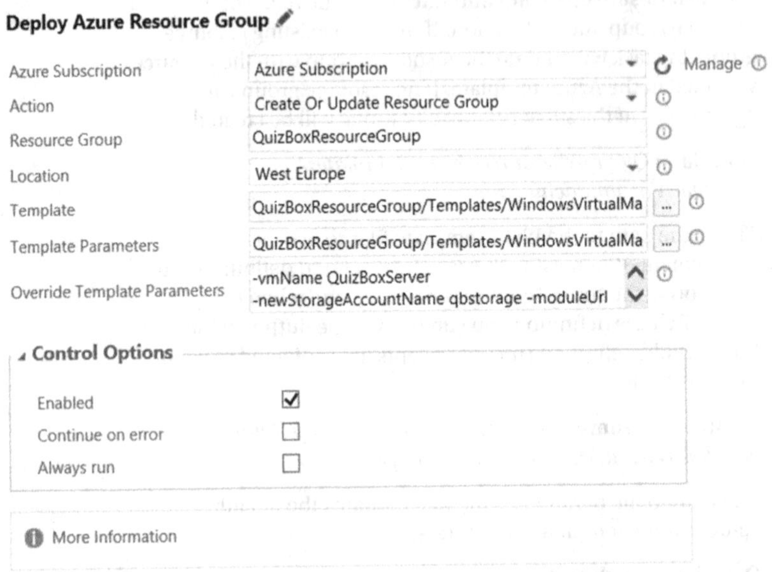

**Deploy Azure Resource Group** ✎

| | | |
|---|---|---|
| Azure Subscription | Azure Subscription ▾ | ↻ Manage ⓘ |
| Action | Create Or Update Resource Group ▾ | ⓘ |
| Resource Group | QuizBoxResourceGroup | ⓘ |
| Location | West Europe ▾ | ⓘ |
| Template | QuizBoxResourceGroup/Templates/WindowsVirtualMa [...] | ⓘ |
| Template Parameters | QuizBoxResourceGroup/Templates/WindowsVirtualMa [...] | ⓘ |
| Override Template Parameters | -vmName QuizBoxServer<br>-newStorageAccountName qbstorage -moduleUrl ⌃⌄ | ⓘ |

**◢ Control Options**

| | |
|---|---|
| Enabled | ☑ |
| Continue on error | ☐ |
| Always run | ☐ |

ⓘ More Information

***Figure 9-23.*** *The Azure Resource Group Deployment task*

Running this build or release (depending on where you are using the task) will now create or update the resource group with all components in it.

## Troubleshooting Deployments

No matter if you deploy an Azure resource group manually or from an automated build, you will need to troubleshoot failed deployments from time to time. You can access the deployment information in the Azure Portal, but generally it is more convenient to use PowerShell to do this. Fetching the information from the last deployment for a particular resource group can be done using the `Get-AzureRmResourceGroupDeployment` cmdlet. Here is an example:

```
PS C:\> Get-AzureResourceGroupDeployment -ResourceGroupName
QuizBoxResourceGroup

DeploymentName    : WindowsVirtualMachine
ResourceGroupName : QuizBoxResourceGroup
ProvisioningState : Succeeded
Timestamp         : 2015-10-10 15:03:58
Mode              : Incremental
TemplateLink      :
Parameters        :
```

```
Name                      Type              Value
===============           ==============    ==========
newStorageAccountName     String            quizboxstorage
adminUsername             String            jakob
adminPassword             SecureString
dnsNameForPublicIP        String            quizboxwebserver
windowsOSVersion          String            2012-R2-Datacenter
_artifactsLocation        String            https://quizboxdev8320.
                                            blob.core.windows.net/
                                            quizboxresourcegroup-
                                            stageartifacts

_artifactsLocationSasToken  SecureString

Outputs          :
```

As you can see, the values of all of parameters that were used in the last deployment are shown here, together with any output from the deployment.

---

■ **Note**    You can define output variables in the template files. These are used to output any results or computation done in the current deployment, so that it can be logged or used in another script.

---

## Managing Environments

The new build and release infrastructure is task-based, meaning that a build or release definition is basically a series of tasks that are executed by an agent. Some of these tasks, the ones that are related to deployment and remote testing, need to know which machines they should connect to and how. Instead of having to enter this information into every task, the available machines are registered separately in TFS and VSO.

---

■ **Note**    This model is different than, for example, an Octopus deploy, in that you don't install agents on every target machine. Instead you have a release agent that runs on some server and then connects to the target servers in order to deploy application bits or run distributed tests.

---

Machines are registered in the Machines tab in the Test hub, as shown in Figure 9-24.

**Figure 9-24.** *The VSO Machines hub*

All machines are added to a machine group, which is a container for grouping related machines together. A machine can be part of multiple machine groups, which makes sense.

---

■ **Note** Even though the machines and machine groups are managed in the Test hub, this doesn't mean that you only can use this for test environments. In the next chapter, you will build a deployment pipeline that deploys the application all the way to production.

---

Figure 9-25 shows the machine group for the QuizBox development environment, where you have registered the web server for the back end and SQL database, and also a Windows 10 test machine from where you will execute your Selenium tests.

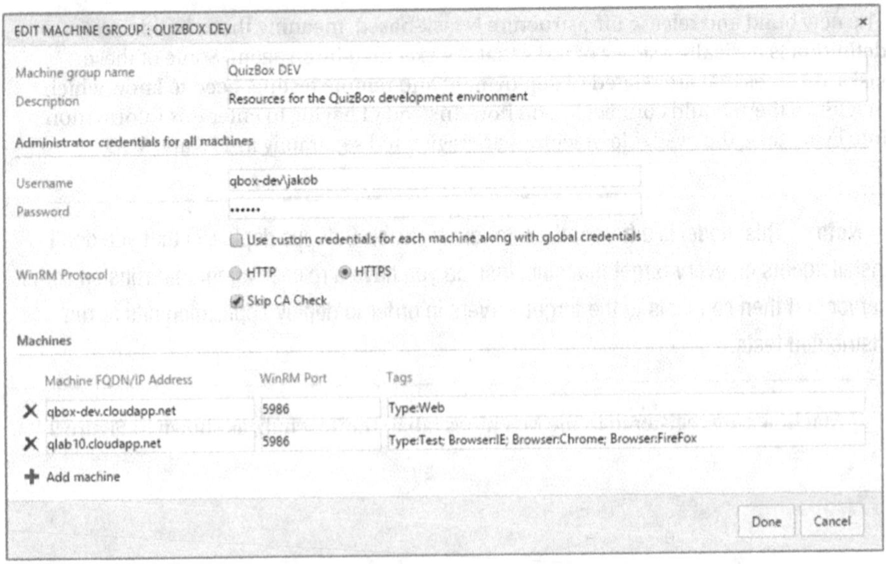

**Figure 9-25.** *QuizBox development environment*

You need to specify the credentials of an account that has administrator privileges on the target machine. You can enter a default set of credentials on the machine group level, and then override it for any machines in the machine group that have alternate credentials.

In addition, you select the WinRM protocol and the port for each machine. In the case of HTTPS, you can check the Skip CA Check checkbox to allow connections to a remote server without a valid SSL certificate. This is handy for internal development and test environments that might not have real SSL certificates, but instead use self-signed ones.

Also, you can use tags when defining machines. This is very handy for larger environments where a lot of servers might be part of the same environment. A common example is setting up a web farm for a large web application, so you have five front-end web servers to which the web application must be deployed. In this case, you can apply a tag to these servers, such as *Type:Web*, and then use this tag in the tasks that need to communicate with these servers. So, to continue with the example of the web farm, you don't have to set up five tasks for deploying to five web servers; you can just create one deployment task and then use the tag to match all servers that have this tag.

Figure 9-26 shows an example of the *IIS Web Application Deployment* task that uses tags to deploy the same web deploy package to all machines that have the tag *Type:Web*.

**Deploy QBox.Web to IIS** ✎

| | | |
|---|---|---|
| Machine Group | QuizBox DEV | ✳ ▾ ↻ Manage ① |
| Select Machines By | ○ Machine Names  ◉ Tags | ① |
| Filter Criteria | Type:Web | ① |
| Web Deploy Package | QBox.Web.zip | ① |
| Web Deploy Parameters File | | ① |
| Override Parameters | | ① |

▲ **Website**

| | | |
|---|---|---|
| Create or Update Website | ▣ | ① |

▲ **Application Pool**

| | | |
|---|---|---|
| Create or Update Application Pool | ▣ | ① |

*Figure 9-26.* IIS Web Application Deployment task

▦ **Note**    There is no validation of the registered machine information done at this point. Any problems with connecting to these machines will turn up when using a build task that tries to access these machines.

Later in this chapter as well in Chapter 10 you will look at many tasks that connect to the machines defined in these machine groups.

# Running Manual Tests

In this section, you are going to look at how to run manual tests using the TFS/VSO web client. You can, of course, also use MTM to do most of these things in a similar way.

---

■ **Note** One advantage of using the MTM client is that you can retrieve much more information about the test session, such as video screen capture, and from the test environments, including IntelliTrace files from web servers used during the test.

You can also record all of the user actions in an *action recording*. This recording can then be used when the tester reruns the test, for instance when verifying a bug fix. The action recording will then allow the tester to "play" the test again, which means the MTM client will simulate all the user actions, so the tester doesn't have to run the entire test again.

---

## Running a Test Case with the Web Test Manager

With the test plan in place and test cases created, you are ready to start running some tests.

1.  Go to the Test Hub in the TFS web client and select a test plan.

2.  Select the test cases to run and press the Run button (Figure 9-27).

Test suite: Regression tests (Suite ID: 502)

Tests    Charts

| ✚ New ▾ | Add existing | ✕ | 🏷 | ↻ | ↱ | ▶ Run ▾ | 🔟 | ⤵ | ✅ | ❌ | ➖ | ✔ | Column options |
|---|---|---|---|---|---|---|---|---|---|---|---|---|---|

| Outcome | ID | Title | Configurat... | Tester |
|---|---|---|---|---|
| ● Active | 504 | Creating a new Quiz question | Windows 8 | Jakob Ehn |
| ● Active | 505 | Enter duplicate question title | Windows 8 | Mathias Ol... |
| ● Active | 506 | Delete existing question | Windows 8 | Mathias Ol... |
| ● Active | 538 | When importing questions from Excel, the questions should be available in the sel... | Windows 8 | Jakob Ehn |
| ● Active | 550 | Export questions should export all questions in the category into an excel file | Windows 8 | Mathias Ol... |

*Figure 9-27. Starting a manual test run*

3.   The Web Test Runner opens and lets you look at the test steps and run through the test case. As you complete a test step, you mark it as passed or failed. If you have started multiple test runs, you navigate between them with the next/prev buttons. It is also possible to add comments and attachments to the test run by pressing the + button (Figure 9-28).

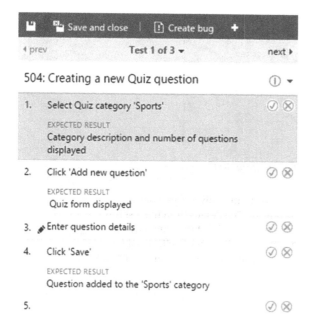

*Figure 9-28. Running a manual test*

4.   You can pass or fail the whole test case if you want to, from the topmost status icon. It is also possible to set other states, including pausing the test (which can be resumed later by you or another tester, from WTM or MTM), as shown in Figure 9-29.

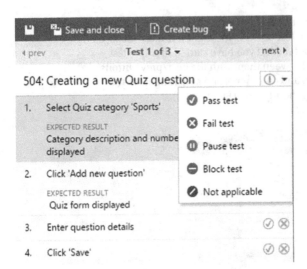

**Figure 9-29.** *Setting the outcome for a manual test*

5.  If a problem is discovered, you can easily report a bug by pressing the Create bug button. The details from the test run are copied over to the bug report. This is just scratching the surface of what can be done when it comes to effective bug tracking with the testing tools, and you will look more into this in the next chapter (Figure 9-30).

New Bug 1*: Not possible to save new quiz                                              ×

Copy template URL

Tags  Add...

**Not possible to save new quiz**

Iteration  QBox\Release 1.0

**STATUS**                                                    **DETAILS**

Assigned To   Type or select a name                    Priority          2
State         New                                      Severity          3 - Medium
Area          QBox                                     Effort
Reason        New defect reported                      Remaining Work
                                                       Activity

**STEPS TO REPRODUCE**  SYSTEM  TEST CASES (1)  TASKS      **ACCEPTANCE CRITERIA**  HISTORY  LINKS (2)  ATTACHMENTS

B  I  U          Category description and number
                 of questions displayed

2.    Passed    Click 'Add new question'

                Expected Result
                Quiz form displayed

3.    Passed    Enter question details

4.    Failed    Click 'Save'

                                              Save    Save and close    Cancel

*Figure 9-30.* *Creating a bug from a manual test run*

# Analyzing Test Results

After a test run is complete (manual or automated), you can look at it in the Runs hub in the web client (Figure 9-31).

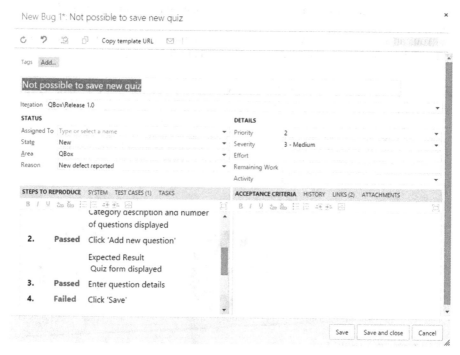

*Figure 9-31.* *Test run results*

The Runs feature has already been covered in Chapter 7 so jump over there for more details.

You can also create your own test result chart from the Test plan view. Click Charts and add charts for test case or test result analysis (Figure 9-32).

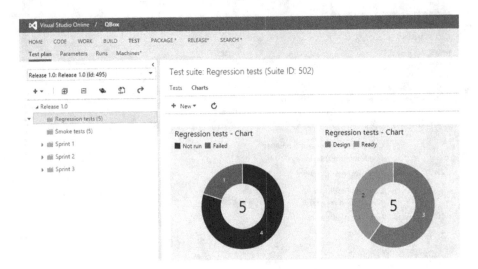

*Figure 9-32. Test result charts*

# Evolving Tests

As a part of the agile process you need to deal with an incremental and iterative development of test assets. As the product goes through the specification-design-implementation-release cycle, the test cases also need to adapt to this flow. Initially you know very little about a new feature and you typically need to run tests against all acceptance criteria defined for the requirement. When a feature has been completed, you should be confident it has been tested according to the test cases and that it works as expected. After that, you only need to run tests to validate changes in the requirement, which means you must have a process for how to know which tests to run.

Another side of the agile story is to look at how to speed up the testing process to keep up with short iterations. If you follow the preceding ideas, you can have techniques to know more about which tests to run. But running all tests manually will probably not be feasible so you need to rethink how you design these test cases.

One way to think about how you can structure your test base is to think of it as a pyramid. Figure 9-33 shows how the types of tests from the testing quadrant can be put in proportion in your specific case.

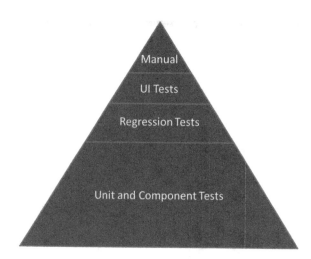

*Figure 9-33.* *Distribution of test types*

Typically you would focus on a big part of unit and component tests because these are the cheapest to implement and maintain. But these tests do not test the system as a whole, so you need to add regression tests to run end-to-end tests as well. Some of the regression tests should be implemented as user interface tests to really simulate how an end user would use the system, but UI tests are more complex to design and maintain, and it is often not practical to have more than a small set of these tests. Most of these tests can and should be automated to give you an efficient way to keep up with the changes in the product.

## Using Test Cases to Track Automated Tests

When you use the test management tools in TFS you have a great way to track your test cases. As the testing evolves and test cases becomes automated tests, it's easy to lose part of the structure you have with the test case. If all you have is code, you don't have an easy way to correlate the automated tests with things like what features they test, that product areas they validate, etc. To get this extra context, you can still use the test cases to manage the tests; all you need to do is connect the automated tests to the test cases. You use Visual Studio to connect an automated test to the test case. Open the test case in Visual Studio and select the Associated Automation tab (Figure 9-34).

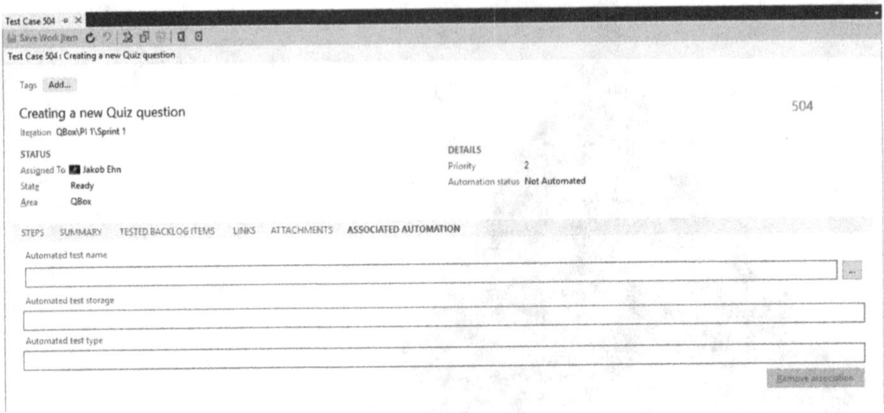

**Figure 9-34.** *Associated automation for a test case*

From the associated test name you can select the test implementing the test case (Figure 9-35). This way you can track back from code what test case (and functionality) the automated test came from and you can also run the automated tests based from a test suite in MTM.

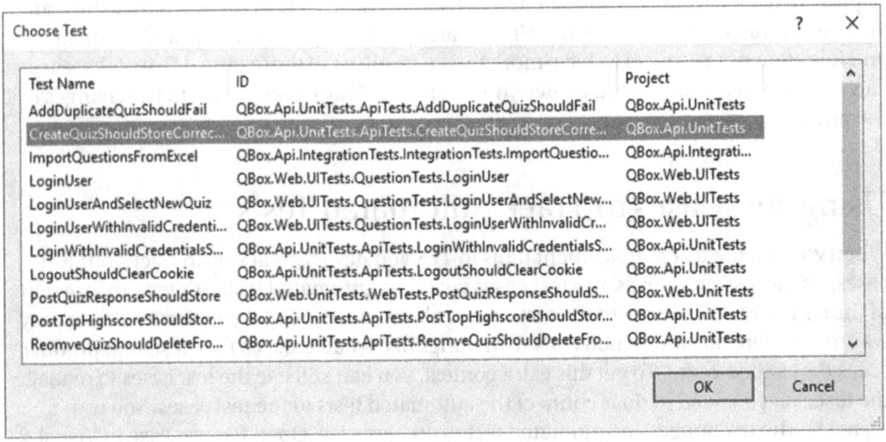

**Figure 9-35.** *Adding a test to a test case*

For more information about using MTM to run automated test, see the MSDN article at https://msdn.microsoft.com/en-you/library/dd380741.aspx.

# Running Automated Tests

Now you are ready to run automated tests. You can do this in lots of different ways, but it is important to keep in mind that these tests run after the system under test has been deployed. In the following example, you are going to use the build system to learn how to use TFS or VSO to orchestrate the AutoTest sequence. In the next chapter, you will see this in a more realistic context where the tests are run as a distinct step in a release pipeline.

Figure 9-36 shows a set of build steps that will build a solution containing tests to run: copy the test files to the test environment, deploy the test agent on the test environment, and finally run the tests on the test machines. This is a significant improvement over previous versions of TFS since you no longer need to set up the test agents in a separate step.

Visual Studio Build
*Build solution **\\*.sln*

Azure File Copy
*AzureVMs File Copy*

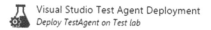

Visual Studio Test Agent Deployment
*Deploy TestAgent on Test lab*

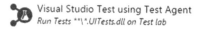

Visual Studio Test using Test Agent
*Run Tests **\\*.UITests.dll on Test lab*

***Figure 9-36.*** *Build steps for an automated test run*

Now let's look at how you configure the activates, including setting up some requirements for the test steps to work.

## Prerequisites

Before you can start running automated tests, you need to think through a few things. You need environments to run your system under test as well as your test system. You also need resources in Azure to integrate the infrastructure. In addition, of course you need to have the system under test deployed onto its environment before you can start testing. This section goes through some of these concerns.

## Environments

To run your automated tests you need two types of environments: one for the system under test where you deploy the system to test, and one for the test system where you manage the test infrastructure and run the tests against the system under test. Potentially you could run your tests on the same server where the application is installed, but this is not recommended because it would require installed software that would not be available in the production environment. The closer the test environments mimic the production environment, the better.

Figure 9-37 shows the QA environment for QuizBox, which is a machine group with four machines: two application servers and two test machines used for running the automated tests.

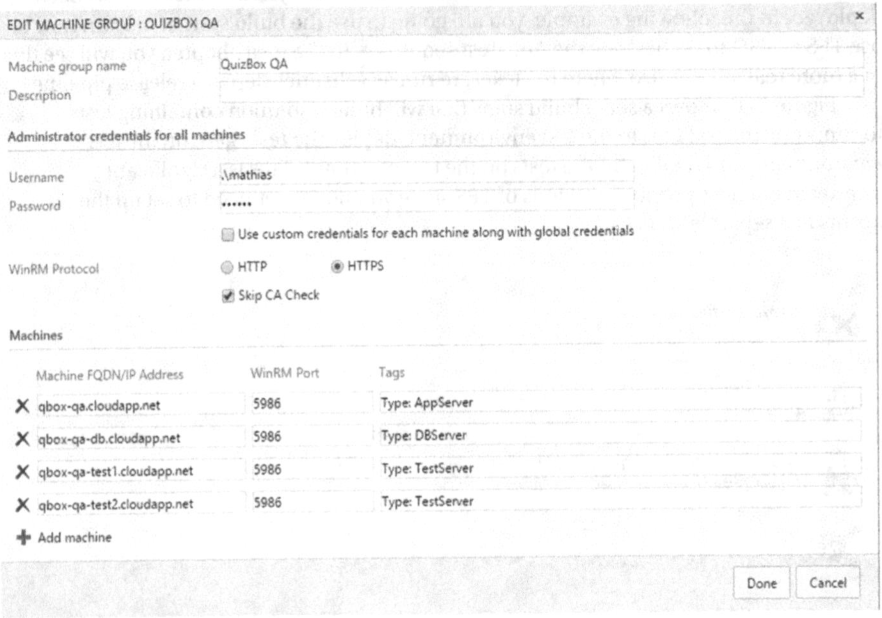

*Figure 9-37.* *System under test environment*

## Azure Subscription

In order to use Azure resources from VSO, you are going to need a service endpoint. This was covered in Chapter 7 so switch back there if you need a refresh.

## Storage Account

When you use Azure as your test environment infrastructure, you need somewhere to stage files to copy from the builds to the environments. For this, you will use an Azure storage account (Figure 9-38).

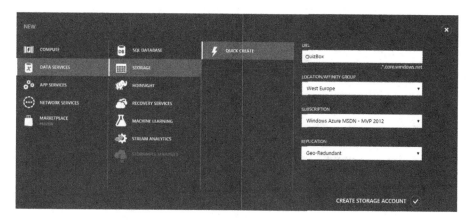

***Figure 9-38.*** *Creating an Azure storage account for QuizBox*

## Load Test Connection

In order to run performance tests as part of a build or release process, you need a service endpoint that connects the test run with the test infrastructure in the cloud. Go to the project admin page in TFS/VSO and select Services. Add a Generic endpoint (Figure 9-39).

***Figure 9-39.*** *Adding a generic endpoint*

Provide the URL for the VSO account that will run the load test. This account will be charged the costs for the test run and it will also hold the test result for the test run analysis. Add a username/password or a personal access token (in which case the username can be blank). Figure 9-40 shows a complete example of a load test connection.

*Figure 9-40. Adding a Cloud Load Test endpoint*

If you want to use a personal access token, here's how to create one: go to your profile settings in VSO (Figure 9-41).

*Figure 9-41. VSO profile settings*

Select the Security hub and add a new token (Figure 9-42).

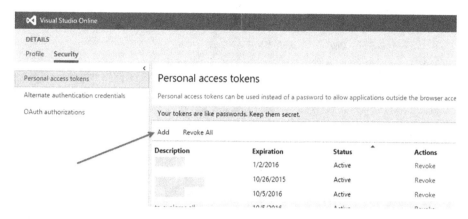

**Figure 9-42.** *Personal access tokens*

When you create a PAT, you can specify how long the token is valid and what scope (capabilities) the service using the PAT will be granted permission for (Figure 9-43).

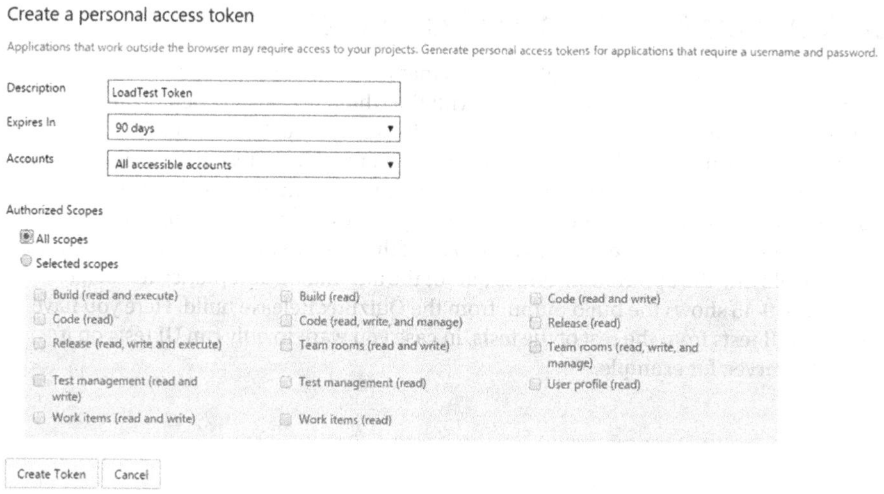

**Figure 9-43.** *Creating a personal access token*

## Variables

In the build steps you use for testing, you need to provide some settings in more than one step. To simplify the maintenance, use shared variables for this, as shown in Figure 9-44, to handle the target folders and authentication details.

Definitions / QBox.BVT | Builds

Build    Options    Repository    *Variables*    Triggers    General    Retention    History

■ Save ▼        🖳 Queue build...      ↺ Undo

List of predefined variables

| Name | Value | | Allow at Queue Time |
|------|-------|---|---|
| system.collectionId | 31b1816a-902d-45a1-b883-832b04138e0e | | ☐ |
| system.teamProject | QBox | | ☐ |
| system.definitionId | 115 | | ☐ |
| ✕ BuildConfiguration | debug | 🔒 | ☑ |
| ✕ BuildPlatform | any cpu | 🔒 | ☑ |
| ✕ storageAccount | quizboxdev | 🔒 | ☐ |
| ✕ remoteDestinationFolder | c:\tests | 🔒 | ☐ |
| ✕ TestUser | .\mathias | 🔒 | ☐ |
| ✕ TestUserPassword | ●●●●●●●●● | 🔒 | ☐ |
| ➕ Add variable | | | |

*Figure 9-44.* *Variables for your automated test steps*

## Deploying the Application and Test Artifacts

Finally, you need to deploy the application so that you have something to run tests against. In Chapter 10, you will be dealing with the whole release and deployment management topic so for now you are simply going to assume that is in place.

You must also deploy the test artifacts to the test machines. Test artifacts include the unit test assemblies, test run settings, and test assembly configuration files. Everything that is needed in order to run the tests on the target test server must be copied or deployed in some way to the server. This is part of the same deployment pipeline that you use for deploying the application, and is part of the automated acceptance test stage.

Figure 9-45 shows the build output from the QuizBox.Release build. Here you have separated UI tests from the rest of the tests, in case you want to only run UI tests on a particular server, for example.

| Summary    Timeline    **Artifacts** | | |
|------|------|------|
| 📁 Installers | Download | Explore |
| 📁 WebDeployPackages | Download | Explore |
| 📁 Scripts | Download | Explore |
| 📁 tests | Download | Explore |
| 📁 database | Download | Explore |
| 📁 uitests | Download | Explore |

*Figure 9-45.* *QuizBox build artifacts*

In this application, all the test projects are part of the same solution so it makes sense to package them together with the application like this. Sometimes the tests might be authored separately from the application. For example, pure UI tests that only exercise the application on the UI level by simulating a user clicking the application are typically not dependent on the application binaries. They only require that the application is installed somewhere where the tests can reach it.

If this is the case, you can set up a different build that produces the test artifacts and then pull in these artifacts from that build definition instead of in the release pipeline. As you will see in the next chapter, a release definition in Visual Studio Release Management can consume artifacts from multiple build definitions.

Usually the test artifacts only have to be copied to the target test machines, so you don't need to run any deployment script to have them installed. Depending on the infrastructure, you can use either the Windows or the Azure file copy task that is available in the Deploy category of the task catalog.

## Windows Machine File Copy

For on-premise servers, or Azure virtual machines that are domain-joined, you can use the *Windows Machine File Copy* task. This task will copy files from a source location to a target using the Windows robocopy tool. This means, among other things, that the SMB protocol needs to be enabled and that the process running the build has sufficient permissions to access the remote machine.

---

■ **Note**    Presently Windows Machine File Copy does not work with a hosted build agent.

---

The most important properties of the task are

- **Source**: The source files to copy. Build variables such as $(Agent.BuildDirectory)\$(Build.Repository.Name) can be used, but not wildcards.

- **Machine group**: Name of the target environment. This is typically already configured but the Manage link will let you jump to the environment view to manage environments if you need to.

- **Select machines by names or tags**: Lets you select a subset of machines in the machine group; for instance you can use the tag "windows 10" to target only Windows 10 clients (assuming you've added the corresponding tag to the environment earlier).

- **Destination folder**: The target for the copy.

- **Copy files in parallel**: If selected, the task will copy files to all machines in the machine group in parallel.

- **Clean target**: If selected, the task will remove all existing files in the destination folder before copying the new files over.

Figure 9-46 shows an example of a completed *Windows Machine File Copy* task.

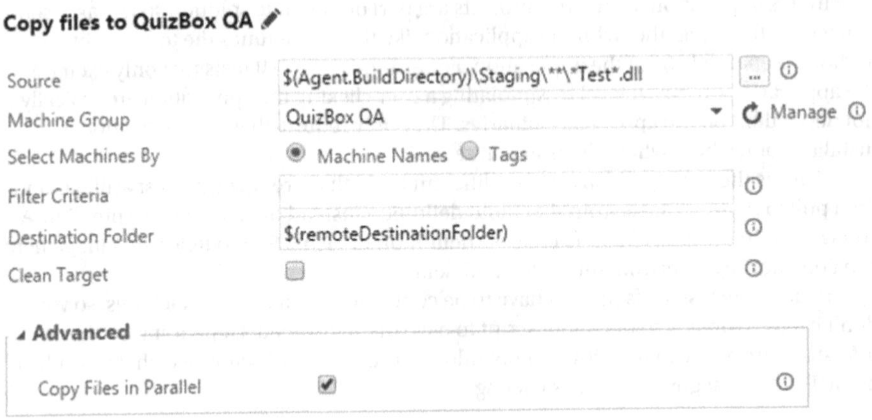

**Copy files to QuizBox QA** 🖊

| | |
|---|---|
| Source | $(Agent.BuildDirectory)\Staging\**\*Test*.dll [...] ⓘ |
| Machine Group | QuizBox QA ▾   ↻ Manage ⓘ |
| Select Machines By | ◉ Machine Names ○ Tags |
| Filter Criteria | ⓘ |
| Destination Folder | $(remoteDestinationFolder) ⓘ |
| Clean Target | ☐ ⓘ |

**⊿ Advanced**

| | |
|---|---|
| Copy Files in Parallel | ☑ ⓘ |

*Figure 9-46.* *Windows Machine File Copy task*

## Azure File Copy

If you are hosting your machines in Azure as standalone machines, it will often not be possible to use the *Windows Machine File Copy* task. In these cases, you can use the *Azure File Copy* task. This task will under the hood use the AzCopy tool to copy the files to blob storage in an Azure storage account, and then it will download and copy the files to the destination folder on the target machine. This means that you do not have to open any other firewall ports than the standard WinRM port.

This task is similar to the previous copy task, with the addition of information needed for the Azure commands.

- **Source**: The source files to copy. Build variables such as $(Agent.BuildDirectory)\$(Build.Repository.Name) can be used, but not wildcards.

- **Storage account**

- **Destination**: You can choose either to copy files to an Azure VM or to a blob. If you copy to a VM, the files will first be copied to the storage account and then to the VM.

  - **Machine group**: Name of the target environment. This is typically already configured but the Manage link will let you jump to the environment view to manage environments if necessary.

  - **Select machines by names or tags**: Lets you select a subset of machines in the machine group; for instance you can use the tag "windows 10" to target only Windows 10 clients (assuming you've added the corresponding tag to the environment earlier).

  - **Destination folder**: The target for the copy.

- When the target is an Azure blob, the following destination parameters are used:

    - Container name

    - Blob prefix

- **Copy files in parallel**: If selected, the task will copy files to all machines in the machine group in parallel.

Figure 9-47 shows a configured *Azure File Copy* task that copies the build result to a target VM using an Azure storage account.

**AzureVMs File Copy** 🖊

| | |
|---|---|
| Azure Subscription | MSDN ▼ ♻ Manage ⓘ |
| Source | $(Agent.BuildDirectory)\$(Build.Repository.Name) ... ⓘ |
| Storage Account | $(storageAccount) ⓘ |
| Destination | Azure VMs ▼ ⓘ |
| Machine Group | QuizBox QA ▼ ♻ Manage ⓘ |
| Select Machines By | ◉ Machine Names ○ Tags |
| Filter Criteria | Type: TestServer ⓘ |
| Destination Folder | $(remoteDestinationFolder) ⓘ |
| Clean Target | ☑ ⓘ |
| Copy Files in Parallel | ☑ ⓘ |

***Figure 9-47.*** *Azure File Copy step*

# Visual Studio Test Agent Deployment

Up until now in TFS you have had to install a central test controller and then local test agents in your environments in order to run automated tests. With TFS 2015, you no longer need to go through that work; the test controller has gone away and you get a build task to deploy the test agent.

The Deploy Test Agent task has three major sections you need to supply (Figure 9-48):

- **Test Machine Group**: Here you get to specify on which machines the agents should be installed. You can use filters in the same way as in the copy tasks earlier.

- **Agent Configuration**: The process that installs the agent will need an account that will run the agent on the test machine. For UI tests, you can also specify that the test agent must run interactively.

- **Advanced**: In this section, you can specify the location of the test agent, which is very useful if the test machine does not have access to the Internet. You can also choose if the test agent should be updated automatically. The Enable Data Collection Only checkbox is used if you want to indicate that this set of machines will not run tests but only use the agent to collect data from testing (such as code coverage data).

**Deploy TestAgent on Test lab** 🖉

**⊿ Test Machine Group**

| | |
|---|---|
| Test Machine Group / Azure Resource Group | Test lab ▾ ℃ Manage ⓘ |
| Select Machines By | ⦿ Machine Names ◯ Tags |
| Filter Criteria | ⓘ |

**⊿ Agent Configuration**

| | |
|---|---|
| Username | $(testUser) ⓘ |
| Password | $(testUserPassword) ⓘ |
| Interactive Process | ☑ ⓘ |

**⊿ Advanced**

| | |
|---|---|
| Test Agent Location | ⓘ |
| Update Test Agent | ☐ ⓘ |
| Enable Data Collection Only | ☐ ⓘ |

***Figure 9-48.*** *Visual Studio Test Agent Deployment step*

# The Visual Studio Test Using Test Agent Task

Finally, there is the test task that runs the tests on remote machines. In Chapter 7, you looked at the Visual Studio Test task that is used to run tests on the build or release agent machine. This is mostly used for pure unit tests that are not dependent on anything external. For running automated integration or UI tests, you need to run tests using the Visual Studio test agent. This is what the *Visual Studio Test using Test Agent* task allows you to do.

In this task, you can select on which machines the tests should run and which tests to run. You can also control how the tests are run, for instance by providing a runsettings file.

---

■ **Note**  In order to use the *Visual Studio Test using Test Agent* task, you *must* precede it with the *Visual Studio Test Agent Deployment* task. The reason for this is that the deploy task is what causes the test agent running on the target machine to start listening for test runs from TFS. So it is required to run this task before every run test task, even if there already is a test agent installed on the target machine.

Note also that the test machine running the Visual Studio test agent must be able to connect back to TFS or Visual Studio Online to be able to publish the test results.

---

This task has the following key elements:

- **Test machine group**: Similar to the previous tasks, used to specify on which machines the tests should be run.

- **Test settings**: This is where you get to control which tests are run and under what circumstances.

  - **Test drop location**: The location of the test files staged on the machine using either of the copy tasks described above.

  - **Test assembly**: Specifies assemblies from which tests will be selected.

  - **Test filter criteria**: Here you can filter tests based on criteria from the test attributes on the test cases.

  - **Platform and configuration**: Reporting fields so you can follow up tests based on the build properties.

  - **Run settings file**: Optional test settings file that allows you to control aspects of the test run, for instance test run parameters.

  - **Override test run parameters**: Use this field to pass in custom values to the tests when they are run. See the section on working with test parameters later in this chapter.

  - **Test configuration**: This field is used for reporting so that you can follow up on which configuration the tests were run. See the section on testing different configurations for information on how to use this parameter.

- **Advanced**: In this section, you can configure the collection of code coverage from the application under test by specifying the machine group for those machines. The machines need to have the test agent deployed for data collection.

Figure 9-49 shows an example of the distributed test task.

271

**Run Tests \*\*\\\*.UITests.dll on QuizBox QA** 🖉

**◢ Test Machine Group**

| | | |
|---|---|---|
| Test Machine Group / Azure Resource Group | QuizBox QA ▾ | ⟳ Manage ⓘ |

**◢ Test Settings**

| | | |
|---|---|---|
| Test Drop Location | $(remoteDestinationFolder) | ⓘ |
| Test Assembly | \*\*\\\*.UITests.dll | ⓘ |
| Test Filter criteria | | ⓘ |
| Platform | | ⓘ |
| Configuration | | ⓘ |
| Run Settings File | Source/QBox.Web.UITests/default.runsettings | ... ⓘ |
| Override Test Run Parameters | webAppUrl=https://quizbox-dev.azurewebsites.net | ⓘ |
| Test Configurations | FullyQualifiedName~Chrome:40;FullyQualifiedName~II | ⓘ |

**◢ Advanced**

| | | |
|---|---|---|
| Code Coverage Enabled | ☑ | ⓘ |
| Application Under Test Machine Group | QuizBox QA ▾ | ⟳ Manage ⓘ |

*Figure 9-49.* *Visual Studio Test using Test Agent step*

# Running Quick Web Performance Tests

It is easy to integrate a load test into the build or release process. When you have gone through and set up a load test connection and created a load test, you can fill out the Quick Web Performance Test task (Figure 9-50). The task has the following key elements:

- **Registered connection**: The load test connection to use for the load test run.

- **Website URL**: Name of the site the load test should hit.

- **Test name**: This is the name of load test to use.

- **User load**: Number of simulated concurrent users.

- **Run duration**: Length of the test run.

- **Load location**: Here you can specify from which region you want the load tests to run from. The default is to use the region where the load test connection account is located.

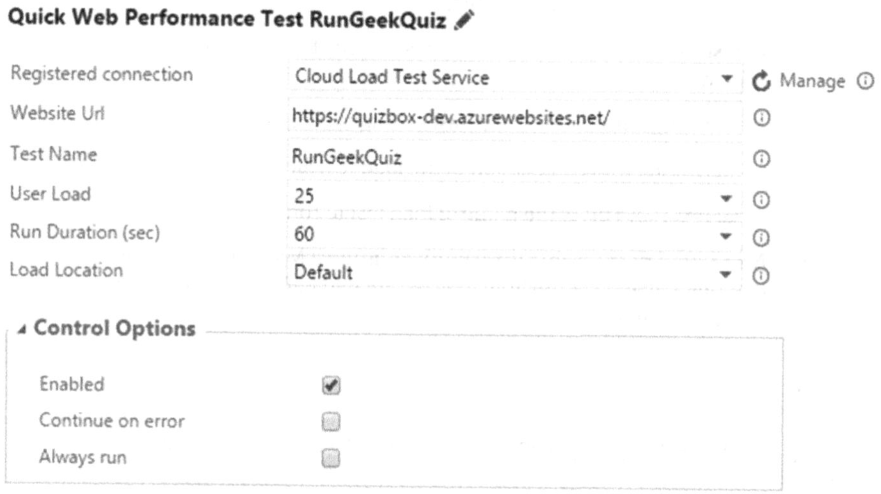

**Quick Web Performance Test RunGeekQuiz** 🖉

| | | |
|---|---|---|
| Registered connection | Cloud Load Test Service ▼ | ↻ Manage ⓘ |
| Website Url | https://quizbox-dev.azurewebsites.net/ | ⓘ |
| Test Name | RunGeekQuiz | ⓘ |
| User Load | 25 ▼ | ⓘ |
| Run Duration (sec) | 60 ▼ | ⓘ |
| Load Location | Default ▼ | ⓘ |

◢ **Control Options**

| | |
|---|---|
| Enabled | ☑ |
| Continue on error | ☐ |
| Always run | ☐ |

*Figure 9-50.* *Cloud-based Web Performance Test step*

# Running Cloud Load Tests

If setting up a quick web test was easy, then running a full load test is just as simple. The big difference is that the load test task will use the configuration setup in the load test, for instance test mix, run length, and user distribution. You can also control the test run using a test settings file, where you can specify deployment items required by the load test. Figure 9-51 shows an example of how to use the load test task.

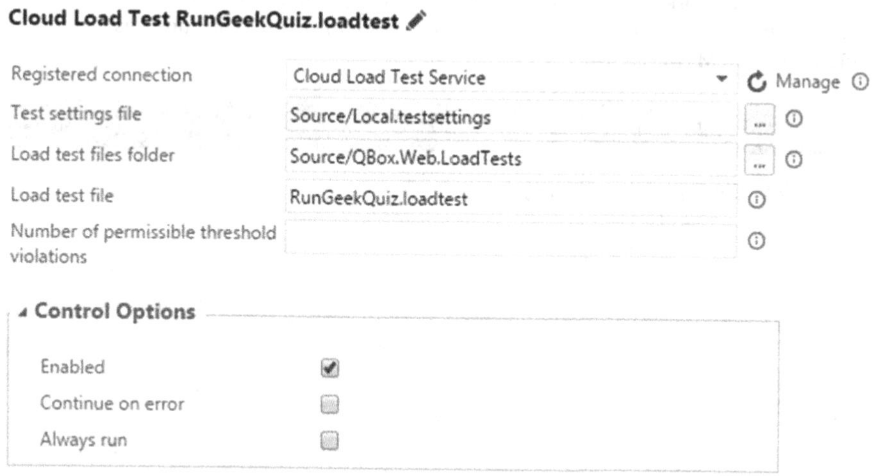

**Cloud Load Test RunGeekQuiz.loadtest** 🖉

| | | |
|---|---|---|
| Registered connection | Cloud Load Test Service ▼ | ↻ Manage ⓘ |
| Test settings file | Source/Local.testsettings | ⋯ ⓘ |
| Load test files folder | Source/QBox.Web.LoadTests | ⋯ ⓘ |
| Load test file | RunGeekQuiz.loadtest | ⓘ |
| Number of permissible threshold violations | | ⓘ |

◢ **Control Options**

| | |
|---|---|
| Enabled | ☑ |
| Continue on error | ☐ |
| Always run | ☐ |

*Figure 9-51.* *Cloud-based Load Test step*

The task has the following key elements:

- **Registered connection**: The load test connection to use for the load test run.

- **Test settings file**: Name of the test settings file to use.

- **Load test file folder**: Location of the load test file.

- **Load test file**: This is the name of load test to run.

- **Number of permissible threshold violations**: Maximum number of times a load test threshold may be violated before the test run is marked as failed.

## Test Results

After the tests have been run, you can analyze the results in several different ways, including in the

- **Test run view**: You looked that this earlier in the chapter and also in Chapter 7.

- **Build result report**: This is covered in Chapter 7.

- **Release result report**: This is covered in Chapter 10.

# Testing Different Configurations

When you have tests that run on different configurations, you want a way to analyze the result per configuration. The new test task has a capability for this based on naming conventions and test configurations.

To get this to work, you need to do a couple of things first. Start by deciding what configurations you want to test. These configurations need to be added as test configurations in MTM (Figure 9-52).

| Test Plan Manager | Test Configuration Manager | Test Case Manager | Shared Steps Manager |
|---|---|---|---|

**Test Configuration Manager**

New   Open   ✕   Manage configuration variables

| ID | Name | Default | State | Configuration variables |
|---|---|---|---|---|
| 40 | chrome | No | Active | |
| 41 | firefox | No | Active | |
| 42 | ie | No | Active | |
| 32 | Windows 8 | Yes | Active | Operating System: Windows 8 |

*Figure 9-52. Test configurations in MTM*

> ■ **Note** Test configurations can't currently be managed in the web client; you must use the MTM client for this.

Then you need to name your tests in a way that makes it possible for the task that runs the tests to map the test to the corresponding test configuration.

Figure 9-53 shows some examples of how you should name the test methods to work with the reporting capability, namely by prefixing the methods with the configuration.

```
[TestMethod]
0 references | Jakob Ehn, 4 days ago | 1 author, 1 change
public void ChromeLoginUser()...

[TestMethod]
0 references | Jakob Ehn, 4 days ago | 1 author, 1 change
public void ChromeViewHighScore()...

[TestMethod]
0 references | Jakob Ehn, 4 days ago | 1 author, 1 change
public void IELoginUserAndSelectNewQuiz()...

[TestMethod]
0 references | Jakob Ehn, 4 days ago | 1 author, 1 change
public void IELoginUserWithInvalidCredentials()...
```

***Figure 9-53.*** *Test methods for different configurations*

With this in place, you can configure the test task. You use the Test Configurations parameter to specify the test case filter. This filter allows you to filter which tests should be executed, and to which test configuration they are mapped. The format for doing so is *<Filter1>:<Id1>;<Filter2>:<Id2>* and so on. There are different types of filters that you can use; one is called *FullyQualifiedName* and is used to match test by the name.

For example, the following test configuration will match all tests that start with either Chrome, Firefox, or IE, and will map each of these to the corresponding test configuration id:

```
FullyQualifiedName~Chrome:40;FullyQualifiedName~FireFox:41;FullyQualifiedName~IE:42
```

> ■ **Note** The id of the test configuration is visible in the MTM client, as shown in Figure 9-52.

You can use *DefaultTestConfiguration:* as a catch all.

Figure 9-54 shows the test task with the test configuration filled out.

**⊿ Test Settings**

| | |
|---|---|
| Test Drop Location | $(remoteDestinationFolder) |
| Test Assembly | **\\*.UITests.dll |
| Test Filter criteria | |
| Platform | |
| Configuration | |
| Run Settings File | Source/QBox.Web.UITests/default.runsettings |
| Override Test Run Parameters | webAppUrl=https://quizbox-dev.azurewebsites.net |
| Test Configurations | FullyQualifiedName~Chrome:40;FullyQualifiedName~I |

*Figure 9-54.* *Specifying test configurations*

Now when the tests are run, you get a nice summary of the outcome by configuration (Figure 9-55).

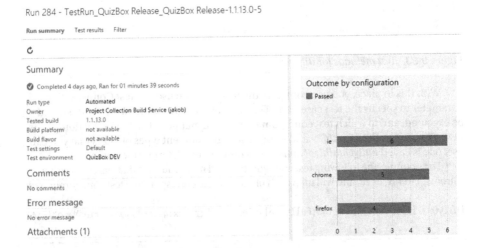

*Figure 9-55.* *Test results, outcome by configuration*

# Parameterizing Test Runs

A common scenario when working with automated tests in different environments is the need to replace parameters. With the test tasks you get a new capability that lets you define parameters with default values in a settings file, which you can override in the task configuration.

To manage test run parameters, you first need a `.runsettings` file in the project. As described in Chapter 8, there is no file template in Visual Studio for a runsettings file so you have to add it as a new XML file.

---

■ **Note**    For more information about the `.runsettings` file, see
https://msdn.microsoft.com/en-you/library/jj635153.aspx.

---

Here is an example of a runsettings file that only contains test run parameters (runsettings can be used for many other things, such as configuring code coverage):

```xml
<?xml version="1.0" encoding="utf-8"?>
<RunSettings>
  <!-- Parameters used by tests at runtime -->
  <TestRunParameters>
    <Parameter name="webAppUrl" value="http://localhost:1156/" />
  </TestRunParameters>
</RunSettings>
```

In this case, you want to be able to replace the URL used in the tests so you add a parameter called webAppUrl.

When a test is run, the TestRunParameters is populated in the TextContext for the test. To use this parameter in your test code, you simply read it from the Properties collection, typically in a TestInitialize method like in the following example:

```csharp
[TestInitialize()]
public void MyTestInitialize()
{
    var url = TestContext.Properties["webAppUrl"].ToString();
    driver = new ChromeDriver();
    driver.Manage().Timeouts().ImplicitlyWait(new TimeSpan(0, 0, 10));
    var page = new HomePage(driver);
    page.GoToHome(url);
}
```

From the *Visual Studio Test* and *Visual Studio Test using Test Agent* tasks, you can now wire this together by selecting the runsettings file and providing the test run parameters overrides for the current environment (Figure 9-56).

| ⬦ Test Settings | | |
|---|---|---|
| Test Drop Location | $(remoteDestinationFolder) | ⓘ |
| Test Assembly | **\*.UITests.dll | ⓘ |
| Test Filter criteria | | ⓘ |
| Platform | | ⓘ |
| Configuration | | ⓘ |
| Run Settings File | Source/QBox.Web.UITests/default.runsettings | [...] ⓘ |
| Override Test Run Parameters | webAppUrl=https://quizbox-dev.azurewebsites.net | ⓘ |
| Test Configurations | FullyQualifiedName~Chrome:40;FullyQualifiedName~II | ⓘ |

***Figure 9-56.*** *Overriding a test run parameter*

---

■ **Note**    This technique is currently only supported when using the MS Test framework.

---

In Chapter 10, you will look at another approach for managing configuration parameters for the application, which can be an alternative to this technique.

# Summary

Testing in a Continuous Delivery process requires an agile approach to testing. You should strive to do your testing work with a focus on quick delivery cycles, which could mean you test feature by feature instead of having a traditional big test effort after development and before the release.

The Visual Studio family provides a coherent suite of tools where you can do test planning, run manual tests, write automated tests at various levels of product QA, and run capacity tests.

The more deliveries you do, the more you should automate the testing to ensure you maintain good quality.

In the next chapter, you will look at release management and how to define the release and deployment process. As a part of that, you will look at how manual and automated testing integrates with the release pipeline.

# CHAPTER 10

■ ■ ■

# Building a Deployment Pipeline

Deploying a modern application can be very complex, with a lot of moving parts and configuration. More often than not, today's applications are distributed and have several kinds of dependencies on web services, databases, service buses, and so on. In addition to the deployment of the actual application, you must also deploy and configure the environments in which the applications will run. We discussed how you can manage your environments in the previous chapter, by keeping the configuration as code inside your source code repository.

If you are looking at shortening your release cycles in the spirit of Continuous Delivery but still want to keep the quality of both the applications and the deployments themselves high, you must make sure that you automate as much as you can. Manual efforts tend to consume a lot of time and resources, and are also prone to errors.

Another desired outcome of automating the building, deployment, and testing of your applications is that it should provide fast feedback about any problems that might have been introduced. However, provisioning test environments and running automated tests can often take a long time to execute, which can potentially slow down the feedback loop. This is one of the purposes of introducing a *deployment pipeline*, where the end-to-end build is split up into different *stages*. The early stages should focus on trying to quickly identify issues and provide feedback. Typical examples here are compilation, running unit tests (not integration or UI tests because they tend to be slower), and perhaps some lighter code analysis for catching technical debt issues.

Let's revisit the image, shown in Figure 10-1, from Chapter 1 that shows an example of a deployment pipeline.

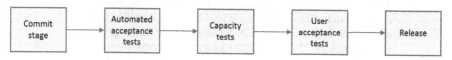

*Figure 10-1.* *Deployment Pipeline Example*

The first stage is often referred to as the *Commit* stage where you compile and publish the binaries that will be used later on in the deployment pipeline. This stage is typically implemented using a build server such as TFS Build or JetBrains Team City.

The later stages in the pipeline can then focus on doing more thorough (and therefore often more time-consuming) verification of the produced build, such as automated UI testing, capacity testing, and manual user acceptance tests. The last stage is deploying the binaries to the production environment and perhaps doing some automated smoke tests to verify the deployment. So, by splitting up all the activities into separate stages, you can make sure that you run the faster verifications early on, while also providing feedback to the team.

In this chapter, you will take a look at the new version of Visual Studio Release Management (VSRM) that will be available in Visual Studio Online at the end of 2015 and on-premise as part of Team Foundation Server during Q1 of 2016. Using VSRM plus the new build system discussed in Chapter 7, you will implement a deployment pipeline for the QuizBox application where you will deploy all your components to different environments, including running automated acceptance testing.

# Visual Studio Release Management

As mentioned in Chapter 2, Microsoft acquired InRelease, a release management tool, from InCycle Software in 2013 and rebranded it as Visual Studio Release Management. InRelease was built specifically for Team Foundation Server and offered support for building a deployment pipeline, with tools for deploying various components such as IIS web sites and SQL databases onto Windows machines.

After the acquisition, Microsoft started adding support for doing deployments using PowerShell DSC, which we discussed in the previous chapter. Also, the integration with Microsoft Azure was considerably improved by letting the users import their Azure subscriptions into the tool, thereby making it easy to select existing Azure virtual machines for deploying applications. Another move against Azure was the announcement of Visual Studio Release Management Service, a hosted version of the release management service that is part of the Visual Studio Online offering.

This version of Visual Studio Release Management is still part of the Visual Studio 2015 suite. However, during 2015 the product team at Microsoft reengineered the release management tool. At the time of this writing, the new version will be available in Visual Studio Online at the end of 2015, and release to Team Foundation Server in Q1 2016.

There are a few reasons why Microsoft decided to do this major overhaul of the release management tool:

- **A simpler Web-based authoring experience:** The InRelease client is a rich client built using WPF. Microsoft, as well as most other SaaS vendors, strives to build most of their offerings with web technology. This makes the toolset more accessible and in general more easy to use. It also enables authoring of release management workflows from any browser and operating system.

- **Better cross-platform support:** Although support for Chef was introduced in one of the Visual Studio 2013 updates, a better cross-platform story was necessary for Release Management. Since the new build system was already on the way, with support for running tasks on agents in Windows, Linux, and OS/X, it was a natural choice for Microsoft to base the Release Management toolset on the same architecture. As you will see later in this chapter, this creates a powerful integration between build and release management and gives you a lot of flexibility in where to add your automations.

---

■ **Note** As with the new build system we covered in Chapter 7, Microsoft will continue to support the existing versions of Visual Studio Release Management, but all new investments will be made to this new version. Therefore, we will use this version as the tool of choice for this book. It should be noted that this is a brand new version, and you should expect to see a lot of changes and new features being released over the next year.

Also, we will use the term *Visual Studio Release Management* in this book to reference this new version. If you read Microsoft documentation at the moment, it will refer to this version as Visual Studio Release Management *vNext*.

---

Let's talk a little about the main concepts in Visual Studio Release Management.

## Release Definitions

In Visual Studio Release Management, a deployment pipeline is realized by creating a *release definition*. You will create at least one release definition for every application that you want to deploy and manage, but you can also create multiple definitions for the same application.

A release definition contains information about *which* application to deploy, *where* the application should be deployed to (environments), and *how* it should be deployed (using tasks). Figure 10-2 shows an example of a release pipeline in Visual Studio Release Management.

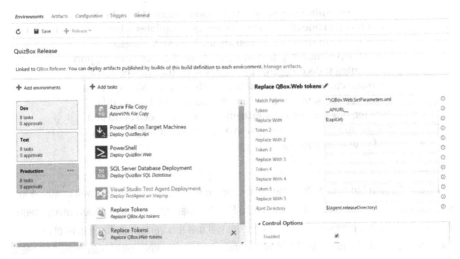

**Figure 10-2.** *A release definition*

Since Visual Studio Release Management is built using the same architecture as the new build system in TFS, you will find the authoring experience very familiar. In fact, the tasks that are available when creating build definitions are often also available for release definitions. This means that you don't have to use a release definition in order to deploy something. For simpler scenarios where you don't have the need of release orchestration, approval workflows, and auditing, creating a build definition that packages and deploys the application is often a suitable solution.

# Releases

When a release definition is triggered, either manually or by the completion of a build, a *release* is started. Every release has a unique name and will start its journey on the first environment in the release definition. During every step of the release, all the output from the different tasks is captured and is available during and after the release as log files. Figure 10-3 shows an example of a release summary, where the release has been deployed to the Dev environment but has not yet entered the Test environment.

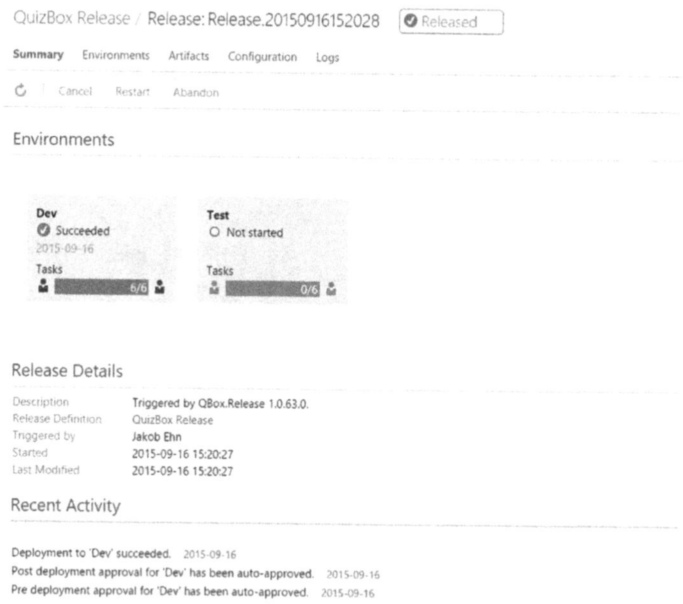

QuizBox Release / Release: Release.20150916152028  ✔ Released

**Summary**  Environments  Artifacts  Configuration  Logs

↻ | Cancel   Restart   Abandon

## Environments

**Dev**
✔ Succeeded
2015-09-16
Tasks
👤 �▓ 6/6 👤

**Test**
○ Not started
Tasks
👤 ▓ 0/6 👤

## Release Details

| | |
|---|---|
| Description | Triggered by QBox.Release 1.0.63.0. |
| Release Definition | QuizBox Release |
| Triggered by | Jakob Ehn |
| Started | 2015-09-16 15:20:27 |
| Last Modified | 2015-09-16 15:20:27 |

## Recent Activity

Deployment to 'Dev' succeeded.   2015-09-16
Post deployment approval for 'Dev' has been auto-approved.   2015-09-16
Pre deployment approval for 'Dev' has been auto-approved.   2015-09-16

*Figure 10-3.*  *Release summary*

# Tasks

A release definition contains a set of tasks that are executed in sequential order, where each task performs some action in the deployment pipeline. Typical examples are deploying a web site, upgrading a database, or running a PowerShell script. Tasks in a release definition use the same manifest and implementation architecture as in TFS build, so you can read more about the details on how tasks work in general and how you can create custom ones in Chapter 7 of this book. Figure 10-4 shows some of the existing deployment tasks that will ship with Team Foundation Server.

*Figure 10-4. Release tasks catalog*

## Machines

A machine refers to an existing machine (virtual or physical) that you want to deploy application bits to, run tests, etc. These machines can either be on-premise machines or running in a cloud, like Microsoft Azure. As long as the release agent is able to connect to these servers (using, for example, WinRM over HTTPS), you can incorporate them into your deployment pipeline. A common example is to deploy a test agent to a machine and then execute a set of tests on that machine. As shown in Figure 10-5, machines are defined by creating *machine groups* that can contain one or more machines.

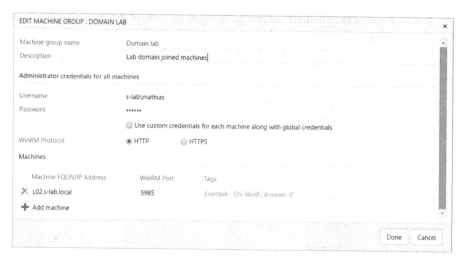

**Figure 10-5.** *Machine groups*

---

■ **Note**  Machines are managed in the Test Hub. You looked at managing machines and machine groups in Chapter 9.

---

# Environments

Environment, on the other hand, is not strictly related to machines or machine groups. The name is a bit confusing and especially so if you have been using previous versions of Visual Studio Release Management.

---

In the previous version of Visual Studio Release Management, *stage* and *environments* were different concepts. In this version, these concepts have been merged together, providing for a simpler authoring experience, at the expense of a bit more confusion when getting started.

---

So, an environment corresponds to a stage in the deployment pipeline. This means that you can have multiple environments (stages) in a deployment pipeline that operate on the same machine groups. For example, you might want to separate the actions of deploying the bits and running smoke tests into two separate stages, both running against the same target servers. You will see this setup later in this chapter when you look at the deployment pipeline for the QuizBox sample application.

Tasks are often linked to machine groups. Many of the tasks in the deployment category are integrated with them and allow you to run the tasks against one or more machines in a machine group. Figure 10-6 shows an example of the *Run PowerShell on Target Machine* task, where the task will execute a script on all machines in the *staging* machine group that has the tag *Web*.

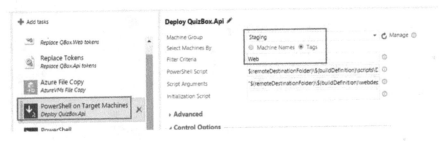

***Figure 10-6.*** *Deployment task*

The ability to use filters like this is powerful and allows you to, for example, deploy a web application to all web servers in a web farm using a single task.

To sum up, an environment is basically a collection of tasks where each task can target one or more machines. This makes an environment a flexible concept because it is not tied to a physical environment.

---

■ **Note**  The product group is planning to add more functionality around how application bits get deployed to different environments. In the current state, as described in this book, there is only the pipeline model, where the application bits must be deployed to every environment in sequential order. Later on, it will be possible to do direct deployments to individual environments in a pipeline.

---

# Implementing a Deployment Pipeline

It is time to get your hands dirty with Visual Studio Release Management by implementing a deployment pipeline where you deploy the QuizBox web application to two different environments, first to development (Dev) and then to production (Prod).

---

■ **Note**  In this sample, you will just deploy the front-end web application of QuizBox to Azure, not all its dependencies. This allows you to focus on the features of the deployment pipeline. Later on, you will look at how you can set up a full deployment pipeline for all the components of the QuizBox application, including web applications, SQL database, running smoke tests, etc.

---

# Verifying the Build Output

You should by now be familiar with how to create a build definition that versions and packages a web application as an artifact, so we won't walk through that in detail here. Figure 10-7 shows the tasks of the stripped-down version of the QuizBox build definition.

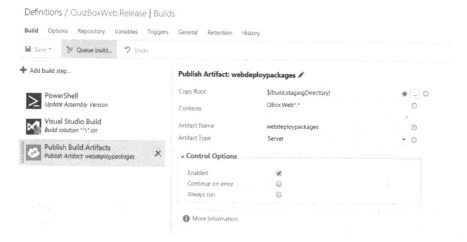

***Figure 10-7.*** *Build artifacts tasks*

You have three tasks in this build definition (all these tasks are described in detail in Chapter 7):

- A *PowerShell* task where you run a script to stamp the AssemblyInfo files with the version number of the build

- A *Visual Studio Build* task that compiles the solution and generates web deploy packages

- A *Publish Build Artifacts* task that grabs the generated web deploy packages and publishes them as build artifacts

When building a deployment pipeline, you need to make sure that the build output contains everything you need and that it is structured properly with meaningful names. When working with deployments, you will find yourself from time to time troubleshooting file paths, and a single character error in one path can take hours to locate! Fortunately, Visual Studio Release Management often supports browsing the build artifacts when authoring the tasks, which makes it a lot easier to enter the correct paths.

In this example, the build creates one build artifact named *WebDeployPackages* that contains the files generated by web deploy, as shown in Figure 10-8.

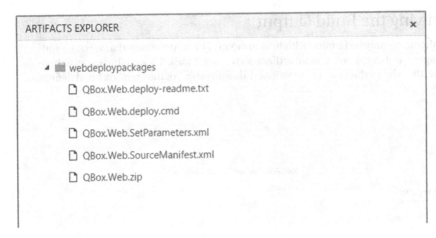

*Figure 10-8.* *Build artifacts structure*

# Creating the Release Definition

As with build definitions, you can use *deployment templates,* which are stored, reusable versions of a release definition. When creating a new release definition, there are default templates available; these are shown in Figure 10-9.

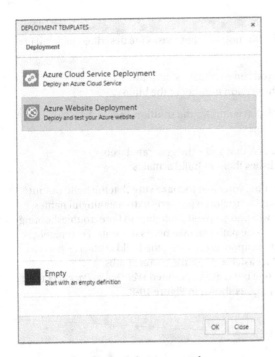

*Figure 10-9.* *Release definition templates*

This list will most likely grow over time, and if you have stored your own deployment templates they will appear in a tab called *Custom*.

In this case, select the *Azure Website Deployment* template, which consists of a *Deploy Website to Azure* task and a *Visual Studio Test* task, as shown in Figure 10-10.

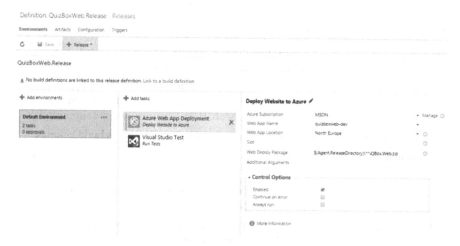

**Figure 10-10.** *Web App deployment release definition*

The template will create one environment called Default Environment (you will change this later) and two tasks, one for deploying the web application as an Azure Web App and a test task that will allow you to run some tests after the deployment.

Note that the deployment task is the same as the one you saw in Chapter 7. Here you can see the advantages of the fact that both the build system and release management are built using the same architecture.

When configuring the release definition, you should also make sure that the release name format is set. This is done under the General tab, as shown in Figure 10-11.

**Figure 10-11.** *Release name format*

In the Release name format field, you can enter the desired name of the releases that are triggered by this release definition. There are several different macros available. In this example, you are using *$(Build.BuildNumber)* and *$(rev:r)*, which will generate release names in the format of

```
Release-1.0.6.0-2
```

where *1.0.6.0* is the build number of the build that is being released, and *-2* is the revision number that is incremented every time the same build is release again.

Table 10-1 lists of all the macros you can use when configuring the release name format.

***Table 10-1.*** *Macros for Configuuring Release Name Format*

| Variable | Description |
|---|---|
| Rev:r | An auto-incremented number with at least the specified number of digits. |
| Date/Date:Mmddyy | The current date, with the default format MMddyy. Any combinations of M/MM/MMM/MMMM, d/dd/ddd/dddd, y/yy/yyyy/yyyy, h/hh/H/HH, m/mm, s/ss are supported. |
| System.TeamProject | The name of the team project to which this build belongs. |
| Release.ReleaseId | The ID of the release, which is unique across all releases in the project. |
| Release.DefinitionName | The name of the release definition to which the current release belongs. |
| Build.BuildNumber | The number of the build contained in the release. If a release has multiple builds, this is the number of the build that triggered the release in the case of continuous deployment, or the number of the first build in the case of a manual trigger. |
| Build.DefinitionName | The definition name of the build contained in the release. If a release has multiple builds, this is the definition name of the build that triggered the release in the case of continuous deployment, or the definition name of the first build in the case of manual trigger. |
| Artifact.ArtifactType | The type of the artifact source linked with the release. For example, this can be Team Build or Jenkins. |
| Build.SourceBranch | The branch for which the build in the release was queued. For Git, this is the name of the branch in the form of refs/heads/master. For Team Foundation Version Control, this is the root server path for the workspace in the form of $/teamproject/branch. This variable is not set in the case of Jenkins artifact sources. |
| Custom variable | The value of a global configuration property defined in the release definition. |

# Linking Artifacts

As mentioned, a key principle of implementing a deployment pipeline is that you should only build and package your binaries and other artifacts once, during the commit stage. The same binaries are then moved through the deployment pipeline and deployed to the different environments and verified by, for example, running automated and manual verification tests. This assures that the binaries that have been tested in all the environments up to the production environment are the same binaries that will be deployed to production. You don't run the risk of introducing hard-to-find errors by recompiling the code for every new environment, and as an extra bonus you potentially save a lot of time as well.

Artifacts can currently be pulled from a build in Visual Studio Online, on-premise TFS, or Jenkins. Select a TFS build by selecting *Build* as the type, as shown in Figure 10-12.

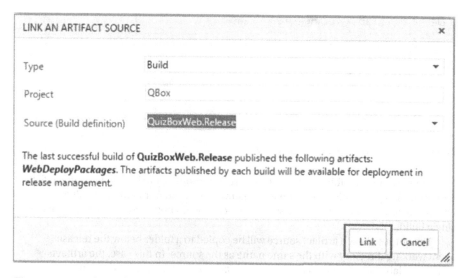

*Figure 10-12. The Link An Artifact Source dialog*

The dialog will then let you select a team project in the current team project collection and a build definition in that team project. When selected, press the Link button to save the artifact source link.

The effect of this is that all artifacts that are produced by the selected build definition will be downloaded at the start of the release. The folder structure will be identical to how the build artifacts are published by the build. As you can see in Figure 10-12, the dialog even dynamically shows the names of the published artifacts of the last successful build. In this case, the name of the artifact is *WebDeployPackages*.

---

■ **Note** In some cases, you might have to consume artifacts from a folder share, for example if you want to integrate another build system like Team City from JetBrains with Visual Studio Release Management. As you can see, there is no option to select this here. Instead, you will have to either refer to this path from the tasks in the pipeline (if they support it) or write a simple PowerShell script that copies the artifact from a network folder to the release agent work directory and run this task in the beginning of each environment.

---

After you have linked an artifact source to the release definition, it will show up on the Artifacts tab, as shown in Figure 10-13.

*Figure 10-13.* *Release definition artifacts*

Note that it is possible to add multiple artifact sources by using the *Link an artifact source* button again. This allows you to consume the output from multiple builds, which can be very handy for larger systems where you do not build everything from one single build.

The output of each artifact source will be copied to a folder below the release agent working directory with the same name as the source. In this case, the artifacts will be available at *$(agent.releaseDirectory)\QuizBoxWeb.Release\*. Note that $(agent.releaesDirectory) is one of the predefined variables of Visual Studio Release Management. You will find a list of the most common ones later in this chapter.

## Configuration Management

To manage the differences in how the applications are deployed and configured in each environment, you need to define and use configuration variables in your release definition. You can then use these variables in your release tasks and inside scripts that are executed by the release agent.

Configuration variables can be defined at different scopes, either in the release definition or in a specific environment.

## Release Definition Variables

Variables defined in the release definition scope are available across all environments. These variables are defined in the Configuration tab of the release definition, as shown in Figure 10-14.

*Figure 10-14.* Release definition configuration variables

In this case, you have defined variables that you can use for all environments, such as when you refer to the name of the build definition, since this value will be the same for any environment. This will reduce duplicate definitions, and you can change these values in one place instead of in every task that uses the corresponding value.

## Environment Variables

More often than not, configuration values will differ depending on the environment to which you are deploying the application. Examples here typically include information like database connection strings, URL-to-back-end service endpoints, local file paths, etc. These configuration variables should be defined at the environment level instead of in the release definition. You can edit environment variables by using the *Configure variables* context menu in the environment, as shown in Figure 10-15.

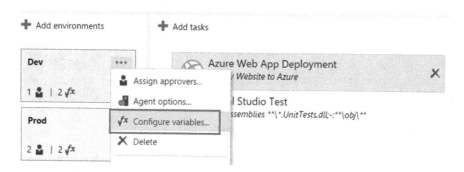

*Figure 10-15.* Configuring environment variables

Environment variables are defined in the same way as for release definition, by entering a name for the variable and a value for the current environment.

In your sample deployment pipeline, you will create two environment variables called *webAppName* and *webAppLocation*, as shown in Figure 10-16. You will then use these variables in the Deploy to Azure task, instead of using hardcoded inline values.

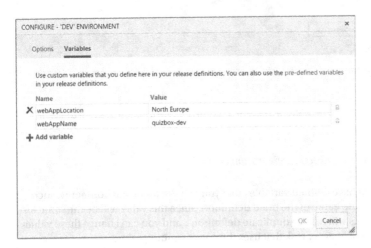

*Figure 10-16.  Configuration variables*

Now, let's go back to the Dev environment and use these variables. In the Azure Web App Deployment task, replace the values in the Web App Name and Web App Location fields with these variables, as shown in Figure 10-17.

*Figure 10-17.  Referencing configuration variables*

Using variables instead of inline values makes it much easier to apply configuration changes across environments, since you can now use the variables view to both get an overview of the values for the different environment and change these values. As Figure 10-18 shows, you can switch to an environment view of the variables (as it will look like once you have created the Prod environment).

Definition: QuizBoxWeb.Release | Releases

Environments    Artifacts    **Configuration**    Triggers    General          | Environment variables |  ▤

⟳    ▣ Save    ＋ Release ▾

View and modify custom variables defined on the environments in this release definition.

|  | Dev | Prod |
|---|---|---|
| webAppLocation | North Europe | North Europe |
| webAppName | quizbox-dev | quizbox-prod |

*Figure 10-18.* *Environment variables view*

Here you can quickly see the different configuration values for all environments and spot if there is anything incorrect. Also, changing, for example, the location for the web apps in all environments does not require you to edit each environment but instead just update these configuration values. Unfortunately, it is currently not possible to add new variables straight from this view; hopefully that will be implemented soon.

# Predefined Variables

Just like with TFS Build, there are several predefined variables available that you can use when authoring tasks and inside any scripts that are executed. Table 10-2 lists some of the more common ones. You refer to them using the $(variableName) syntax, such as $(Agent.Name).

*Table 10-2.* *Predefined Variables*

| Variable | Scope | Description |
|---|---|---|
| Release.DefinitionName | Global | The name of the release definition to which the current release belongs. |
| Release.ReleaseName | Global | The name of the current release. |
| Release. ReleaseId | Global | The identifier of the current release record. |
| Agent.Name | Agent | The name of the agent as registered with the agent pool. This is likely to be different from the machine name. |
| Agent.HomeDirectory | Agent | The folder where the agent is installed. This folder contains the code and resources for the agent. |
| Agent.RootDirectory | Agent | The root directory for this agent, used to synchronize with the source. |
| Agent.WorkingDirectory | Agent | The working directory for this agent. By default this is $(Agent.RootDirectory)_work. |
| Agent.ReleaseDirectory | Agent Release | The local path configured for the agent, where all folders for a specific release definition are created. It will be $(Agent.RootDirectory{hash of collection of definition identifier and repository URL}. |

Also, it is possible to refer to Windows environment variables in the same way. For example, $(temp) will return the TEMP path as defined on the machine running the release agent.

---

■ **Note**  It is currently not possible to define variables in terms of another variable. So for example, the following variable definition does not work:

*DeploymentPath $(agent.releasePath)\installpath*

---

## Environments and Machines

For this first sample, you will deploy the application as an Azure Web App. This means that you don't need to configure any machines for this pipeline.

Every environment has its set of tasks and approval workflow. In general, you should strive to keep the deployments as similar as possible across all environments. If you deploy to dev and test environments using one particular technology and to production using another, the risk of the production deployment failing will be much higher since you haven't tested it properly before. It is very common that for every production release there have been tens or hundreds of deployments to the development and test environments before. If you use the exact same deployment tasks and scripts, you can be much more confident that the production deployment will run successfully.

When the dev environment has been configured, you can take advantage of the Clone environment functionality. This will copy the entire environment, including tasks, options, and approval workflow, into a new environment.

Let's rename your environment to Dev instead, to match your fictive development environment. Then, as shown in Figure 10-19, use the clone option to create a Prod environment.

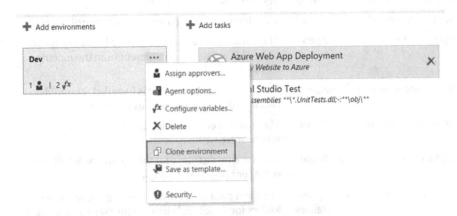

***Figure 10-19.** Cloning an environment*

> ■ **Note** This is a pure copy operation. If you, for example, added a new task to the Dev environment afterwards, you would have to update the other environment as well.

## Continuous Deployment

If you want the deployment pipeline to be triggered automatically whenever a build completes, you can use the Triggers tab to configure this. As shown in Figure 10-20, you can select which artifact source should trigger the release (in case you have multiple artifacts sources linked) and you can select the target environment for the triggered releases.

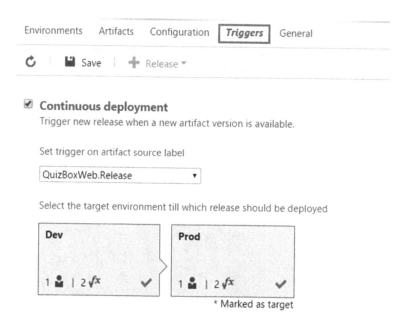

*Figure 10-20.* *Configuring continuous deployment*

# Running a Release

Now it's time to actually start deploying your application. You can trigger a release by either queuing the QuizBoxWeb.Release build definition, or starting a release manually, as shown in Figure 10-21.

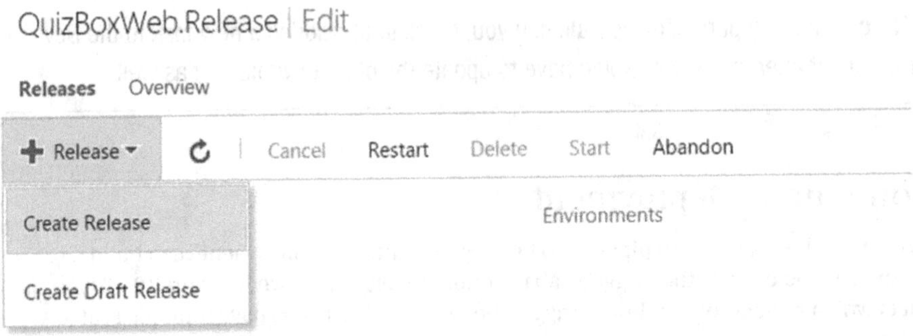

## QuizBoxWeb.Release | Edit

**Releases**   Overview

**+ Release ▾**   **Ċ** |   Cancel   Restart   Delete   Start   Abandon

Create Release                                    Environments

Create Draft Release

**Figure 10-21.**  *Creating a release*

Selecting the Create Release option is the standard operation, and it will trigger a new release based on the selected release definition. In the dialog shown in Figure 10-22, you can set a description for this particular release, assign the target environment, and select which build should be picked.

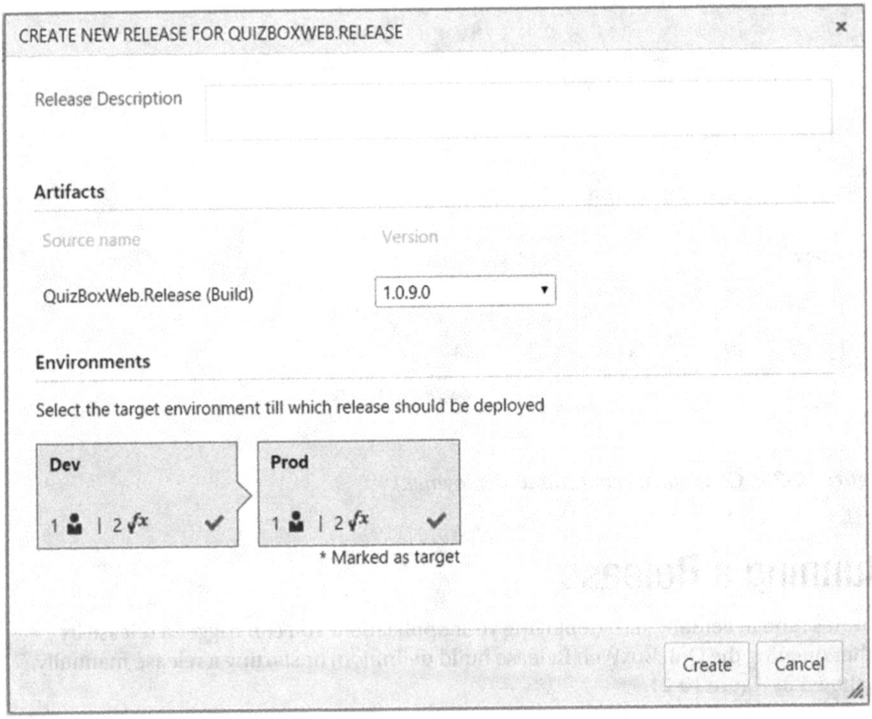

CREATE NEW RELEASE FOR QUIZBOXWEB.RELEASE                                    ✕

Release Description

### Artifacts

Source name                          Version

QuizBoxWeb.Release (Build)           1.0.9.0                ▾

### Environments

Select the target environment till which release should be deployed

Dev                    Prod

1 👤 | 2 √x      ✔     1 👤 | 2 √x      ✔
                       * Marked as target

Create        Cancel

**Figure 10-22.**  *Starting a release*

Selecting a target environment means at which environment the deployment pipeline will stop. You might not want to run every build through the whole pipeline (e.g. all the way to production), but maybe just push a new build to the dev environment to showcase sometime. One way to do this is to select the Dev environment as the target in the Create Release dialog.

By default, the latest successful build will be selected for new releases. This is often what you want, but selecting a previous build could be useful in a rollback scenario, where you identified a problem with the latest deployment and where redeploying the previous version is possible.

When the release is started, the release summary page is shown; it contains overall status information about the current release. As you can see in Figure 10-23, the summary page shows how far down the pipeline the release has reached, which artifacts that were consumed, information about which work items were linked to the build being depoyed, and a summary of all steps up until the current point in time.

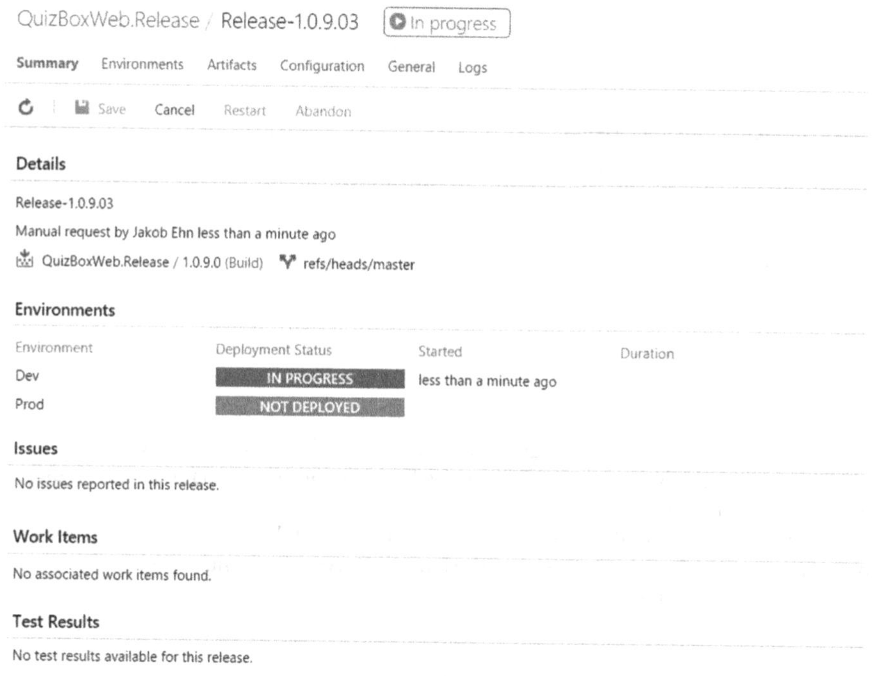

***Figure 10-23.*** *Release summary*

You can also see a summary of any tests that have been executed during the deployment pipeline. In Figure 10-23, you can see that a set of tests has been executed in the Dev environment. Clicking the link will show the same test run summary page as you saw in Chapter 7 when you looked at running tests from a build definition.

# Tracking Releases

A deployment pipeline can be a lengthy process. A single release can sometimes last for days due to approvals and manual smoke testing being a part of the pipeline.

Releases can be tracked at two different levels in Visual Studio Release Management. First, by selecting *All release definitions* in the Explorer view and then selecting the Overview tab, you will get a dashboard view of all release definitions and how far in the deployment pipeline the latest release of each definitions has reached. Figure 10-24 shows an example where you can see the status of three different release definitions.

*Figure 10-24.   Release overview*

In Figure 10-24, you can see that the latest release of the QuizBoxWeb.Release definition has been released successfully to the Dev environment and is currently being released to the Prod environment.

To get an overview of the release activity, you can select the Releases tab instead. This view, shown in Figure 10-25, shows the latest releases with some overview information about each release.

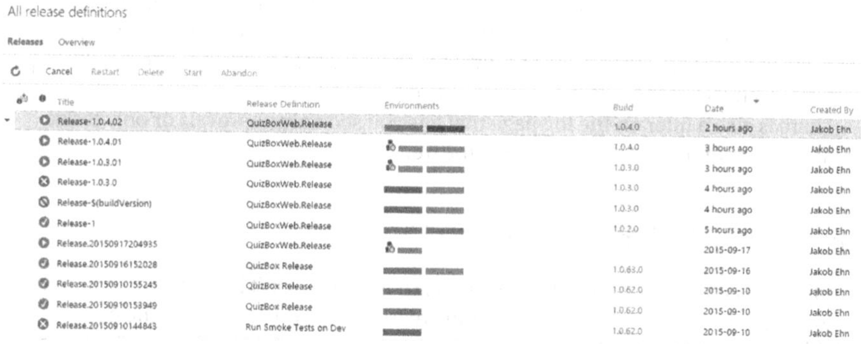

**Figure 10-25.** *Release activity*

In Figure 10-25, you will note that some of the releases have an approval icon in front of the environments. This indicates that an approver was specified and the release is paused while waiting for this approval to be granted.

Using the State filter at the top right of the screen, you can filter the releases by stage. For example, you can show only releases that are in progress or have been released.

Selecting a single release definition will show the release history for that particular definition. From both views, you can see details of a release by selecting it from the list view. From here the summary page discussed previously will be shown.

To see more details of a release, switch to the Log tab. Here every step of each environment that has been executed is displayed in a tree view, as shown in Figure 10-26. By selecting a specific step you can see all the log output from that particular step.

**Figure 10-26.** *Release log*

This view is what you will use when it is time to troubleshoot failed deployments. For more efficient searching, especially for larger releases, you can download the log output from either a specific step or for the entire release. This allows you to quickly search through all log files using a decent text editor.

There is also a filter on the log page that lets you see only approvals or only tasks. By default, both of these will be shown in the tree view.

## Controlling Release Flow

A running release can be canceled at any time, so that you won't have to wait for a release that you might know already will fail for some reason. Figure 10-27 shows the options available for a running release.

*Figure 10-27.* *Release flow*

Once the release is canceled, there are two options:

- Abandon: This will permanently stop the release and no further work or changes can be done with that release.

- Restart: If you cancel the release, or if the release failed, you have the option to restart it from the start in the current environment. This can be very handy since it allows you to fix some problem that might have caused the release to fail (maybe a server was temporarily down) and rerun the release without having to restart the entire pipeline.

Restarting a release will create a new section in the log view, as shown in Figure 10-28, to separate the previous deployment from the running deployment.

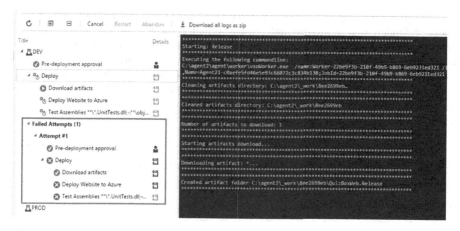

***Figure 10-28.*** *Restarted release*

As you can see in Figure 10-28, the first deployment failed and is shown in the *Failed Attempts* section.

# Creating a Draft Release

In some cases, you might want to try out different changes to a release definition to see how this affects the deployment. Instead of creating a copy of the release definition, you can instead trigger a *draft release.* This will instantiate a new release with all the configuration values and linked artifacts as usual, but the release will not start until you tell it to start. Figure 10-29 shows an example of a draft release that has been created but not yet started.

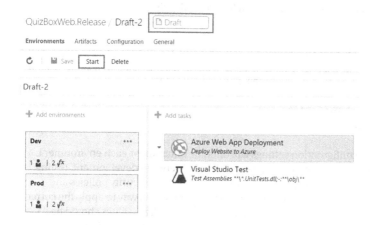

***Figure 10-29.*** *Draft release*

This gives you an opportunity to edit the values for the release without affecting the release definition. Changes to this draft release only affect this release. You can change the properties of any task and the environment options such as approvals and which linked artifacts that should be used. You can also disable tasks by clearing the Enabled checkbox, which lets you effectively try out a changed pipeline process for this particular release.

When the draft release is started, by using the Start button shown in Figure 10-29, the release will start just like a regular release and you can no longer change anything about it. A running release is always immutable.

---

■ **Note** In previous releases of Visual Studio Release Management, it was possible to skip stages when creating a draft release. Currently this is not possible in this version of Visual Studio Release Management.

---

# Configuration Management

Modern enterprise or SaaS applications are almost always implemented using a distributed architecture. A typical e-commerce application usually consists of several web sites, external and internal web services, multiple data stores including both relational and document databases, and perhaps a mobile application developed for the different mobile platforms. Connecting these systems together often results in a lot of configuration for each individual component. The front-end web site needs to know how to connect to the back-end order web service and so on.

These settings can be stored in different places. One very common solution in the Microsoft .NET world is to store them in .NET configuration files. For example, every ASP. NET web application has a corresponding web.config file where all application-specific settings can be stored. In the QuizBox sample, the front-end web application has the URL to the back-end Web API web service in the web.config file, like so:

```
<applicationSettings>
  <QBox.Web.Properties.Settings>
    <setting name="ApiUrl" serializeAs="String">
      <value>http://qbox-dev.cloudapp.net/api</value>
    </setting>
  </QBox.Web.Properties.Settings>
</applicationSettings>
```

Of course, these configuration settings will often be different for each environment. URLs, paths, and user account names can very well differ between development, testing, and production environments due to various reasons such as IT security policies and differences in network topologies, to mention a few. So you need a way to apply the correct values for these configuration settings for each environment. These values should be replaced as part of the deployment, meaning that you can store the values in Visual Studio Release Management and keep them out of source control where they do not belong.

■ **Note** At the time of writing, there is no out-of-the-box support for token replacement in, for example, configuration files in Visual Studio Release Management. The product team is actively working on it and there will be a solution for it when it is shipped with Team Foundation Server in Q1 2016. In this chapter, we show how token replacement can be implemented by the use of a custom release task.

## Implementing Token Replacement

When implementing a strategy for replacing tokens in various configuration files, you need to decide on a naming convention for these tokens. The most important thing is to select a format that is very unlikely to collide with any other reserved tokens. The previous version of Visual Studio Release Management used a convention for variables where they were pre- and post-fixed with __, as in __*SomeVariable*__, so it makes sense to use the same format when using this new version. So the convention will be that you replace all tokens that you find in the format __*Variable*__ with the value of *$(Variable)*.

Doing token replacement in a set of files is a perfect job for PowerShell. Here is a PowerShell script that accepts a SourcePath parameter that can either point to a specific file or to multiple file using a search pattern:

```
[CmdletBinding(DefaultParameterSetName = 'None')]
param
(
    [String] [Parameter(Mandatory = $true)] $SourceFiles
)

import-module "Microsoft.TeamFoundation.DistributedTask.Task.Common"
import-module "Microsoft.TeamFoundation.DistributedTask.Task.Internal"

$patterns = @()
$regex = '__[A-Za-z0-9.]*__'
$matches = @()

$matchingFiles = Find-Files -SearchPattern $SourceFiles
foreach ($file in $matchingFiles)
{
    $matches = select-string -Path $file -Pattern $regex -AllMatches | % {
    $_.Matches } | % { $_.Value }
    ForEach($match in $matches)
    {
        $matchedItem = $match
        $matchedItem = $matchedItem.Trim('_')
        $matchedItem = $matchedItem -replace '\.','_'
```

```
    (Get-Content $file) |
    Foreach-Object {
        $_ -replace $match,(get-item env:$matchedItem).Value
    } |
    Set-Content $file -Force
  }
}
```

The script runs through all files that match the search pattern and replaces any tokens that have the __Variable__ pattern with the corresponding environment variable value.

---

■ **Note** This script uses the *Find-Files* PowerShell function that is defined in the *Microsoft. TeamFoundation.DistributedTask.Task.Common* PowerShell module. These modules are currently only available when running scripts inside a task; you cannot import them from a regular script. In the future, you can expect to find these libraries packaged separately to make it easier to use them from regular PowerShell scripts as well.

---

A release task is packaged and uploaded in the same way as a build task. You can go back to Chapter 7 for details on how to package and upload a task that uses this script. Figure 10-30 shows an example where this task is used in a release definition.

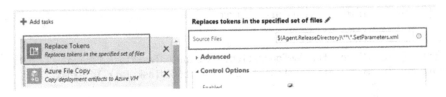

***Figure 10-30.*** *Replace tokens task*

In this example, you match all *\*.SetParameters.xml* files located anywhere the agent release directory and replace the tokens found inside these files.

Placing this task at the beginning of every environment lets you do token replacement before any other tasks are executed.

# Approvals

Auditing releases and deployment is important for many companies. Part of this is assigning a group of people to be responsible for approving if a deployment should be allowed to continue or not. Approval is built into Visual Studio Release Management, and is scoped to environments. In every environment you can configure pre- and post-approvals. Pre-deployment approvals are used to verify that the environment is ready to be deployed to. Even if the application bits have been approved for deployment, the environment might not be ready. Post-deployment approvals are used to validate a deployment to an environment by, for example, running some manual tests against the deployed application.

## An Approval Scenario

Let's walk through a typical scenario where approvals are used. Assuming that you have three environments (Dev, QA, and Prod), you want to protect the QA and Prod environment so that not everyone can deploy a new build to those environments. Often there is a different set of people that "own" these environments; perhaps a QA team is in charge of when things are deployed to the test environment. Likewise, there is usually an IT operations team that controls the production environments. It might even be completely locked down so that no one can log onto these server.

The Dev environment often doesn't need any approvers; they just want to get every check-in built and deployed to this environment to have the latest bits out. When the version running on the Dev environment is determined to be stable enough, the QA team can trigger a deployment to the QA environment by approving the Dev environment.

When the build is in the QA stage, more thorough testing is done, both automated and manual. You might also perform load testing here if you don't have a separate pre-production environment. After the build has been verified and is considered to be ready for production, the QA team approves the build. This will move the deployment along to the pre-approval step of the production environment, waiting for it to be approved by the IT operations team.

As shown in Figure 10-31, in this scenario you would use the pre- and post-deployment approval steps in the QA environment and assign them to the QA team. In the production environment, you would assign the pre-approval step to the Ops team. You might also use the post-approval step in the production environment as a way of formalizing any manual verification tests that should be done after a deployment to production.

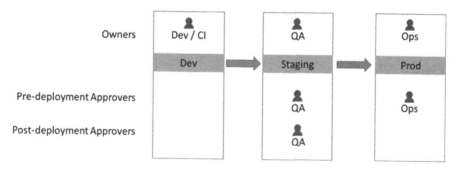

*Figure 10-31. An approval scenario*

## Assigning Approvers

As mentioned, approvers are assigned to environments. This is done by clicking the context menu in the environment and selecting *Assign approvers*, as shown in Figure 10-32.

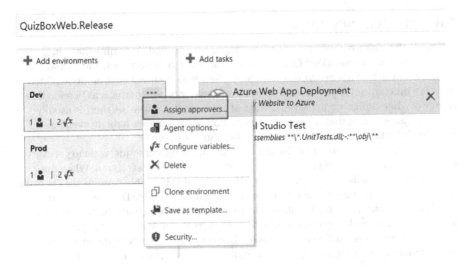

*Figure 10-32. Assigning approvers*

For each environment you can assign a pre-deployment and post-deployment approver, as shown in Figure 10-33. By default both these are set to automated, which means that no approval will be done and the deployment will continue to the next step. In this example, the pre-deployment step is automated, but the QA team is assigned as post-deployment approvers.

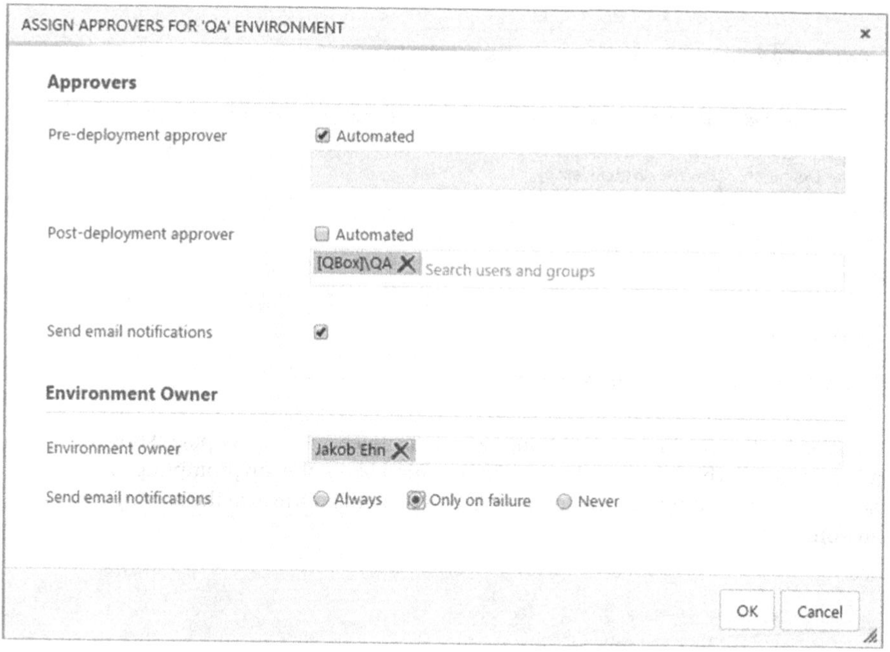

*Figure 10-33. Pre- and post-deployment approvers*

You can also set the environment owner here. The environment owner can manage the environment and can receive notifications about the deployments being done to the environment. In the above example, we only send a notification in case of a failure.

# Approving a Release

When the deployment pipeline reaches an environment that needs approval, it sends an email to every person that is assigned as approver for that particular environment. The email contains information about the release and a link to the release summary page that will show a notification message that the release needs to be approved, as shown in Figure 10-34.

**Release-1.0.9.05** - Pending pre-deployment approval in Dev

You are requested to accept (or refuse) a pre-deployment approval in the following deployment :

| | |
|---|---|
| Release Definition: | QuizBoxWeb.Release |
| Release: | Release-1.0.9.05 |
| Target Environment: | Prod |
| Environment: | Dev |

Click here to view the approval request.

***Figure 10-34.** Approval notification mail*

Clicking the link in the email brings you to the release summary page, shown in Figure 10-35, which now contains an information bar at the top prompting that the release needs your approval for the pre-deployment approval of the Deploy Dev environment.

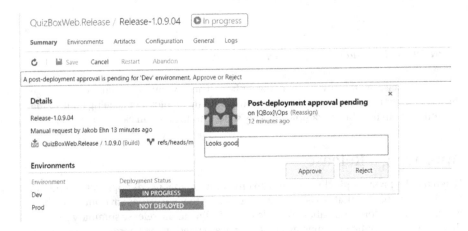

***Figure 10-35.** Approving a release*

When either approving or rejecting a release, the approver has the option to fill out a comment about the decision. Although not required, it is good practice to always log any relevant information here for later.

When assigning multiple approvers, either as users or as a group, every person must approve the release before it continues. If one person rejects the approval request, the release will fail and stop.

# Securing the Deployment Pipeline

Visual Studio Release Management uses the same permission model as the rest of Team Foundation Server. Several different permissions are defined that can be granted or denied to users and groups at various scopes. This means that you can, for example, set some general permissions at the team project level, and then override them for specific release definitions or even specific environments within a release definition.

The different permissions that can be set are listed in Table 10-3.

***Table 10-3.*** *Permissions*

| Permission | Description | Scopes |
|---|---|---|
| Administer release permissions | Can change any of the other permissions | Project, Release definition, Environment |
| Delete release definition | Can delete release definition(s) | Project, Release definition |
| Delete release environment | Can delete environment(s) in release definition(s) | Project, Release definition, Environment |
| Edit release definition | Can create/edit release definition(s), configuration variables, triggers, and artifacts | Project, Release definition |
| Edit release environment | Can edit environment(s) in release definition(s) | Project, Release definition, Environment |
| Manage release approvers | Can add or edit approvers for environment(s) in release definition(s) | Project, Release definition, Environment |
| Manage releases | Can edit the configuration in releases, and can start/stop and restart/release deployments | Project, Release definition |
| Queue releases | Can create new releases | Project, Release definition |
| View release definition | Can view release definition(s) | Project, Release definition |
| View releases | Can view releases belonging to release definition(s) | Project, Release definition |

## Example: Locking Down the Production Environment

A common scenario is that you want to make sure that only the IT operations team can author the resources in the production environments, while the rest of the team only has read access. Let's walk through the steps to implement this in the deployment pipeline you just created.

You need to separate the different users by adding them to different teams. In this sample, you have three groups, Developers, QA, and Ops, as shown in Figure 10-36.

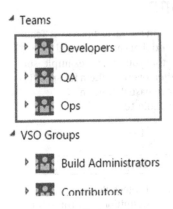

**Figure 10-36.** *QuizBox teams*

Select the *Prod* environment, and select *Security* from the context menu, as shown in Figure 10-37.

**Figure 10-37.** *Environment security*

Add the two team groups (Developers and QA) and then set all permissions to Deny, as shown in Figure 10-38.

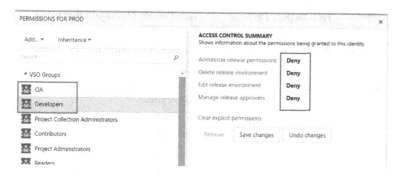

*Figure 10-38.* *Deny permissions*

Now, when a member of the Developers or QA team browses to the Prod environment, all details will be visible but not editable, as shown in Figure 10-39.

*Figure 10-39.* *Locked down Prod environment*

# Deployment Pipeline for QuizBox

Now that you have taken a good look at the functionality available in Visual Studio Release Management, it is time to look at how you have applied the tools and processes from this and previous chapters to implement a deployment pipeline for the QuizBox application.

Table 10-4 lists the components that make up the QuizBox application and which deployment technologies you selected for each component.

***Table 10-4.*** *QuizBox Components*

| Component | Package | Deployment Technology |
|-----------|---------|----------------------|
| QuizBox Front Web | Web Deploy Package | Web Deploy command line using PowerShell |
| QuizBox Backend Web | Web Deploy Package | Web Deploy command line using PowerShell |
| Quizbox SQL Database | DACPAC | `Sqlcmd.exe` using remote PowerShell |
| QuizBox Admin Tool | Windows Installer (MSI) | `MsiExec.exe` using remote PowerShell |
| QuizBox Unit Tests | | Visual Studio Test Runner |
| QuizBox UI Acceptance Tests | | Selenium, executed using Visual Studio Test Runner |

# Deployment Pipeline Overview

Before diving into the details of each step in the deployment pipeline, let's take a step back and look at an overview of the deployment pipeline for QuizBox. A schematic overview is shown in Figure 10-40, where each stage/environment is shown with a summary of the main steps within each stage.

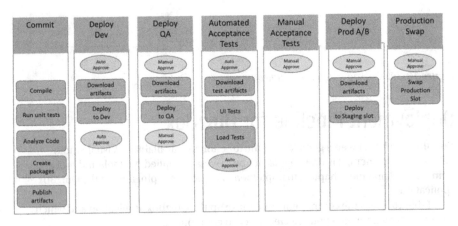

***Figure 10-40.*** *Deployment pipeline overview*

Note again that we are using the term *stage* here instead of *environment*, which is the term in Visual Studio Release Management. As you can see in the figure, you have multiple environments that all affect the physical QA environment.

# Commit Stage

The commit stage is where you compile and package the binaries that will be deployed and verified through the deployment pipeline. The commit stage is usually implemented using an automated build system. In your case, you use TFS Build for this. In previous chapters, you learned how to use TFS Build to compile, test, package, and publish the binaries and artifacts.

The output of the commit stage is a set of artifacts that will be consumed by the later stages in the pipeline. You can select different options when it comes to storing these artifacts. What is important is that it is permanent (e.g. the artifacts are not deleted) and versioned so that you can uniquely identify the artifacts for a specific build. Usually you use the build number as part of the path or URI to the artifacts.

In this case, you use the built-in TFS storage for publishing the build artifacts. The build artifacts structure of the QuizBox.Release build is shown in Figure 10-41.

| Summary | Timeline | **Artifacts** | | |
|---|---|---|---|---|
| Installers | | | Download | Explore |
| WebDeployPackages | | | Download | Explore |
| Scripts | | | Download | Explore |
| tests | | | Download | Explore |
| database | | | Download | Explore |
| uitests | | | Download | Explore |

*Figure 10-41. QuizBox release build artifacts*

# Deploying to Dev

The first "real" stage in the QuizBox deployment pipeline is where the application is deployed to a development environment. Since the QuizBox release definition is set to be triggered every time a new artifact is pushed by the linked build, this means that every time you queue a QuizBox.Release build definition and it finishes successfully, it will trigger a new release that will be automatically deployed to the Dev environment.

Let's recap what the development environment looks like for QuizBox. It consists of an Azure Web App where the front-end web application is running, and an Azure VM where the back-end web service, the SQL database, and the QuizBox BackOffice application are running.

Your goal is to automate as much as possible using your deployment pipeline. This means that you will make sure that the VM is configured so that the necessary dependencies are installed and configured, any inbound ports are opened, and so on.

Figure 10-42 shows the tasks in the Deploy Dev environment.

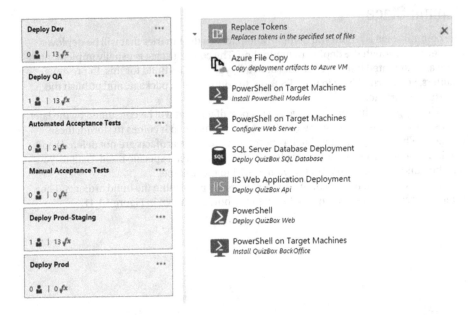

**Figure 10-42.** *Deploy Dev environment*

Let's walk through each task in detail to see what is going on.

## Replacing Tokens

You start off by doing a token replacement, as discussed previously in this chapter. In this case, you need to replace some configuration settings in the QuizBox Web API and the QuizBox front-end web application, such as the database connection information. Using the technique discussed in Chapter 7, you have tokenized the publish profiles, which means that the tokens will end up in the *.SetParameters.xml files that are used when deploying the web deploy package. See Figure 10-43.

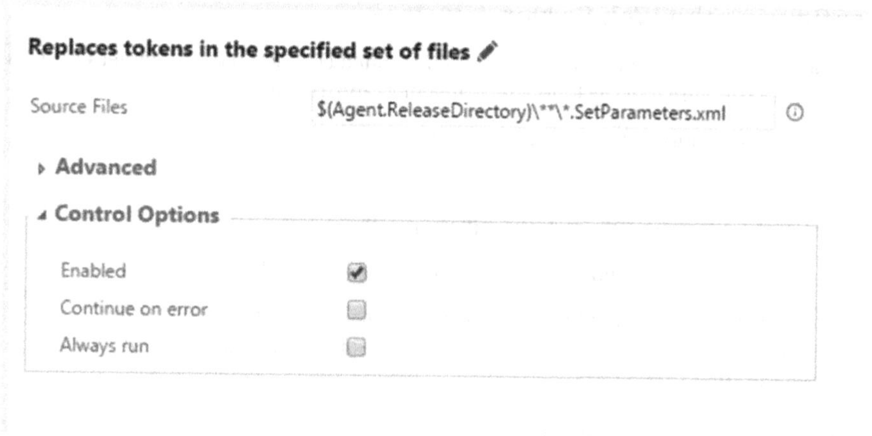

**Replaces tokens in the specified set of files** ✏

| | |
|---|---|
| Source Files | $(Agent.ReleaseDirectory)\*"\*.SetParameters.xml  ⓘ |

▸ **Advanced**

◢ **Control Options**

| | |
|---|---|
| Enabled | ☑ |
| Continue on error | ☐ |
| Always run | ☐ |

*Figure 10-43.* *Replace tokens*

## Azure File Copy

To be able to run scripts and installers on the Azure VM, you need to copy these files to the server. To do this, use the Azure File Copy task that uses an Azure storage account as an intermediary storage, as shown in Figure 10-44.

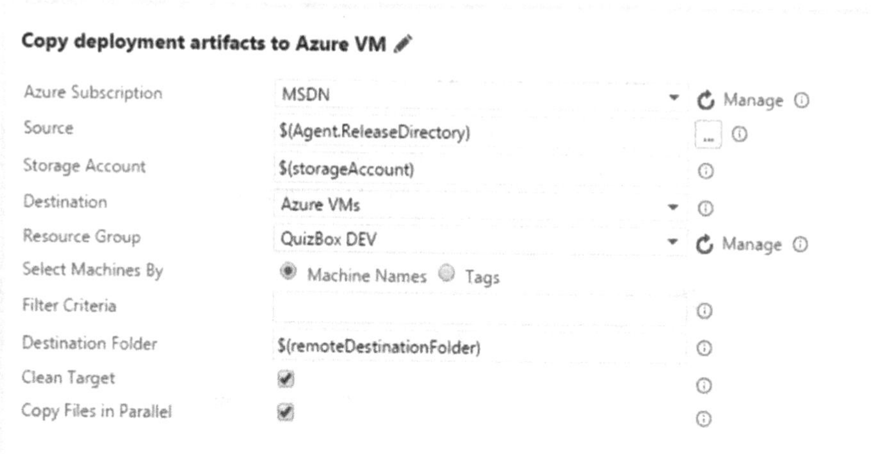

**Copy deployment artifacts to Azure VM** ✏

| | | |
|---|---|---|
| Azure Subscription | MSDN | ▾  ↻ Manage ⓘ |
| Source | $(Agent.ReleaseDirectory) | … ⓘ |
| Storage Account | $(storageAccount) | ⓘ |
| Destination | Azure VMs | ▾ ⓘ |
| Resource Group | QuizBox DEV | ▾  ↻ Manage ⓘ |
| Select Machines By | ⦿ Machine Names ◯ Tags | |
| Filter Criteria | | ⓘ |
| Destination Folder | $(remoteDestinationFolder) | ⓘ |
| Clean Target | ☑ | ⓘ |
| Copy Files in Parallel | ☑ | ⓘ |

*Figure 10-44.* *Azure File Copy task*

Specify the name of the Azure storage account where the files should be copied to, and the local path on the VM where the files should end up. Beneath the surface, this task takes care of running a process on the VM that will download the files from the storage account onto the VM.

## Configuring the Web Server

This is a Remote PowerShell task that runs a PowerShell DSC script on the target VM. This DSC script makes sure that the following is installed and/or configured:

- IIS (including IIS Management tools)

- ASP.NET 4.5

- A folder where the web site will be installed

- An application pool and a web site for the back-end web site

The PowerShell DSC script is shown below. It uses the *xWebAdministration* PowerShell module, which is part of the PowerShell Gallery and is available at www.powershellgallery.com/.

```
Configuration QuizBoxApiWebSite
{
        Import-DSCResource -ModuleName xWebAdministration

        Node $env:COMPUTERNAME
        {
                WindowsFeature WebServerRole
                {
                        Ensure = "Present"
                        Name = "Web-Server"
                }

                WindowsFeature AspNet45
                {
                        Ensure = "Present"
                        Name = "Web-Asp-Net45"
                        DependsOn = "[WindowsFeature]WebServerRole"
                }

                WindowsFeature WebMgmtConsole
                {
                        Name = "Web-Mgmt-Console"
                        Ensure = "Present"
                        DependsOn = "[WindowsFeature]WebServerRole"
                }

                xWebAppPool QuizBoxApiAppPool
                {
                        Ensure = "Present"
                        Name = "QuizBoxApi"
                        State = "Started"
                        DependsOn = "[WindowsFeature]AspNet45"
                }
```

```
File WebSiteRoot
{
        Type = 'Directory'
        DestinationPath = $DestinationPath
        Ensure = "Present"
        DependsOn = "[xWebAppPool]QuizBoxApiAppPool"
}

xWebsite QuizBoxApiSite
{
        Ensure = "Present"
        Name = "QuizBoxApi"
        PhysicalPath = $DestinationPath
        State = "Started"
        ApplicationPool = "QuizBoxApi"
        BindingInfo      = MSFT_xWebBindingInformation
        {
                Protocol            = "HTTP"
                Port                = 80
        }

        DependsOn = "[File]WebSiteRoot"
}
    }
}
```

```
QuizBoxApiWebSite -Verbose
```

Figure 10-45 shows how to execute this script, using the *Run PowerShell on Target Machines* task.

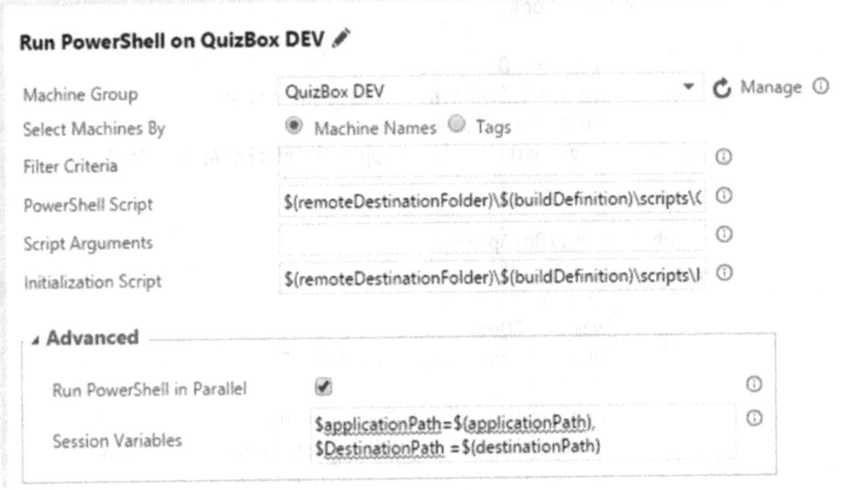

**Run PowerShell on QuizBox DEV** ✎

| | | |
|---|---|---|
| Machine Group | QuizBox DEV ▼ | ↻ Manage ⓘ |
| Select Machines By | ◉ Machine Names ○ Tags | |
| Filter Criteria | | ⓘ |
| PowerShell Script | $(remoteDestinationFolder)\$(buildDefinition)\scripts\C | ⓘ |
| Script Arguments | | ⓘ |
| Initialization Script | $(remoteDestinationFolder)\$(buildDefinition)\scripts\I | ⓘ |

▲ **Advanced**

| | | |
|---|---|---|
| Run PowerShell in Parallel | ☑ | ⓘ |
| Session Variables | $applicationPath=$(applicationPath), $DestinationPath =$(destinationPath) | ⓘ |

*Figure 10-45. Run PowerShell on target machine*

The task also uses an initialization script that copies the xWebAdministration PowerShell module files to the correct location on the target server. This script is as follows:

```
# Copy DSC modules into system modules folder
$customModulesDirectory = Join-Path $env:SystemDrive "\Program Files\
WindowsPowerShell\Modules"
$customModuleSrc = Join-Path $applicationPath "xWebAdministration"

Copy-Item -Verbose -Force -Recurse -Path $customModuleSrc -Destination
$customModulesDirectory
```

Note that in the task you must supply the arguments to the script explicitly. Since these scripts are executed on the remote server, you cannot rely on the variables defined in Release Management to be automatically available inside the scripts. Therefore you need to supply these variables explicitly.

## SQL Server Database Deployment

For the QuizBox sample application, you are using a local SQL Server Express that is installed on the same virtual machine where the back-end web service is running. To deploy and update the QuizBox database onto this SQL Server instance, use the *SQL Server Database Deployment* task, which makes it easy to deploy SQL Server DACPAC files. As shown in Figure 10-46, you can select different ways to connect to the SQL Server. You can select Server, which means that you enter information into the server, database, username, and password fields. This is the approach that you have used here. You can also enter a specific connection string, or you can use a SQL Server publish profile.

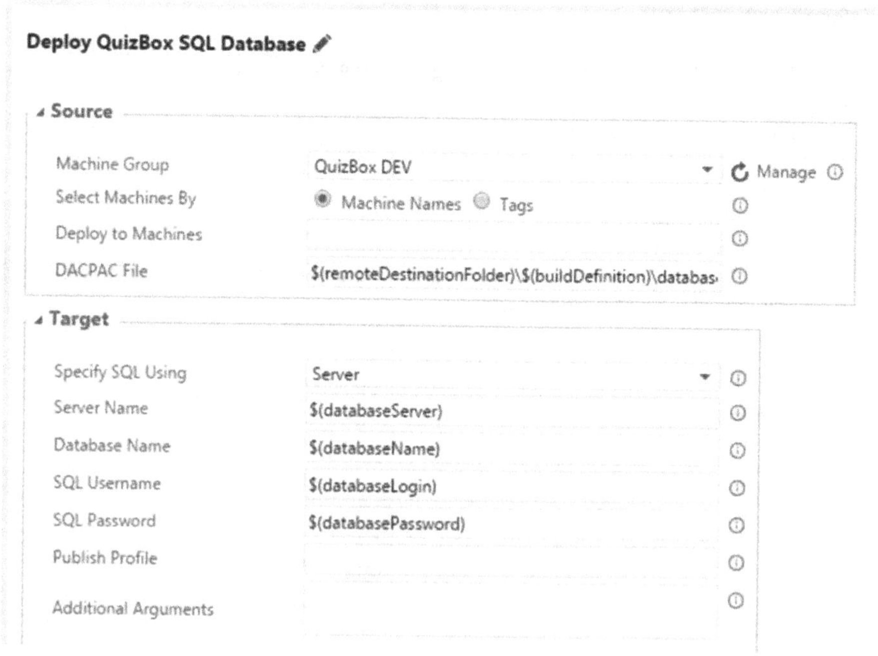

**Deploy QuizBox SQL Database** 🖉

▲ Source

| | | | |
|---|---|---|---|
| Machine Group | QuizBox DEV | ▼ ↻ Manage ⓘ | |
| Select Machines By | ⦿ Machine Names ○ Tags | ⓘ | |
| Deploy to Machines | | ⓘ | |
| DACPAC File | $(remoteDestinationFolder)\$(buildDefinition)\databas· | ⓘ | |

▲ Target

| | | |
|---|---|---|
| Specify SQL Using | Server | ▼ ⓘ |
| Server Name | $(databaseServer) | ⓘ |
| Database Name | $(databaseName) | ⓘ |
| SQL Username | $(databaseLogin) | ⓘ |
| SQL Password | $(databasePassword) | ⓘ |
| Publish Profile | | ⓘ |
| Additional Arguments | | ⓘ |

*Figure 10-46.* *Deploy SQL Database*

## PowerShell on Target Machines

To deploy the QuizBox back-end Web API REST service, use web deploy. This service is running on the IIS installed on the virtual machine, and since you do not want to enable remote web deploy to this server, you need to run this on the server. This is done by running a PowerShell script using the *PowerShell on Target Machines* task, where you specify the local path to the script that you want to execute and supply the necessary parameters.

The PowerShell script that is used is very simple. You basically just run the QuizBox.Api.deploy.cmd file, which is a file that is generated by web deploy during the build process. Before executing this file, set the working directory to the path that you supply to this script. In general, it is a good idea to execute scripts from their working directory, so that any relative paths get resolved correctly.

```
[CmdletBinding()]

param(
        [Parameter(Position=1)]
        [string]$workingDirectory
)
```

```
if( $workingDirectory)
{
        Write-Verbose -Verbose ("Setting working directory to " +
$workingDirectory)
        Set-Location $workingDirectory
}

.\QBox.Api.deploy.cmd /Y
```

Figure 10-47 shows how the script is executed in the deployment pipeline, using the *Run PowerShell on Target Machine* task.

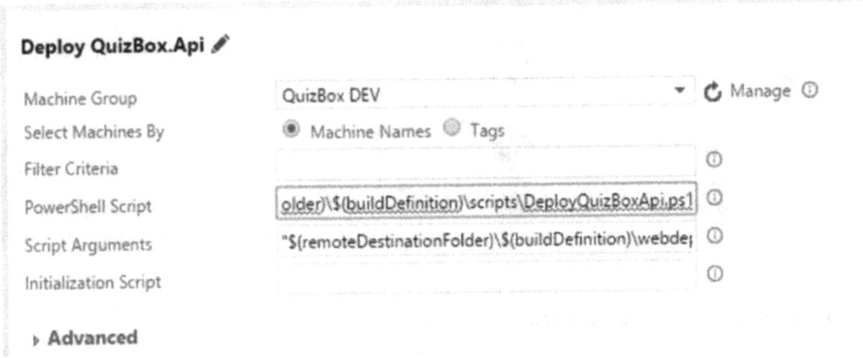

**Deploy QuizBox.Api** 🖉

| | |
|---|---|
| Machine Group | QuizBox DEV ▼ ↻ Manage ⓘ |
| Select Machines By | ◉ Machine Names ○ Tags |
| Filter Criteria | ⓘ |
| PowerShell Script | older)\$(buildDefinition)\scripts\DeployQuizBoxApi.ps1 ⓘ |
| Script Arguments | "$(remoteDestinationFolder)\$(buildDefinition)\webde| ⓘ |
| Initialization Script | ⓘ |

‣ **Advanced**

*Figure 10-47.* Run QuizBox API deployment script

## PowerShell

The QuizBox front-end web application is running as an Azure Web App. This means that you can deploy it straight from the server where the release agent is running; you don't have to go through the QuizBox VM server. Therefore, use the standard PowerShell task in order to run the corresponding PowerShell script.

---

■ **Note** There is a custom task available for deploying Azure Web App (*Deploy Azure Web App*), as you have seen before. A downside with this task is that it does not support parametrization using the SetParameter files, so you can't substitute the necessary parameters as part of the deployment. The task internally uses the Publish-AzureWebSite PowerShell function from the Azure PowerShell library, and this is where the limitation is. That is why you're using a regular PowerShell script here.

---

The PowerShell script is similar to the previous script, except that you must explicitly pass the necessary credentials in order to deploy the web app to the Azure subscription.

```
[CmdletBinding()]

param(
        [Parameter(Position=1)]
        [string]$publishUrl,
        [Parameter(Position=2)]
        [string]$userName,
        [Parameter(Position=3)]
        [string]$password
)

.\QBox.Web.deploy.cmd /Y "/M:$publishUrl" /u:$userName /p:$password /a:Basic
```

Figure 10-48 shows how the script is executed from the deployment pipeline.

**Deploy QuizBox Web** ✎

| | |
|---|---|
| Script filename | QBox.Release\scripts\DeployQuizBoxWeb.ps1 |
| Arguments | "https://quizbox-dev.scm.azurewebsites.net:443/msdep |

◢ **Advanced**

| | |
|---|---|
| Working folder | QBox.Release\WebDeployPackages |

*Figure 10-48.* *Deploy QuizBox Web task*

## Installing QuizBox BackOffice (MSI)

Finally, let's deploy the back office application. This is a desktop application, packaged into a Windows Installer MSI using Windows Installer XML (WiX), as you saw in Chapter 7. For simplicity, you will install this on the server mainly to show how it can be done. Normally, the MSI should either be published to a location from where the end users can download it, or it should (preferably) be packaged into a ClickOnce application and published to a web server.

To deploy this, use msiexec.exe on the target server to run the installation. Pass the /qn parameters to run the installation in silent mode. Be careful not to run anything that would display a UI during its execution since that would block the deployment process.

Here is the PowerShell script that is used to deploy the MSI:

```
[CmdletBinding()]
param(
        [Parameter(Position=1)]
        [string]$msiPath,
        [Parameter(Position=2)]
        [string]$installLocation
)

Function CheckExitCode([int]$code)
{
        if( $code -eq 0 ) {
                Write-Verbose -Verbose "Installation finished with
                ExitCode: $code"
        }
        else {
                throw "Installation failed with ExitCode: $code"
        }
}

$logPath = Split-Path $msiPath
$logPath = Join-Path $logPath "install.log"
$arguments = "/i ""$msiPath"" /qn /lv ""$logPath"" INSTALLDIR=""$installLoc
ation"""
Write-Verbose -Verbose $arguments
$result = (start-process msiexec "$arguments" -Wait -PassThru).ExitCode
CheckExitCode($result)
$logOutput = Get-Content $logPath | Out-String
Write-Verbose -Verbose $logOutput
```

Also, use the log switch (/ln) to direct all log output to a file. This file is then read and written to the output stream, so that all output is available in the release log for verification and troubleshooting.

For completeness, Figure 10-49 shows how the script is executed using the *Run PowerShell on Target Machine* task.

**Figure 10-49.** *QuizBox BackOffice script*

# Deploying to QA

Your QA physical environment is identical to the development environment. The main difference with regards to QA is that you will perform automated acceptance testing and, if they complete successfully, also do manual testing.

Since the topology itself is identical, we won't repeat all of the deployment tasks here. The only difference is the values of the environment variables.

# Automated Acceptance Tests

Now you have reached the stage where you want to perform automated acceptance testing. These tests should cover as much as possible of the existing functional requirements, often in the form of regression tests. This can be a mixture of unit tests that test on the API level and UI tests that exercise the actual application by launching it and performing user actions.

In this case, you will run a set of web tests using the Selenium test framework. You will execute the tests across three different browsers: Internet Explorer, Google Chrome, and Firefox. The tests will be executed on a separate client machine, a Windows 8.1 VM running in Azure. This machine will have the three browsers installed but nothing else, and it will run the tests against the QuizBox front-end web application deployed as an Azure Web App.

You will also execute a set of cloud load tests, which are standard Visual Studio load tests that are executed using the Microsoft Azure infrastructure. The set of tasks in this environment is shown in Figure 10-50.

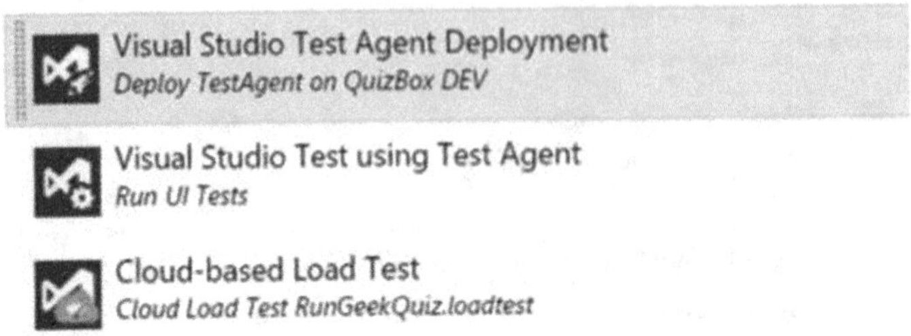

**Visual Studio Test Agent Deployment**
*Deploy TestAgent on QuizBox DEV*

**Visual Studio Test using Test Agent**
*Run UI Tests*

**Cloud-based Load Test**
*Cloud Load Test RunGeekQuiz.loadtest*

*Figure 10-50. Automated Acceptance Tests environment*

## Deploying the Test Agent

To be able to run tests on a target machine, there needs to be a Visual Studio test agent installed on the machine. Deploying the test agent can be done automatically using the *Deploy Test Agent* task. This task, shown in Figure 10-51, will download the test agent software from either the public download URL over at Microsoft MSDN or from a network path that can be supplied to the task. After downloading the software, it will be copied to the target machine and then configured and started.

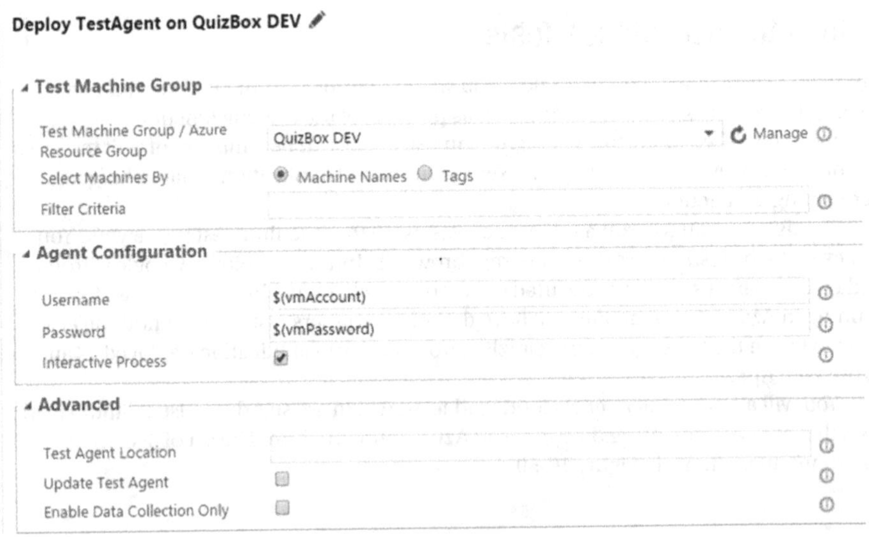

**Deploy TestAgent on QuizBox DEV** 🖉

▲ **Test Machine Group**

| | | |
|---|---|---|
| Test Machine Group / Azure Resource Group | QuizBox DEV | ▼ 🔄 Manage ⓘ |
| Select Machines By | ◉ Machine Names  ○ Tags | |
| Filter Criteria | | ⓘ |

▲ **Agent Configuration**

| | | |
|---|---|---|
| Username | $(vmAccount) | ⓘ |
| Password | $(vmPassword) | ⓘ |
| Interactive Process | ☑ | ⓘ |

▲ **Advanced**

| | | |
|---|---|---|
| Test Agent Location | | ⓘ |
| Update Test Agent | ☐ | ⓘ |
| Enable Data Collection Only | ☐ | ⓘ |

*Figure 10-51. Deploy Test Agent task*

Since you are going to run UI tests with this agent, you configure it to run as an interactive process. You also need to pass the credentials to use for the agent. Here you have declared these as environment variables.

If you check the *Update Test Agent* checkbox, the task will check for any updates to the agent, even if the agent is already installed.

## Running Tests on the Target Machine

After the test agent is deployed, you can execute the tests by using the *Run Tests on Target Machine* task (see Figure 10-52). In this task, you need to supply the test agent with information about where the tests are located and which of the test assemblies to execute. You also pass the path to the run settings file that specific your runtime test parameters. You then override the values for this environment in the *Override Test Run Parameters* field. For more information about the run settings file, see Chapter 9.

| ◢ **Test Machine Group** | | |
|---|---|---|
| Test Machine Group / Azure Resource Group | QuizBox DEV | ▼ ⟳ Manage ⓘ |

| ◢ **Test Settings** | | |
|---|---|---|
| Test Drop Location | $(remoteDestinationFolder)\$(buildDefinition)\uitests\ | ⓘ |
| Test Assembly | **\*test*.dll | ⓘ |
| Test Filter criteria | | ⓘ |
| Platform | | ⓘ |
| Configuration | | ⓘ |
| Run Settings File | QBox.Release\uitests\default.runsettings | ... ⓘ |
| Override Test Run Parameters | webAppUrl=https://quizbox-dev.azurewebsites.net | ⓘ |
| Test Configurations | FullyQualifiedName~Chrome:40;FullyQualifiedName~IE:42;FullyQualifiedName· | ⓘ |

| ◢ **Advanced** | | |
|---|---|---|
| Code Coverage Enabled | ☐ | ⓘ |
| Application Under Test Machine Group | | ▼ ⟳ Manage ⓘ |

***Figure 10-52.*** *Run Tests on Target Machine task*

Make sure that all of the dependencies of the test assemblies are included in the set of files that are copied to the target machine. In this case, for example, you must have the different web drivers available and also the run settings file.

---

■ **Note** In order to use the *Run Tests on Target Machine* task, you *must* precede it with the *Deploy Test Agent* task. The reason for this is that the deploy task is what causes the test agent running on the target machine to start listening for test runs from TFS. So it is required to run this task before every *Run Test* task, even if there already is a test agent installed on the target machine.

---

## Cloud-Based Load Tests

To run the *Cloud-Based Load Tests* task you need to specify a connection to a Visual Studio Online account. This is done using the administration page, as was shown in Chapter 9. In addition, you enter the path to the test settings file and where the load tests are located, as shown in Figure 10-53.

**Cloud Load Test RunGeekQuiz.loadtest** ✏

| | | |
|---|---|---|
| Registered connection | Cloud Load Test Service ▼ | ↻ Manage ⓘ |
| Test settings file | QBox.Release\loadtests\default.testsettings | ... ⓘ |
| Load test files folder | QBox.Release\loadtests\ | ... ⓘ |
| Load test file | RunGeekQuiz.loadtest | ⓘ |
| Number of permissible threshold violations | | ⓘ |

***Figure 10-53.*** *Cloud-Based Load Tests task*

To control if the load test is considered successful or not, you can enter a threshold limit in the *Number of permissible threshold violations* field. This number is very hard to get right and will vary from project to project. You need to continuously evaluate this setting to find the right threshold.

Currently, the results of a cloud-based load tests is not visible in the release summary. You will see the ID of the load test run in the output log, and you can use this to locate it from the Load Test Manager in Visual Studio. Figure 10-54 shows an example of the summary page of a load test run, available in Visual Studio.

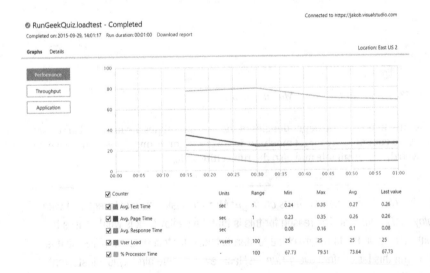

***Figure 10-54.*** *Load Test summary in Visual Studio*

■ **Note**   Authoring performance and load tests and using the Load Test Manager are features of Visual Studio Enterprise only.

## Manual Acceptance Tests

This is a special stage, in that you have not defined any tasks in this environment! So, what is the reason for this empty environment? Obviously the deployment pipeline would work without this environment, but the reason for having this as a separate stage is that the status of the deployment pipeline becomes much more visible. The process of running manual acceptance tests can be a very long process, sometimes several days, so having a visible indication that the deployment pipeline is in this stage is valuable.

Figure 10-55 shows an example where you can see that release *QuizBox. Release-1.1.1.0-2* is currently in manual acceptance testing. If this was just part of the post-deployment approval step for the previous environment, it would not be as clear.

*Figure 10-55.*   *Release overview*

Of course, this is a matter of taste and preferences. You can also use the post-approval step to signal that the QA team should do their manual acceptance testing in order to validate and approve it for release into production.

## Deploying to Production A/B

Finally, the QuizBox application should be deployed to its production environment. The binaries have moved through the entire pipeline and have been deployed and verified. At this stage, you should have confidence that the deployment to production will be successful.

There are a few differences in the production environment compared to QA and development. For example, you are running an instance of SQL Server instead of SQL Express in production, so the connection information will be slightly different. But the rest of the settings and topology are similar, so we won't repeat all the steps here again.

Another difference, however, is that the QuizBox team wants to perform A/B testing in production. To do this, you want to be able to publish a new feature to a subset of users to see how the new feature is being used. So for QuizBox, this means that you need to deploy two versions of the front-end web site, one version where the new feature is available and one version where the regular functionality is available. Then you need a way to measure this.

Since you are using Microsoft Azure for the front-end web application, you can use the following two technologies to implement A/B testing: *deployment slots* and *traffic routing*.

A deployment slot in the context of an Azure Web App is a parallel instance of the web site that runs completely independent of the original site (see Figure 10-56). This site can be accessed by appending the name of the deployment slot to the host name of your web app, like *https://webappname-**deploymentslotname**.azurewebsites.no*.

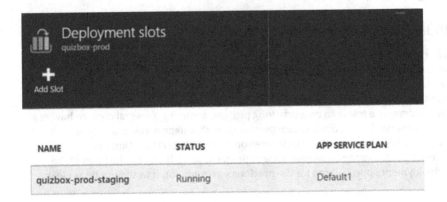

*Figure 10-56.* *Deployment slots*

---

■ **Note**    Deployment slots are only available in the Standard or Premium app service plans.

---

In this example, there is a deployment slot for quizbox-prod called *staging*, and it is accessible via the URL ***http://quizbox-prod-staging.azurewebsites.net***.

When you created a deployment slot, you can deploy new versions of the web application to it, which means that you can try out the new functionality by going to the staging URL instead of the real one. Once the staging functionality is determined to be ready to be rolled out to everyone, you can *swap* the deployment slot so that everything that is deployed to the staging slot immediately and automatically becomes available in the production URL.

Now that you have a staging deployment slot for your production site, how can you direct user traffic to it? This is where traffic routing can help. By default, all traffic for an Azure Web App is routed to the main production site. By using the Traffic Routing blade (shown in Figure 10-57), you can change this behavior. By adding your staging deployment slot and configuring the amount of traffic that should be directed to it, you effectively enable A/B testing.

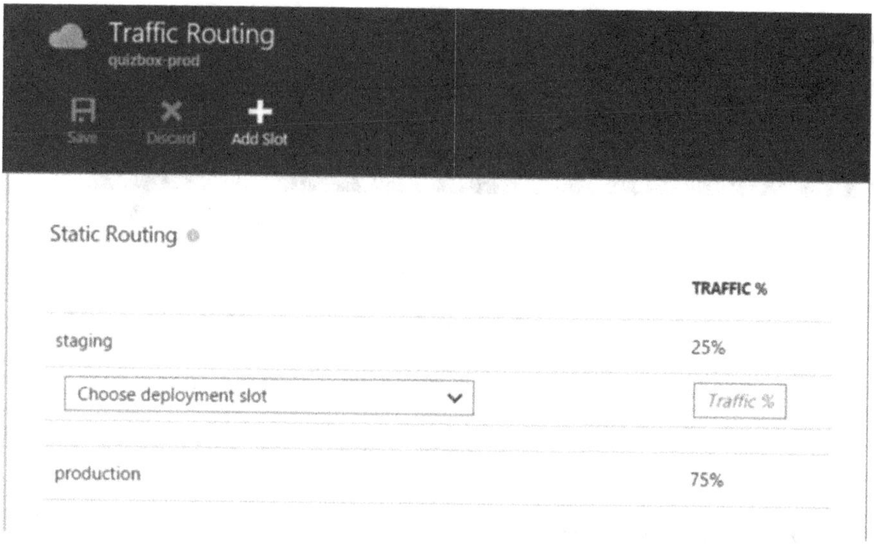

*Figure 10-57. Traffic routing*

Now 25% of the traffic will, at random, be directed to the staging version of the QuizBox web application, and the other 75% of the traffic will return the production site. Note that as a single user, all requests during the entire session will be directed to the same site (using affinity cookies). But the next session for that same user might very well be served from the other site. This is a foundation for true A/B testing, since you want to learn how users are responding to the new functionality compared to the existing one. In the next chapter, where we discuss Application Insights, you will see how to collect information based on these different sites and how to visualize it.

## Production Swap

The last stage in the deployment pipeline takes care of swapping the production slot so that the latest version becomes available for all users. Swapping a deployment slot can be done through the Azure Portal. On the page of the deployment slot site you can find the Swap button located in the toolbar, as shown in Figure 10-58.

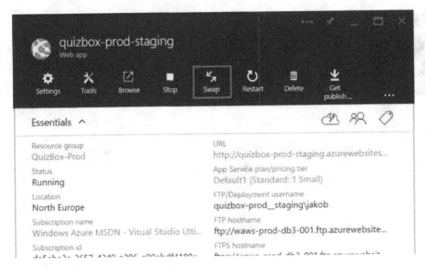

*Figure 10-58. Swapping deployment slots*

In your deployment pipeline you naturally want to automate this step. This can be done using the following short Azure PowerShell script:

```
[CmdletBinding()]

param( [Parameter(Position=1)]
       [string]$webAppName)

Switch-AzureWebsiteSlot -Name $webAppName -Force
```

When using the `Switch-AzureWebsiteSlot` cmdlet with only the name of the web app, it will assume that there is only one deployment slot for this web app and do a swap between them. If you have multiple deployment slots, you must specify which slots that should be swapped

Run this script using the Azure PowerShell task, shown in Figure 10-59.

*Figure 10-59. Running the Azure PowerShell script*

Running an Azure PowerShell script must always be done in the context of an Azure subscription. Here you have connected the task to a subscription called MSDN that is registered in this instance of TFS. This will allow you to run scripts against this subscription without any further authentication.

# Summary

In this chapter, you looked at the concept of a deployment pipeline and then examined how the latest version of Visual Studio Release Management can be used to implement such a pipeline. You took an in-depth look at how to configure a deployment pipeline in practice using the QuizBox sample application. You should now have a good understanding of the functionality available in Visual Studio Release Management and how it integrates with the new build system and how you can use it to deploy applications both to on-premise servers and to Microsoft Azure.

In the next chapter, you will look at how to use Application Insights to gain insights into your applications and your users.

# CHAPTER 11

■ ■ ■

# Measure and Learn

As mentioned in Chapter 1, it is important from the very start of a project to consider things like how your application is going to be monitored in test and production, and what telemetry will be needed to understand how your users are using your application.

Getting feedback and metrics from your applications in production allows you to gain insights that will help you to not just detect and diagnose issues, but, if done right, prioritize your future investments. Doing things like A/B testing where you deploy a new feature to, say, half of your users and then measure in what degree the new feature is being used allows you to invest your resources in things that really matter.

---

■ **Note**    A practice related to this is *hypothesis-driven development* (www.drdobbs.com/ architecture-and-design/hypothesis-driven-development/229000656), where development is seen more as a series of experiments that you use to determine if your expected outcome is achieved. Read more about it at www.thoughtworks.com/insights/ blog/how-implement-hypothesis-driven-development.

---

Analytics should not just be about solving problems once they have happened; they should be an integrated part of the development cycle. When gathering requirements for a new user story or feature, you should always consider how you measure the success of the new or changed feature.

In this chapter, you will take a look at Application Insights, an analytics platform that gives you a full picture ("360-degree view") of your applications and services. Monitoring the performance and issues in production combined with alerts allows you to diagnose bottlenecks and quickly react to issues. In addition, by sending telemetry events you can understand who your users are and if they are using the application in the way that you intended.

Last, you will take a look at how the QuizBox application uses Application Insights to gain insights to the different parts of the application and its users.

# Application Insights

Application Insights was originally released in preview back in the Visual Studio 2013 timeframe as an instrumenting service, with the back end and user portal hosted in Azure as part of the Visual Studio Online portal. Later, the portal was completely rewritten to be part of the new Azure Preview Portal (also known as Ibiza); it contained a large amount of new features and a broader support of platforms. At the //Build conference in 2015, Application Insights went into public preview with a pricing plan based on the telemetry volume of the measured applications. At this moment, Application Insights is free up to 5 million data points per month.

Application Insights is an analytics platform that support many application platforms, including iOS, Android, and Java, and brings together Application Performance Management (APM) and Usage Analytics into a coherent set of services. It is part of the Azure Portal as a separate resource that can be added with other resource into a resource group. Figure 11-1 shows where you can find these resources in the portal.

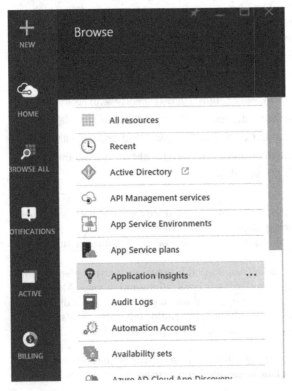

***Figure 11-1.*** *Application Insights in the Azure Portal*

Creating an Application Insights resource is straightforward. Give it a name and a resource group, and select from which kind of application you are planning to send telemetry. You can see the available selections in Figure 11-2.

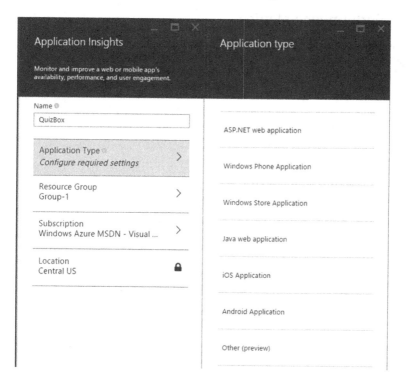

***Figure 11-2.*** *Creating an Application Insights resource*

The selection you make here affects the default selection of charts for the newly created resource. Also, the guidance that is available at different places for Application Insights is affected by your choice. You are free to change which charts and metrics should be displayed for the resource. Also note that even though an application type is selected for the resource, you can send telemetry from different types of applications into the same Application Insights resource. We will talk in more detail later in this chapter about different options for grouping and segmenting Application Insights resources.

# Detecting and Diagnosing Issues

Determining if your applications are running and performing well is of the uttermost importance to any organization. Being able to quickly diagnose and respond to production issues is a competitive advantage, and should be considered and planned for right from the beginning of the project.

Application Insights helps in several ways with this. Here we list some of the key features.

## Monitoring Performance Metrics

Application Insights by default tracks many different performance metrics, such as browser page load time, server response time, number of server requests, and failed requests. An overview of the most important performance metrics is available on the start page of the Application Insights resource, as shown in Figure 11-3.

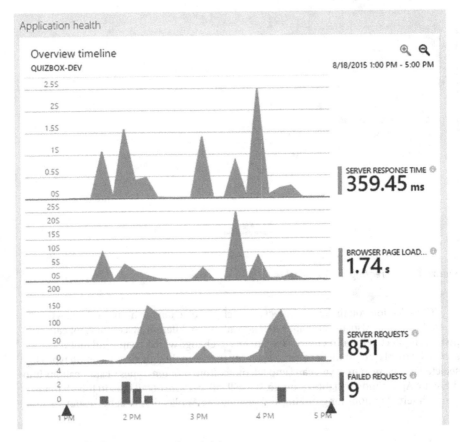

*Figure 11-3. Performance overview metrics*

The overview page gives a quick glimpse of the performance and throughput on both the server and the client (in case of web applications or devices) and the number of successful and failed requests. From here, you can drill down to learn more about performance and you can diagnose any issues that have occurred recently.

> ■ **Note** Depending on the pricing plan, Application Insights stores raw data up to 30 days, with the option to continuously export the data. The aggregated data is only deleted when using the free plan, and it is deleted after 13 months.

## Detecting Exceptions

After adding the Application Insights SDK to your web project, or installing the Status Monitor application on the web server, you can start reporting exceptions back to Application Insights, together with the stack trace and other detailed information. As with other requests sent to AI, you can view it with the rest of the telemetry of the session. This allows you to see what actions the user performed that led up to the point of failure.

Figure 11-4 shows how the detailed information about an exception is shown, and how you can select related telemetry for the same request or the same session to understand the root cause of the exception.

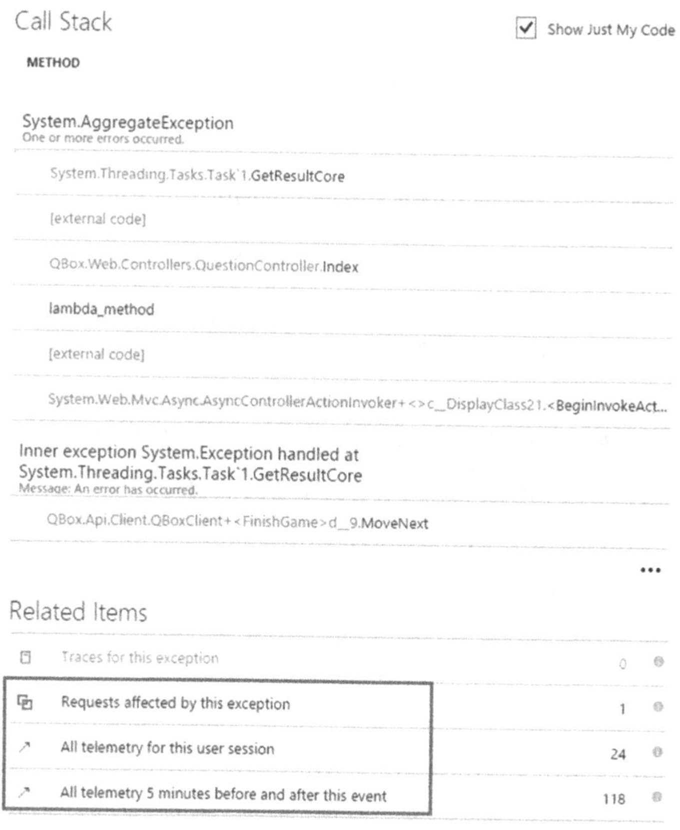

*Figure 11-4.  Diagnosing exceptions*

It is also possible to report exceptions explicitly by using the SDK. This allows you to report exceptions that are caught, and you can ask the user for any extra information about what they did and pass this along as additional information. It should also be noted that, for web applications running on IIS, most exceptions that originate from the server are caught by IIS, and won't be sent to Application Insights automatically. Therefore you need to add a few lines of code to report these exceptions. The following code shows an example of how this can be set up for an ASP.NET MVC 5 application:

```
public class MvcApplication : System.Web.HttpApplication
{
    protected void Application_Start()
    {
        AreaRegistration.RegisterAllAreas();
        FilterConfig.RegisterGlobalFilters(GlobalFilters.Filters);
        RouteConfig.RegisterRoutes(RouteTable.Routes);
        BundleConfig.RegisterBundles(BundleTable.Bundles);
        RegisterGlobalFilters(GlobalFilters.Filters);
    }

    public static void RegisterGlobalFilters(GlobalFilterCollection filters)
    {
        filters.Add(new AiHandleErrorAttribute());
    }
}

public class AiHandleErrorAttribute : HandleErrorAttribute
{
    public override void OnException(ExceptionContext filterContext)
    {
        if (filterContext != null && filterContext.HttpContext != null &&
        filterContext.Exception != null)
        {
            //If customError is Off, then AI HTTPModule will report the exception
            //If it is On, or RemoteOnly (default) - then we need to
            explicitly track the exception
            if (filterContext.HttpContext.IsCustomErrorEnabled)
            {
                var ai = new TelemetryClient();
                ai.TrackException(filterContext.Exception);
            }
        }
        base.OnException(filterContext);
    }
}
```

Here you use an MVC attribute class that overrides the OnException method, and in it you report the exception to AI using the TrackException method.

Depending on which web framework you are using, there are different places where you need to add hooks for handling unhandled exceptions and report them to Application Insights.

## Availability Monitoring

Measuring the availability is often done using "outside-in" testing, where external clients are configured to continuously send requests to different parts of the application. The requests can either be simple (a.m. ping requests) or more complex where a longer scenario is validated.

Application Insights supports availability tests in the form of *URL ping tests* for detecting if a specific URL is accessible and also *multi-step tests* that can for example log in to a web site and perform a few actions to verify that the application is functional. An example of a multi-step test is a web performance test, which is authored using Visual Studio 2015 Enterprise. Using it, you can create complex tests that verify different scenarios.

---

■ **Note**    There is a limit when running web performance tests in Application Insights. They can't have more than 100 steps and they can't run longer that 2 minutes.

---

Availability problems can sometimes be caused by network failures or bottlenecks on different datacenters, causing problems only in some regions in the world. To be able to verify if your application is available from different areas of the world, availability tests in Application Insights support multiple test locations, as shown in Figure 11-5. In the example, there is a URL ping test for the start page of QuizBox that will be requested only from the test location in Stockholm, Sweden. If you only have users from Sweden, you might not be interested about the availability from other parts of the world.

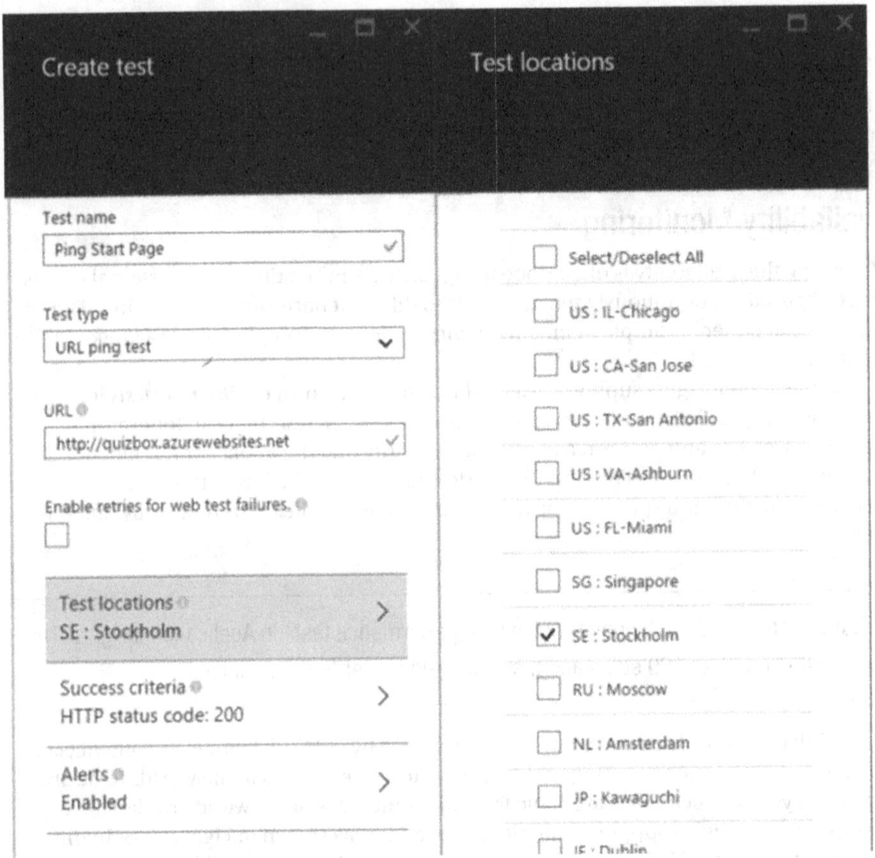

**Figure 11-5.** *Creating a URL ping test*

These availability tests can be scheduled to be executed at a certain interval. The results are plotted on a chart, which you can drill down into for more details, as shown in Figure 11-6.

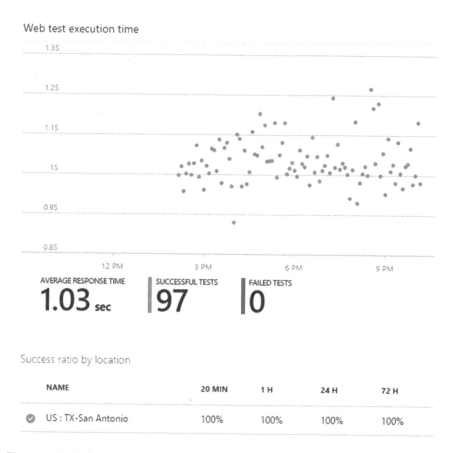

*Figure 11-6.* *Web test chart*

# Alerts

The AI portal is great for getting a quick overview of the status of the application and for diagnosing issues, but you can't rely on members of the operations team spending all their time in the portal. By setting up alerts, the team can be notified when something happens out of the ordinary.

Availability tests are one thing that can generate alerts, but you can also configure custom alerts to be triggered for events that you might be interested in, such as when

- The number of exceptions exceeds a certain limit

- The average response time is greater than a certain threshold

- The amount of memory goes low

Figure 11-7 shows an example where an alert email will be sent to the Ops team at QuizBox if the average server response time over the last 5 minutes exceeds 0.8 seconds.

*Figure 11-7.* *Custom alerts*

Use these alerts extensively to stay on top of issues in production. By acting on trends (for example, if memory consumption over time exceeds a certain limit) you can fix problems before they become critical.

## Diagnosing Dependency Issues

Problems that occur in an application can often be caused by external dependencies, such as SQL database or remote web services. Understanding where the bottlenecks are is important and can be time consuming when you don't have any tracing information.

Application Insights can automatically detect external dependencies for you, and show you how much time is spent waiting for the dependencies to complete.

Currently, the out-of-the-box dependency monitoring supports ASP.NET web applications and services plus Java web apps, and tracks calls to the following types of dependencies:

ASP.NET:

- SQL databases

- ASP.NET web and WCF services that use HTTP-based bindings

- Local or remote HTTP calls

- Azure DocumentDb, table, blob storage, and queue

Java:

- Calls to a database through a JDBC driver, such as MySQL, SQL Server, PostgreSQL, or SQLite

On the overview blade, the average duration of each dependency is displayed, as shown in Figure 11-8.

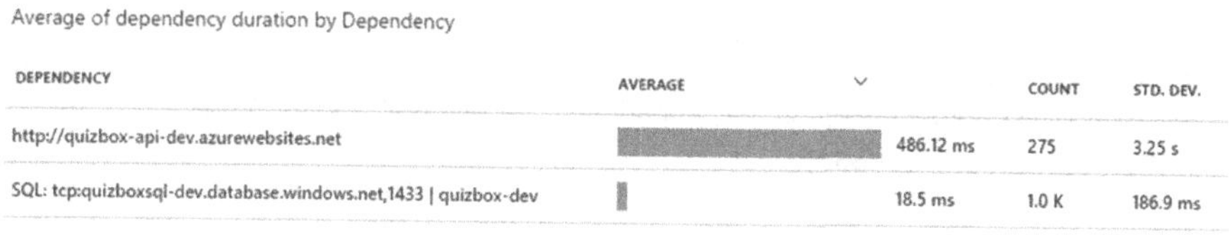

Average of dependency duration by Dependency

| DEPENDENCY | AVERAGE | ∨ | COUNT | STD. DEV. |
|---|---|---|---|---|
| http://quizbox-api-dev.azurewebsites.net | | 486.12 ms | 275 | 3.25 s |
| SQL: tcp:quizboxsql-dev.database.windows.net,1433 \| quizbox-dev | | 18.5 ms | 1.0 K | 186.9 ms |

*Figure 11-8.* *Diagnosing dependencies*

Drilling down into requests, you can also see details on requests to the external dependencies to find out where the time is spent, as shown in Figure 11-9.

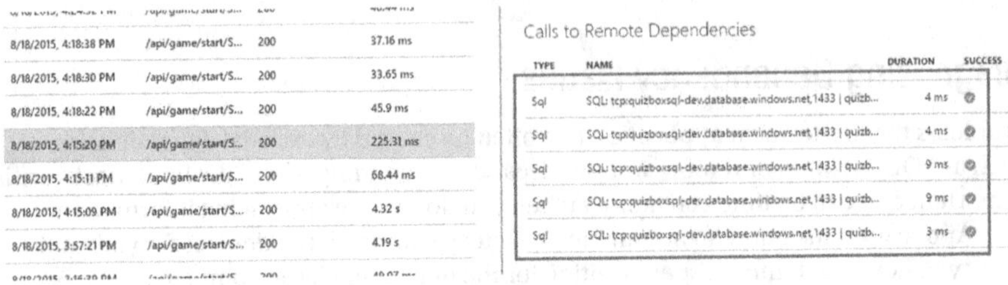

*Figure 11-9.* *Calls to remote dependencies*

If you have other external dependencies that are not picked up automatically by Application Insights but you want to track, it is possible to implement custom dependency tracking. There is a TrackDependency API that allows you to send information about the duration of the calls to a specific dependency.

Here is a short example that measures the duration of a call to a certain dependency (the someDependency object) and then sends it to Application Insights using the TrackDependency method:

```
var success = false;
var startTime = DateTime.UtcNow;
var timer = System.Diagnostics.Stopwatch.StartNew();
try
{
    success = someDependency.Call();
}
finally
{
    timer.Stop();
    telemetry.TrackDependency("myDependency", "myCall", startTime,
    timer.Elapsed, success);
}
```

# Understanding Your Users

Knowing that your application is performing well in production is important, but so is understanding your users and how they are using the application.

Application Insights provides plenty of analytics out of the box that help you understand the usage.

When selecting the Usage tile in Application Insights, graphs showing overview information about users, user sessions, and page views are shown. Figure 11-10 shows an example.

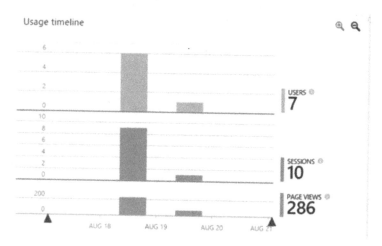

**Figure 11-10.** *Usage information*

The *Users* graph shows the number of distinct users, where each point is a single day. For web applications, users are counted by using cookies. For device applications, you will need to supply a unique user identification to have these graphs light up.

The *Sessions* graph shows the number of unique sessions over the same period of time. By comparing this to the number of unique users, you can calculate your number of returning users.

The *Page Views* graph shows how many pages that have been requested. This gives you an indication of how much of the application the users have gone through during their sessions. For example, it is common for new users to explore many parts of an application to learn about it, but after a while they know what they are interested in and how to quickly get there. So it is common to see higher page activity when introducing new features or when there are many new users coming in.

Drilling down into these graphs gives you detailed information, and you can filter the information on specific metrics.

# Knowing Your Users

Understanding where your users come from and which browsers, operating systems, or devices they are using can be very important. All this information is available automatically, and Figure 11-11 shows examples of this.

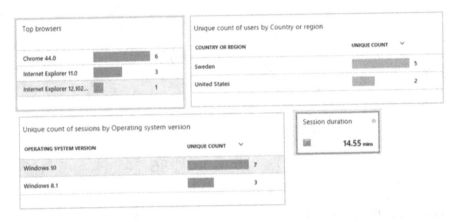

**Figure 11-11.** *User information*

Demographic information is important because it can indicate the need for supporting additional languages and other culture-specific information. It can also provide support when deciding on where to focus your marketing investments. Browser statistics are obviously helpful from a technical point of view because they show which browser you must be able to support for your web applications.

To understand more about how the users are using the application, you can drill down into the Page View graph (shown in Figure 11-12). This will show you information about which pages are the most visited, but also session-related information such as which pages are the most common entry and exit points of the application. This helps you understand where users are entering your application and also where they often drop off. Analyzing this information helps you understand at which point you might be losing users. If you are running an e-commerce site, you can use this to find ways to make more users proceed all the way to the checkout.

Activity by Page name

| PAGE NAME | PAGE VIE... ∨ | USERS | SESSIONS |
|---|---|---|---|
| Index - QuizBo | 106 | 7 | 10 |
| Quiz Question - QuizBo | 101 | 6 | 9 |
| Home Page - QuizBo | 49 | 7 | 10 |
| All questions answered - QuizBo | 24 | 5 | 8 |
| - QuizBo | 6 | 2 | 2 |

Unique count of sessions by Entry page ◉

| ENTRY PAGE | UNIQUE COUNT ∨ |
|---|---|
| Home Page - QuizBo | 3 |
| Quiz Question - QuizBo | 3 |
| Index - QuizBo | 1 |

Unique count of sessions by Exit page ◉

| EXIT PAGE | UNIQUE COUNT ∨ |
|---|---|
| All questions answered - QuizBo | 2 |
| Index - QuizBo | 2 |
| Quiz Question - QuizBo | 2 |
| Home Page - QuizBo | 1 |

*Figure 11-12.* *Usage information*

# Correlating Telemetry Information

As you saw in the previous section, the instrumentation key is what identifies a particular resource in Application Insights. However, since an application is typically deployed to multiple environments on its way to production, by default all telemetry data will go into the same resource in Application Insights. So if you run a load test in your staging environment, you will see a large increase of the number of users, which will affect the data about your actual users.

## Segmenting by Environment

A common way to solve this is to set up different resource groups for the different environments (for example, Dev, Test, and Production) and create an Application Insights resource in each resource group. This way, there is one instrumentation key for each environment, which will be applied during deployment. You don't have to create different resource groups for each environment, but doing so means you can manage all the alerts, billing, permissions, and other Azure resources in one place.

---

■ **Note**    If you are not hosting your applications in Azure, you can still use this approach in order to separate the telemetry and diagnostics for your different environments. The resource groups will then only contain the Application Insights resource.

---

## Tagging

The above approach works very well when you want to completely separate the telemetry from different environments, and it should be the default setup for most applications. However, sometimes you need to compare or correlate telemetry between your environments. You might deploy your application to multiple locations on premise and want to compare or aggregate telemetry data from them.

This can be solved by tagging all the telemetry that is sent with something that identifies the thing that you want to filter or group on. You can use the version number of the application, as you will see later in the section about QuizBox. If you are running the application in multiple environments, you can pass in the name of that environment. This way you will be able to use the Metric Explorer and Diagnostic Search in Application Insights to analyze and compare the data coming from multiple sources.

The easiest way to make sure that the tag is always sent is to create a custom initializer that is passed when creating the `TelemetryClient` object.

```
public class QuiBoxContextInitializer : IContextInitializer
{
    public void Initialize(TelemetryContext context)
    {
        context.Properties["Environment"] = Properties.Settings.Default.
        CurrentEnvironment;
    }
}

TelemetryClient = new TelemetryClient(new TelemetryConfiguration()
{
        ContextInitializers = { new QuiBoxContextInitializer()}
})
{
        InstrumentationKey = Settings.Default.InstrumentationKey
};
```

In this code, you implement a custom initializer that define a property called Environment, by reading the value from the configuration file. At application startup, when you create the TelemetryClient, you pass an instance of this initializer. As a result, all information passed through using this client object will also send the name of the current environment.

In the Application Insights portal you can then use the Metric Explorer and Search to segment and filter your data by this property.

Another usage of this approach is when you are running multiple versions of the same applications at the same time, for example when using A/B testing. Application Insights defines a standard telemetry attribute for application version. When looking at chart detail for any metrics, you can then group the information by application version to compare and filter the information.

# Instrumenting the Applications

There are a few options available to start using Application Insights on your applications. The first is to add one of the Application Insights SDK that are available for the different platforms and application types. This SDK will by default give you a range of standard diagnostic and usage telemetry. In addition, you can use the API to create custom telemetry to track usage or diagnose other problems.

Another option for ASP.NET web applications running on IIS is to install the *Application Insights Status Monitor* tool that can dynamically instrument any running ASP.NET application and send data to Application Insights. This is a standalone tool that is installed using the Web Platform Installer, and it lets you monitor web applications that are already running without rebuilding and, more importantly, redeploying them. It also adds support for dependency diagnostics, discussed previously in this chapter. This information is not available when only using the SDK.

When running the Application Insights Status Monitor on your web server, it will list all ASP.NET web applications that are available. You then select a web application and either point it to an existing Application Insights resource in your Azure subscription or create a new one. Figure 11-13 shows what this looks like.

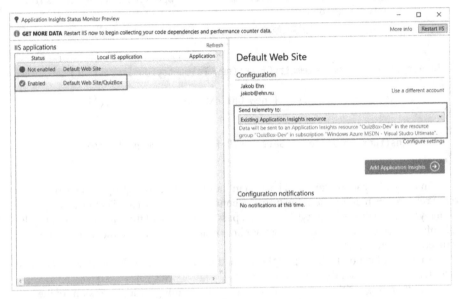

*Figure 11-13. Instrumenting ASP.NET applications in the Status Monitor*

Note that you need to restart IIS to begin collection telemetry from the application that you selected.

If you are running your web applications as an Azure Web App, you cannot use the Status Monitor tool. To get the same rich diagnostic information you need to install an Application Insights extension to your Web App.

To install the extension, select the Web App resource in the Azure Portal and then click the *Tools* button. From there, select *Extensions*, *Add* and select Application Insights from the list of extension, as shown in Figure 11-14. After a short period of time the extension will start sending additional diagnostic information to Application Insights.

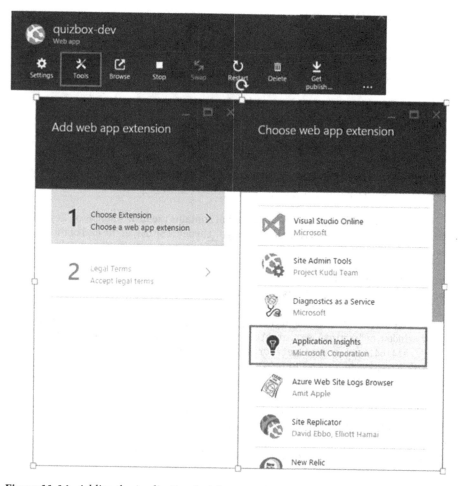

*Figure 11-14. Adding the Application Insights extension*

When you create an Application Insights resource in Azure, either from Visual Studio or from the portal, it will generate a unique instrumentation key. This is what identifies this particular resource, and it must be configured in every client application that wants to send data to Application Insights.

By default, when using the Visual Studio Application Insights extension to add AI to a project, the instrumentation key will be located in the configuration file for Application Insights, called ApplicationInsights.config. Here is an excerpt from this file is shown with the iKey marked.

```
</TelemetryInitializers>
<!--
  Learn more about Application Insights configuration with
  ApplicationInsights.config here:
  http://go.microsoft.com/fwlink/?LinkID=513840

  Note: If not present, please add <InstrumentationKey>Your
  Key</InstrumentationKey> to the top of this file.
-->
<!-- This key is for Application Insights resource 'QBox.Web' in resource group
'QuizBox-Dev' -->
  <InstrumentationKey>7ff9a227-13d5-421b-90a8-fde6d05c492c</InstrumentationKey>
</ApplicationInsights>
```

For ASP.NET web applications, a script that contains the instrumentation key will also be added to the shared layout master page _Layout.cshtml, at the end of the <head> element:

```
<script type="text/javascript">
var appInsights=window.appInsights||function(config){
    function s(config){t[config]=function(){var i=arguments;t.queue.push
    (function(){t[config].apply(t,i)})}}var t={config:config},r=document,
    f=window,e="script",o=r.createElement(e),i,u;for(o.src=config.url||
    "//az416426.vo.msecnd.net/scripts/a/ai.0.js",r.getElementsByTagName(e)
    [0].parentNode.appendChild(o),t.cookie=r.cookie,t.queue=[],i=["Event",
    "Exception","Metric","PageView","Trace"];i.length;)s("track"+i.pop());return
    config.disableExceptionTracking||(i="onerror",s("_"+i),u=f[i],
    f[i]=function(config,r,f,e,o){var s=u&&u(config,r,f,e,o);return
    s!==!0&&t["_"+i](config,r,f,e,o),s}),t
}({
    instrumentationKey: "7ff9a227-13d5-421b-90a8-fde6d05c492c"
});

window.appInsights=appInsights;
appInsights.trackPageView();
</script>
```

We recommend that you extract this instrumentation key into a separate application setting in your configuration file, and then use code in one place to read it.

> ■ **Note**    See the section about the QuizBox sample application later in this chapter for how this can be implemented.

This way, there is only one place that needs to be updated as part of the deployment of the application. Later in this chapter, you will learn how to set the instrumentation key during deployment to an environment.

# Managing Application Insights in the Deployment Pipeline

We already talked about instrumentation keys and how they are what identifies a particular Application Insights resource. When it comes to managing these keys across the different environments and/or installations, the deployment pipeline is the natural place to do this.

Every time you deploy your application to a particular environment you must make sure that you supply the correct instrumentation key as part of the deployment. The key should be located as a separate application setting (as described earlier in this chapter), which means you can use the same technique to replace these values as with the rest of the application-specific settings. In Chapter 10, you learned how to replace tokens during a deployment to a particular environment; you can use the same technique for replacing the instrumentation key in your deployment pipeline. In the next section, you will look at the QuizBox application and how you can accomplish this.

# Sample Application

The QuizBox application has multiple components in the same application. It has a front-end web application and a back-end web application. In addition, there is the mobile application with its own user interface.

There are a few alternatives available for instrumenting this application. You could create a separate Application Insights resource for every component (e.g. every application or service gets its own instrumentation key). This would provide a clean separation between the components, put would also make it harder to get an overview of the entire application.

Instead, let's use the same iKey for all components, thereby aggregating all the information about the application in the same resource.

## Instrumenting QuizBox

Since you want to share the same iKey across all components, you must create a separate Logger class that encapsulates access to the instrumentation key. This class, partly shown below, is then referenced by the different applications:

```
public class Logger
{
    private static TelemetryClient TelemetryClient { get; set; }

    static Logger()
    {
        TelemetryClient = new TelemetryClient
        {
            InstrumentationKey = Settings.Default.InstrumentationKey
        };
    }
}
```

As you can see, this class reads the instrumentation key from the configuration file. Applying the correct iKey for each environment is done in the deployment pipeline. To do this, you simply create an environment variable called instrumentationKey in every environment that contains deployment steps, and then supply the corresponding value. The environment variables for QuizBox are shown in Figure 11-15.

Definition: QuizBox Release : Releases

Environments   Artifacts   **Configuration**   Triggers   General

↻   💾 Save   ➕ Release ▾

| | Deploy DEV | Deploy QA | Deploy PROD-Staging |
|---|---|---|---|
| apiUrl | http://qbox-dev.cloudapp.net/api | ✳ http://qbox-qa.cloudapp.net/api | http://qbox-prod.cloudapp.net/api |
| applicationPath | c:\deploy\QBox.Release\scripts | c:\deploy\QBox.Release\scripts | c:\deploy\QBox.Release\scripts |
| backOfficeInstallLocation | c:\quizbox\ | c:\quizbox | c:\quizbox\ |
| databaseLogin | quizbox | quizbox | quizbox |
| databaseName | QuizBox | QuizBox | QuizBox |
| databasePassword | ••••••• | ⊕ ••••••• | ••••••• ⊕ |
| databaseServer | .\SQLEXPRESS | .\SQLEXPRESS | localhost |
| destinationPath | c:\wwwroot_quizboxapi | c:\wwwroot_quizboxapi | c:\wwwroot_quizboxapi |
| instrumentationKey | 7ff9a227-13d5-421b-90a8-fde6d05c492c | fd631724-fefb-4e09-bf61-b5583a0dbb76 | a8e2fe76-2d4f-4f0f-a381-253a694ffd8c |
| vmAccount | .\jakob | .\qa | .\jakob |
| vmPassword | ••••••• | ⊕ ••••••• | ••••••• ⊕ |
| webSite | QuizBoxApi | QuizBoxApi | QuizBoxApi |
| webSiteName | Default Web Site | Default Web Site | Default Web Site |

*Figure 11-15. Instrumentation key environment variables*

# Dependency Analysis

As mentioned, QuizBox consists of multiple components. From the perspective of each component, the other components can be seen as external dependencies. These dependencies are automatically tracked by Application Insights when using either the Status Monitor application when running on IIS, or using the Application Insights extension when running in an Azure web site.

Using this feature, it was easy to determine which component was performing badly and if failures were caused by internal components or external dependencies. See Figure 11-16.

| Average of dependency duration by Dependency | | | | |
| --- | --- | --- | --- | --- |
| DEPENDENCY | AVERAGE | ∨ | COUNT | STD. DEV. |
| http://quizbox-api-dev.azurewebsites.net | | 833.66 ms | 64 | 4.34 s |
| SQL: tcp:quizboxsql-dev.database.windows.net,1433 | quizbox-dev | | 10.71 ms | 368 | 60.37 ms |

*Figure 11-16. Dependency duration*

# Usage Analysis

To be able to analyze how your users are using the QuizBox application, let's add some custom telemetry in addition to what you get out of the box.

For instance, you want to be able to determine which of the game categories are popular and maybe over time see how this popularity relates to marketing campaigns or current events. Application Insights will log requests to the URL that starts a new game, but you don't get information about which category was selected. To do so, use the TrackEvent method to track this information.

```
TelemetryClient.TrackEvent(selectedCategory);
```

In this code, you track an event with the same name as the category. This will make it easy to view and track the popularity of the categories using the Filter mechanism, as shown in Figure 11-17.

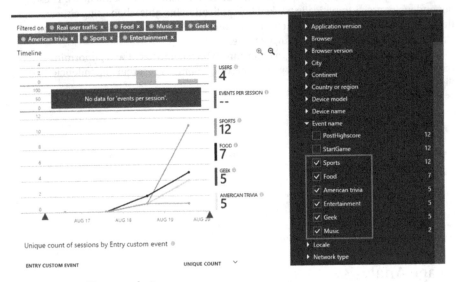

**Figure 11-17.** *Usage analysis*

Here you can see the popularity of the available categories over time.

---

■ **Note** If your application uses a REST notation for all URLs, you get a lot of this information automatically, since each function corresponds to a specific URL. But in cases where you have single-page application (SPA), you will need to add custom events to track extra information. Also, note that for POST requests, no additional information is tracked except the URL itself. If you want to track extra information for POST requests, use the `TrackEvent` or `TrackMetric` methods.

---

## A/B Testing

At one point, QuizBox got a new feature where the users can select a random category. To determine if this new feature is being used, you can perform A/B testing, in which two versions of the same application are deployed in parallel. Tracking the usage is done by adding a new event for the random category, so that it can be compared to the normal behavior where the users select a category. In addition, make sure that you pass the version number on every request. This can be done by adding the assembly version to the `TelemetryContext` at the start of the application.

```
static Logger()
{
    TelemetryClient = new TelemetryClient
    {
        InstrumentationKey = Settings.Default.InstrumentationKey,
    };
    TelemetryClient.Context.Component.Version = Assembly.
    GetExecutingAssembly().GetName().Version.ToString();
}
```

Comparing these metrics can be done by grouping on the application version property, as shown in Figure 11-18.

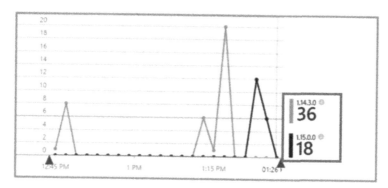

*Figure 11-18.* *Grouping on an application version*

# Summary

In this chapter, you learned about the importance of measuring your applications and your users in order to discover both how the applications are behaving in the wild and how your users are actually using them. This allows you to quickly react to any issues that occur, hopefully before the majority of the users are affected by them, and also to get insights into what parts of your application are actually used and if new features are being well received by your users.

All this information can be used to continuously improve your applications and to help you prioritize the work that goes into the product backlog.

# Index

# Get the eBook for only $5!

Why limit yourself?

Now you can take the weightless companion with you wherever you go and access your content on your PC, phone, tablet, or reader.

Since you've purchased this print book, we're happy to offer you the eBook in all 3 formats for just $5.

Convenient and fully searchable, the PDF version enables you to easily find and copy code—or perform examples by quickly toggling between instructions and applications. The MOBI format is ideal for your Kindle, while the ePUB can be utilized on a variety of mobile devices.

To learn more, go to www.apress.com/companion or contact support@apress.com.

All Apress eBooks are subject to copyright. All rights are reserved by the Publisher, whether the whole or part of the material is concerned, specifically the rights of translation, reprinting, reuse of illustrations, recitation, broadcasting, reproduction on microfilms or in any other physical way, and transmission or information storage and retrieval, electronic adaptation, computer software, or by similar or dissimilar methodology now known or hereafter developed. Exempted from this legal reservation are brief excerpts in connection with reviews or scholarly analysis or material supplied specifically for the purpose of being entered and executed on a computer system, for exclusive use by the purchaser of the work. Duplication of this publication or parts thereof is permitted only under the provisions of the Copyright Law of the Publisher's location, in its current version, and permission for use must always be obtained from Springer. Permissions for use may be obtained through RightsLink at the Copyright Clearance Center. Violations are liable to prosecution under the respective Copyright Law.

Printed in the United States
By Bookmasters